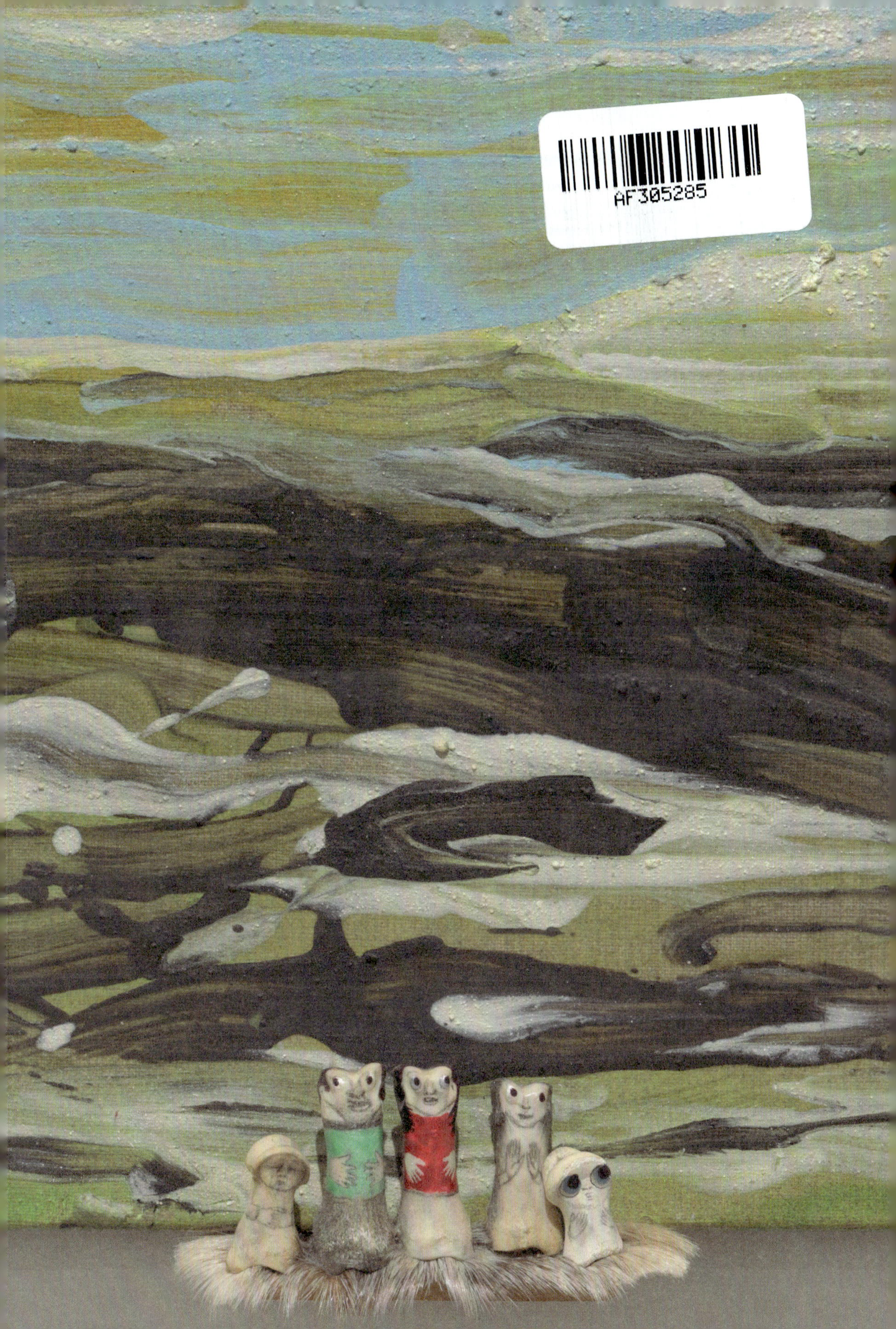

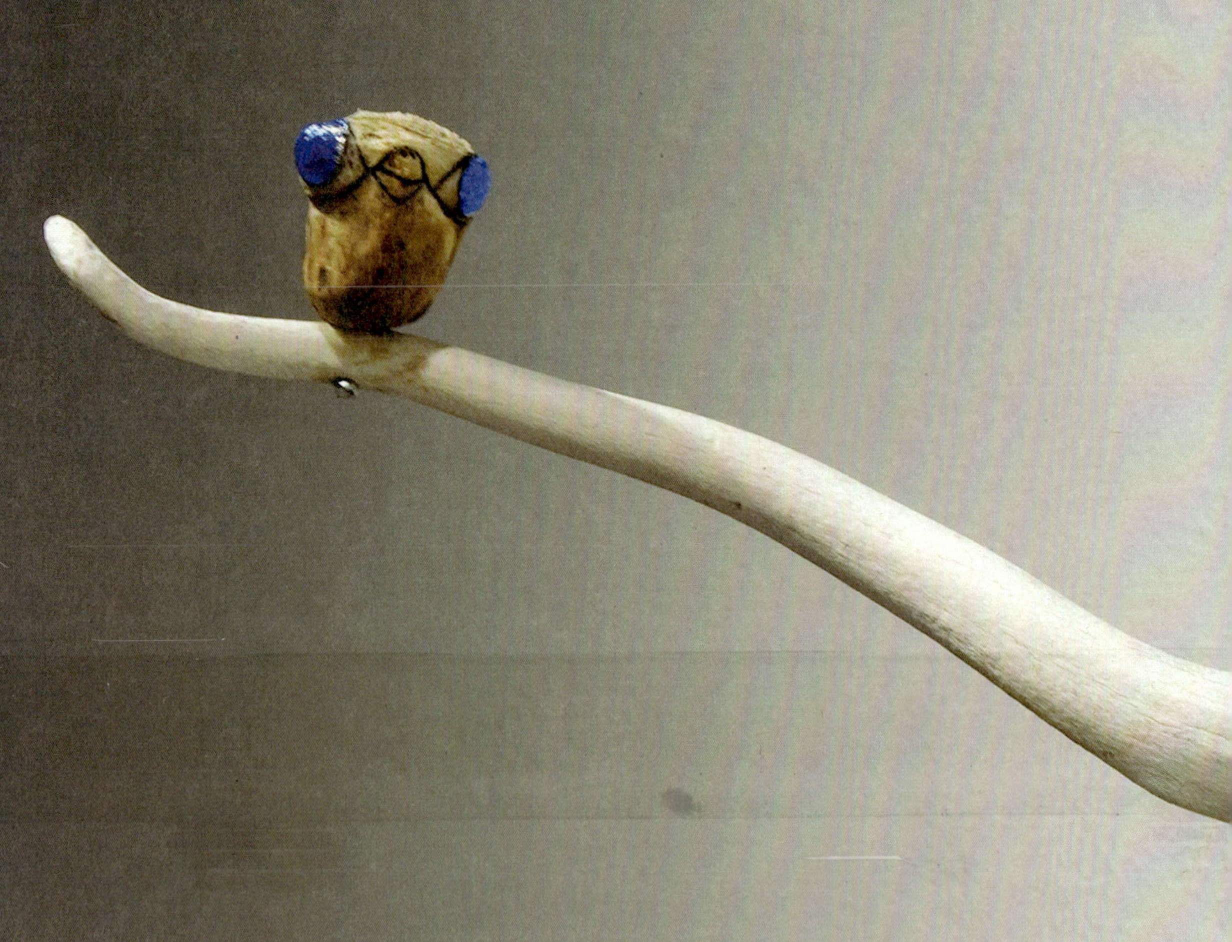

Cover:
Rádjajohtin I
Pacing the Borders I
2014

Previous page:
Geasi vuordin
Waiting for Summer
2007

This page:
Lottelávlunmuorra I
A Bird's Singing Tree I
2008

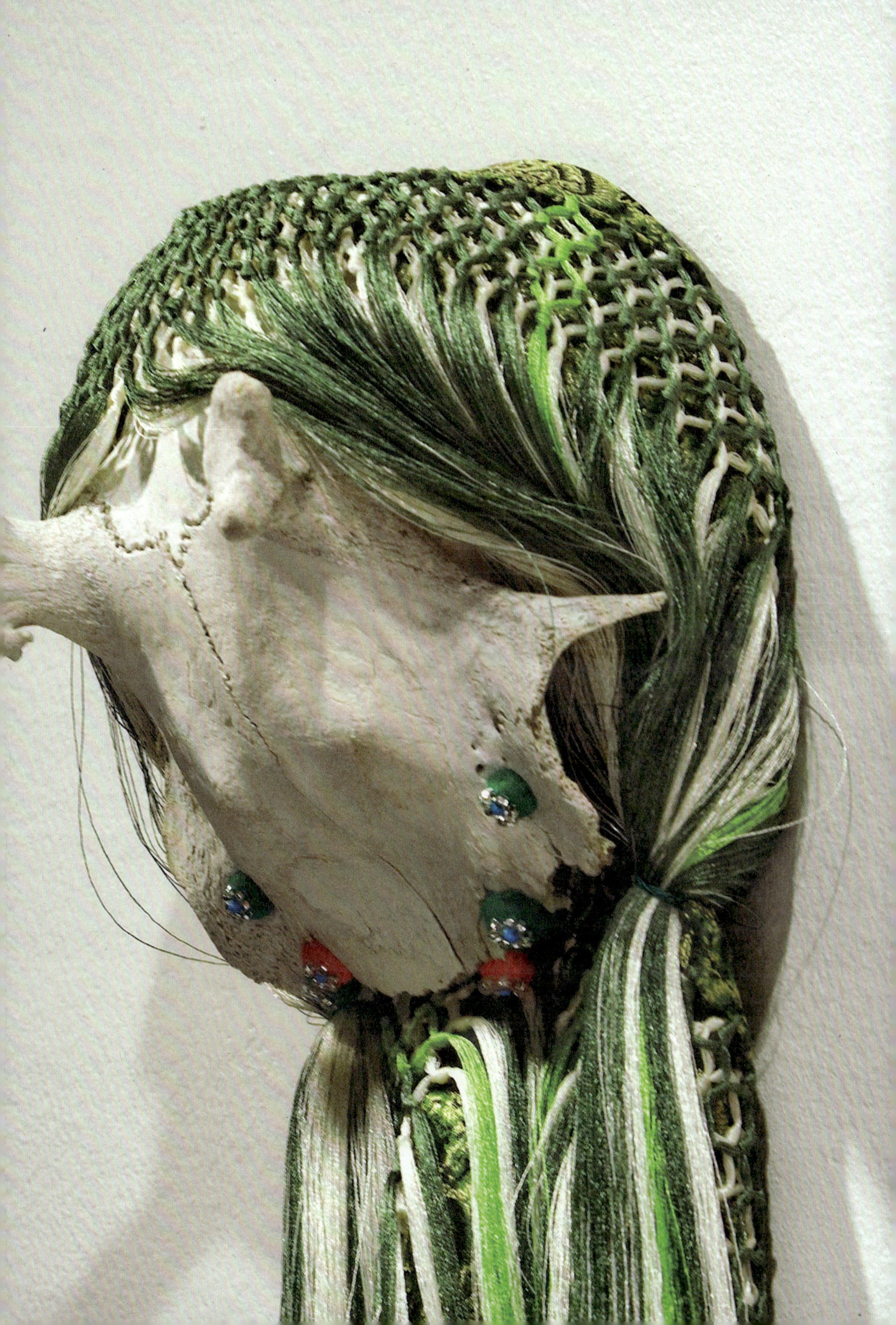

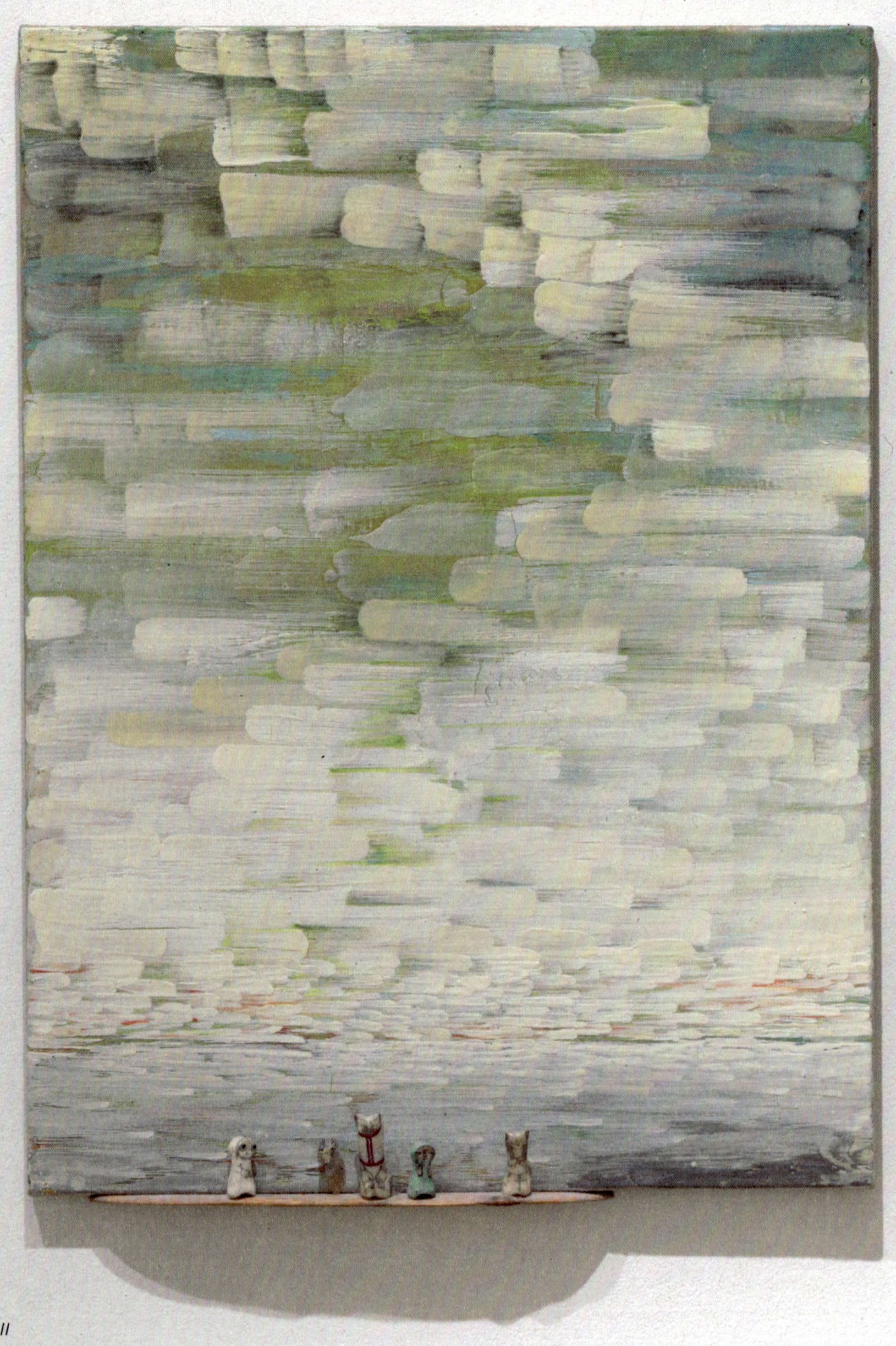

Murku II
Fog II
2008

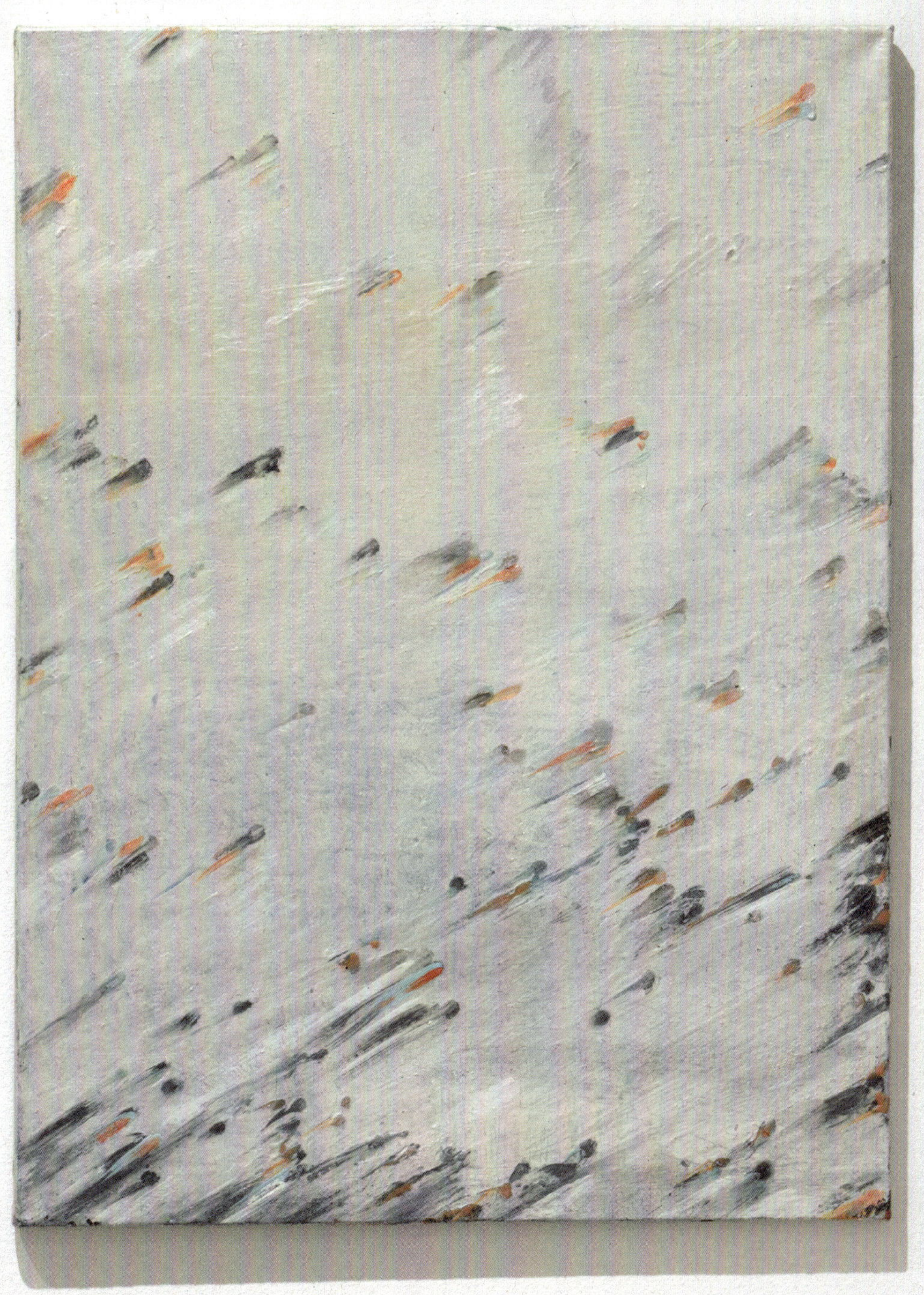

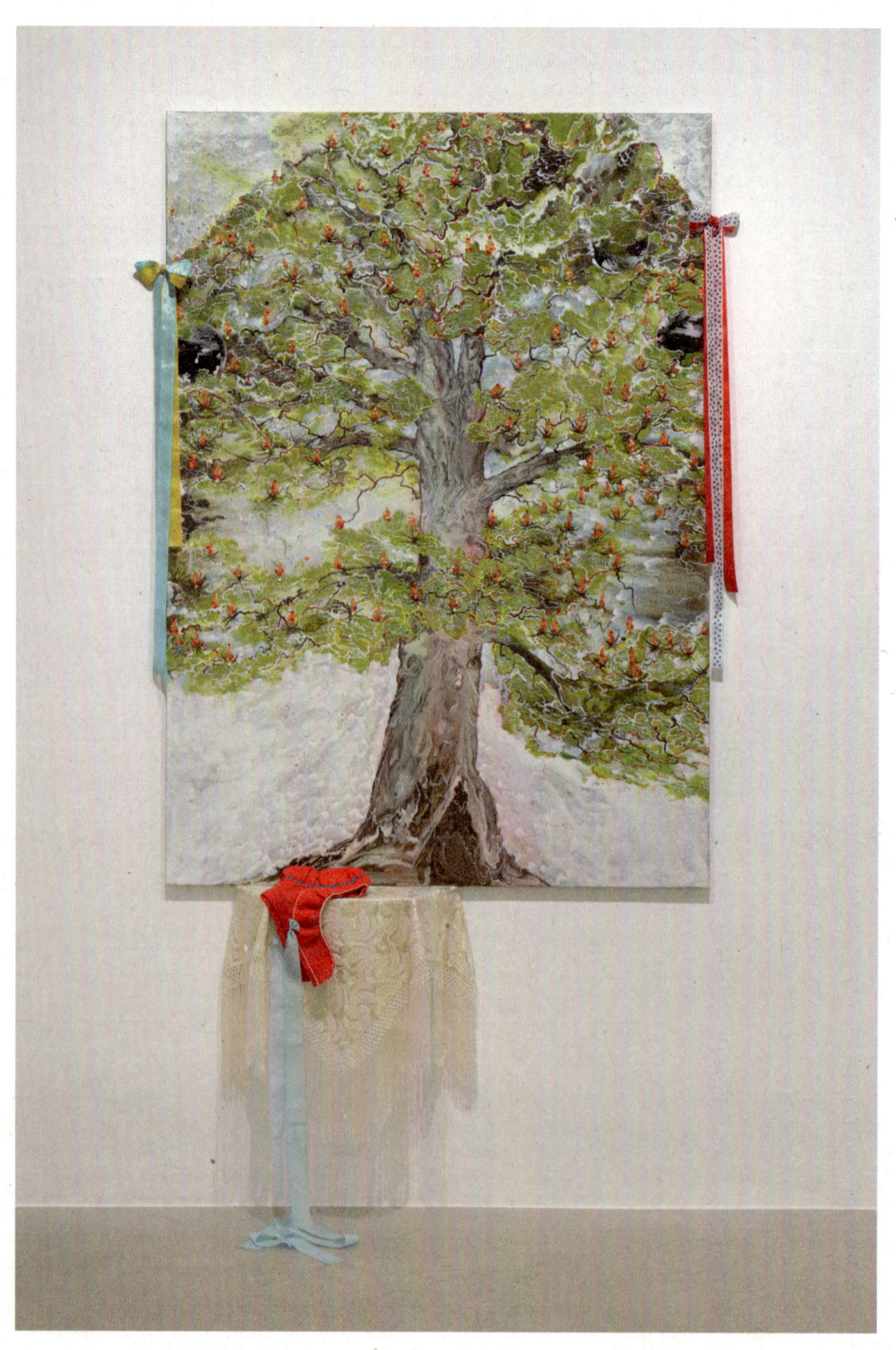

Áhku Dálkkasbeahci
Áhkku's Medicine-pine
2009

6   **Outi Pieski**

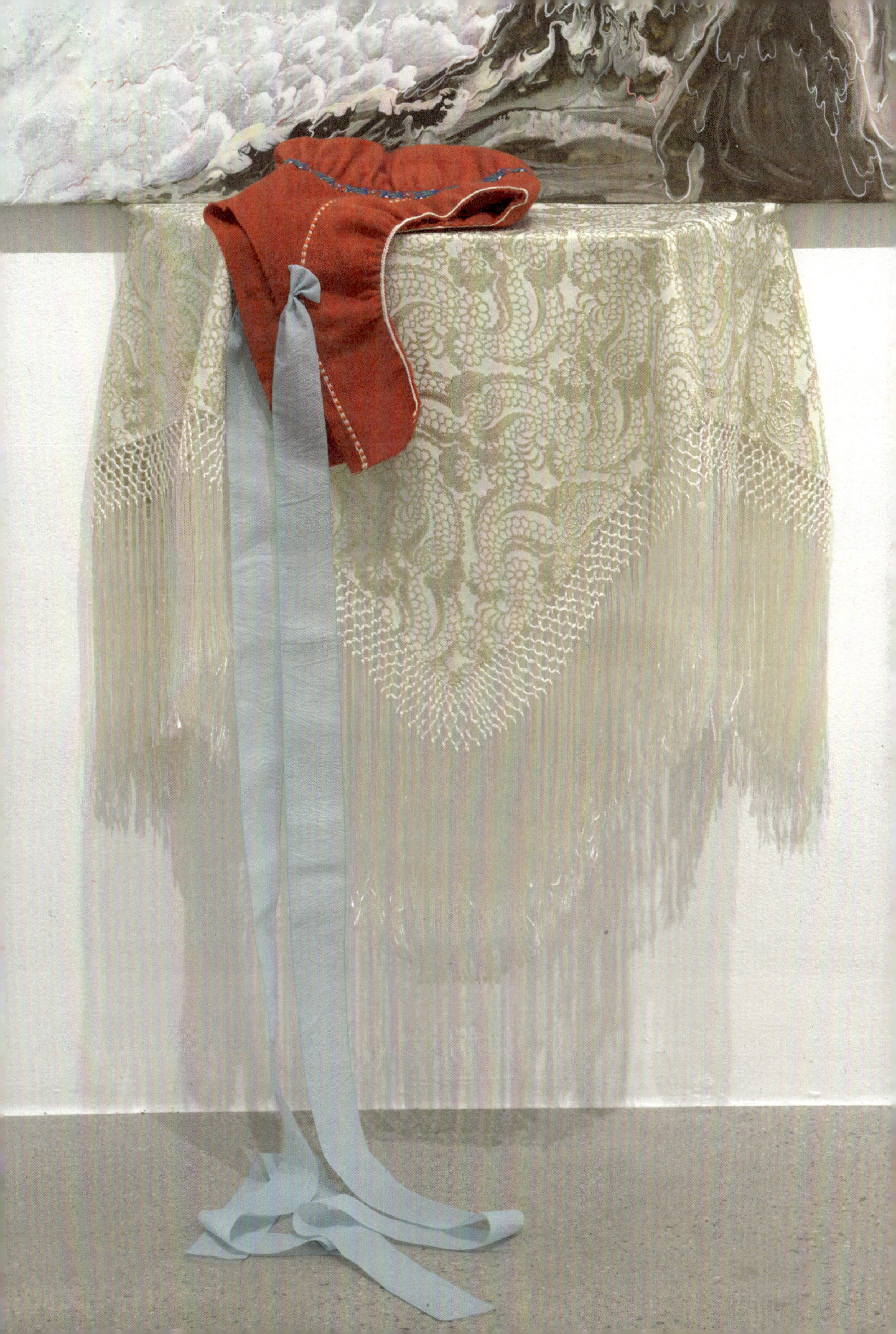

Giisavárri
Giisavárri Fell
2009

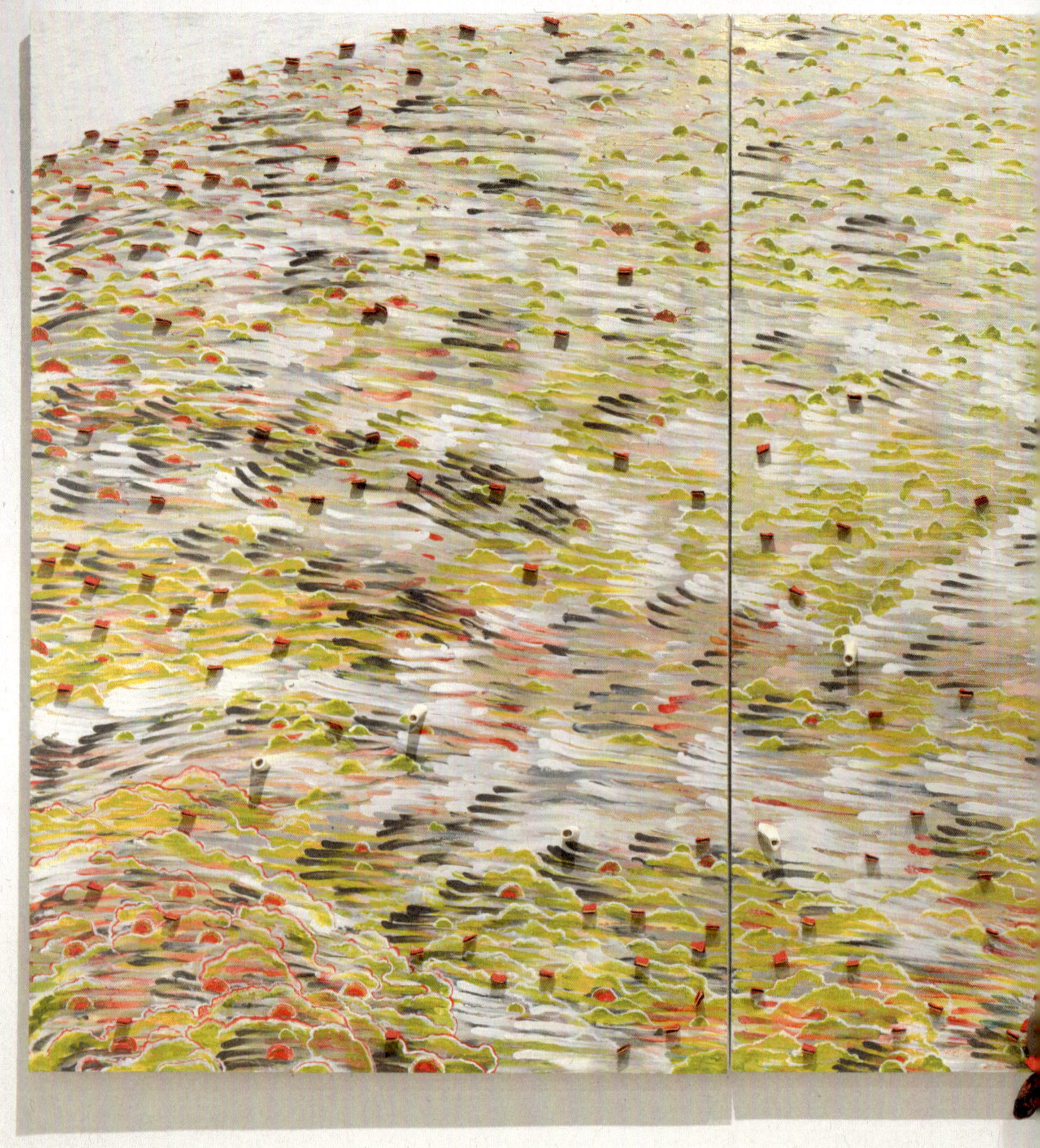

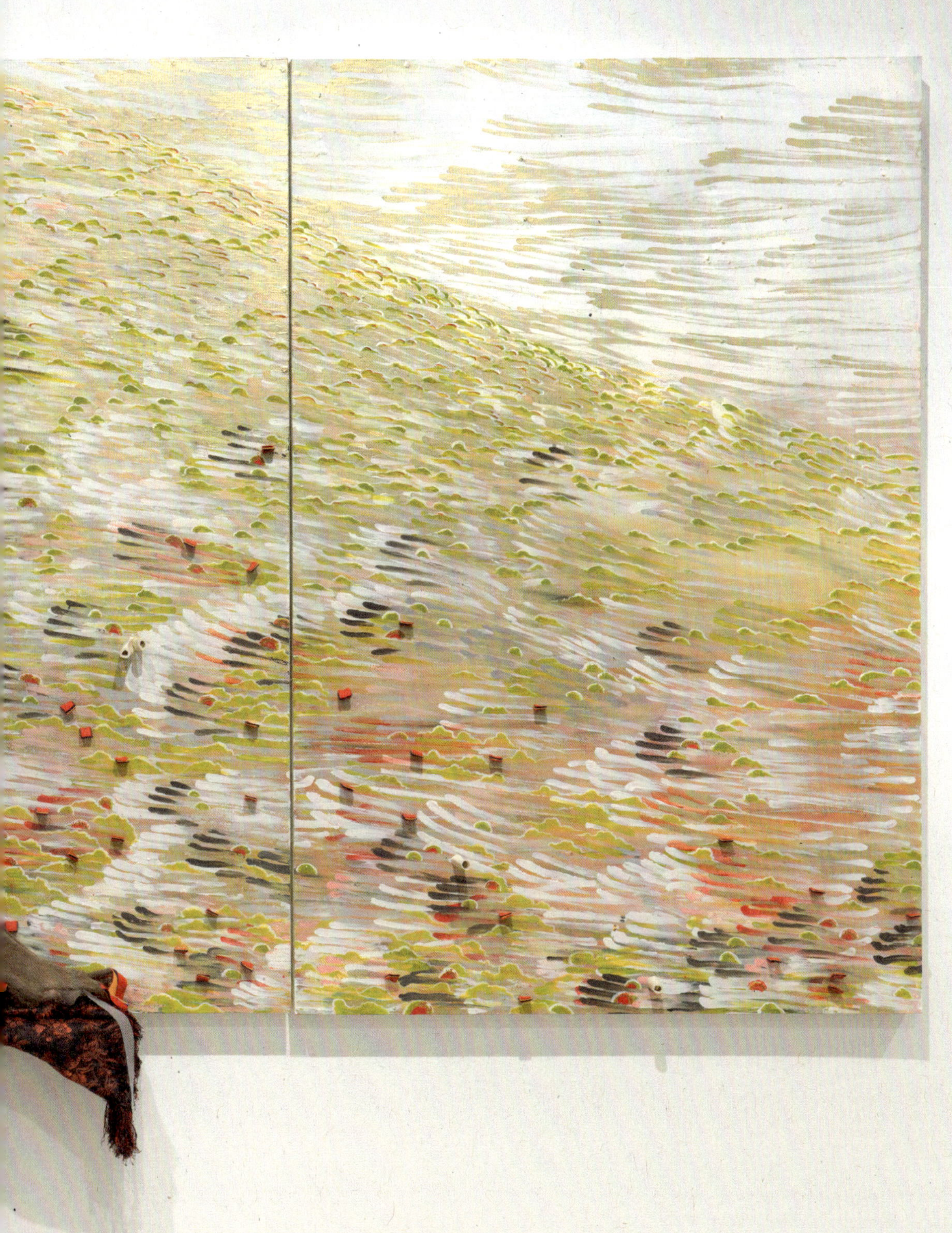

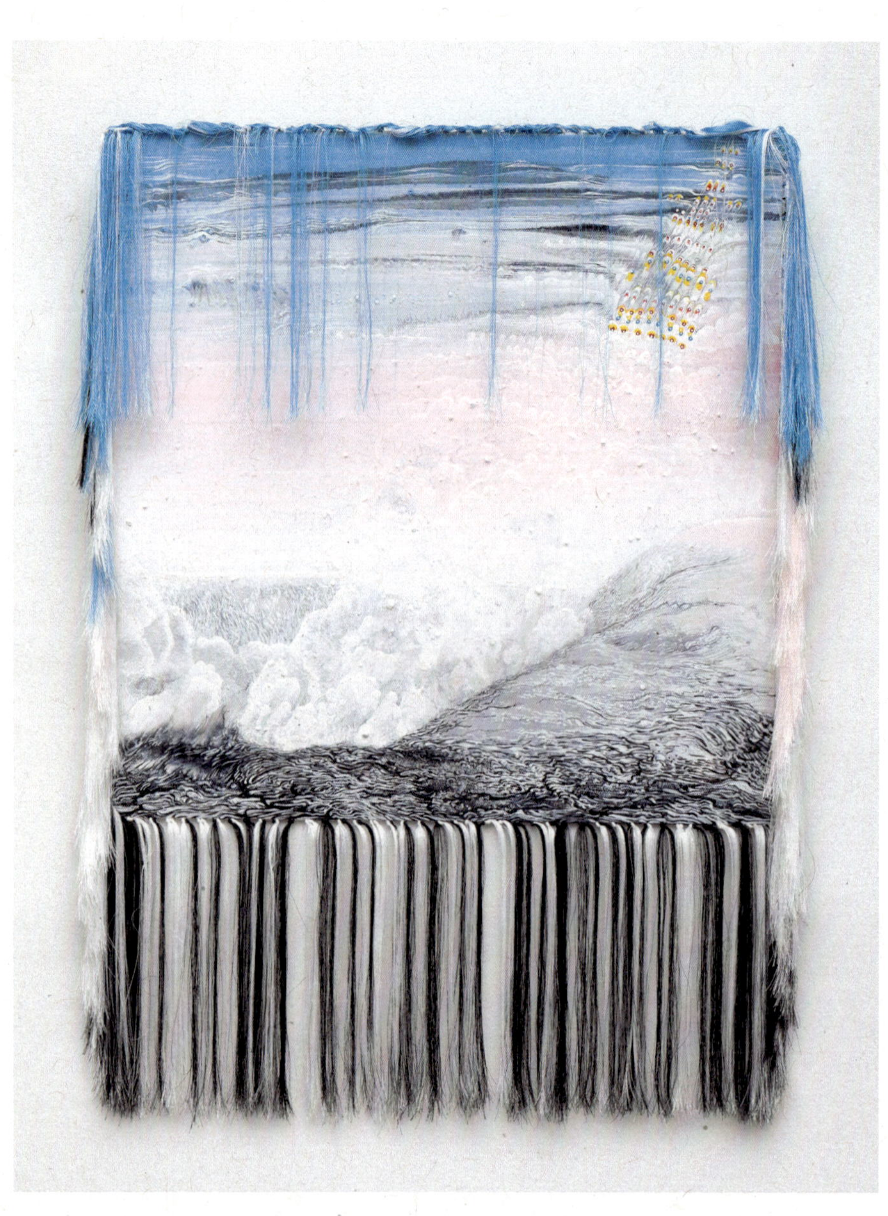

Nuvvos Áilegas feaskkir
The Corridor of Nuvvos Áilegas
2013

10   **Outi Pieski**

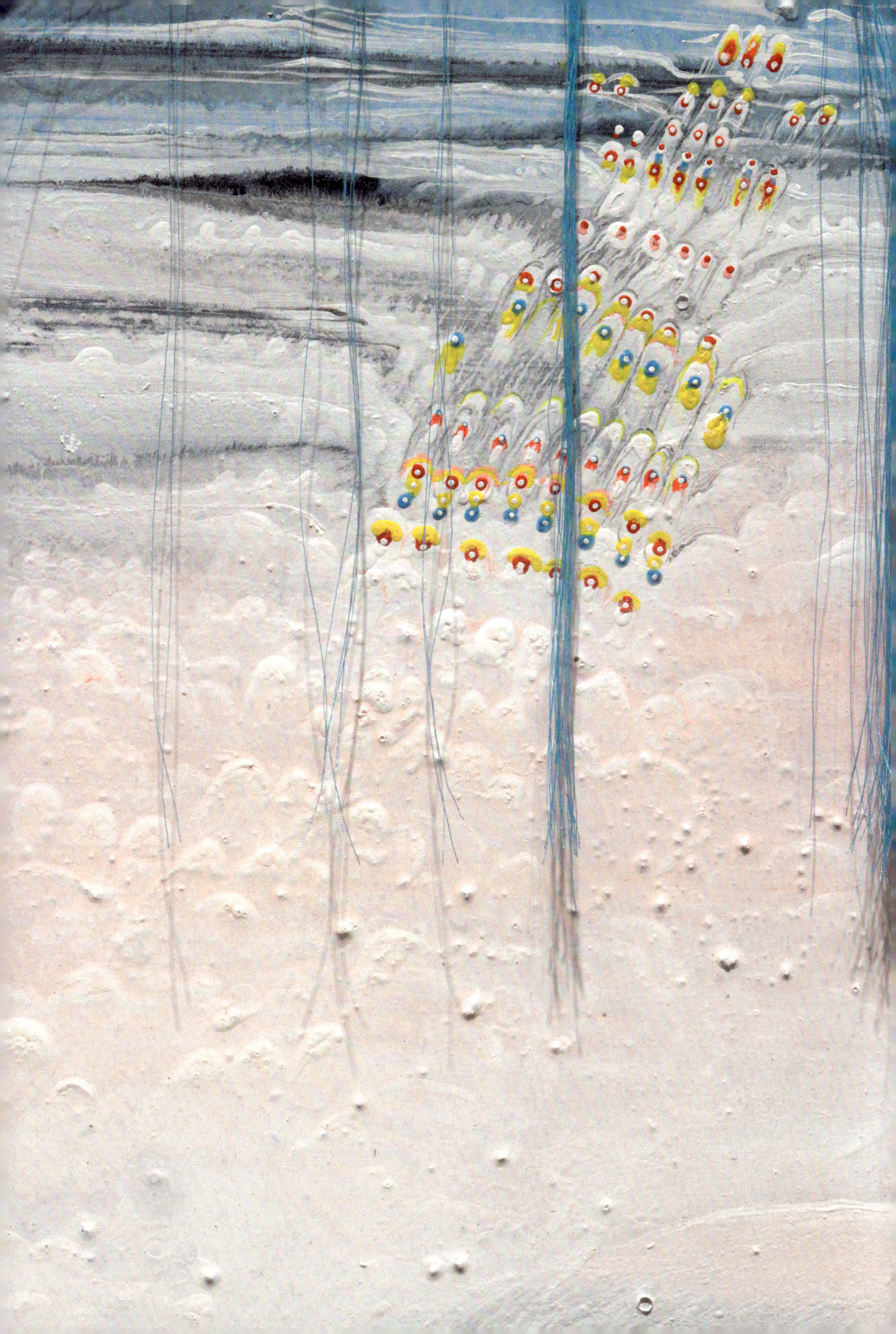

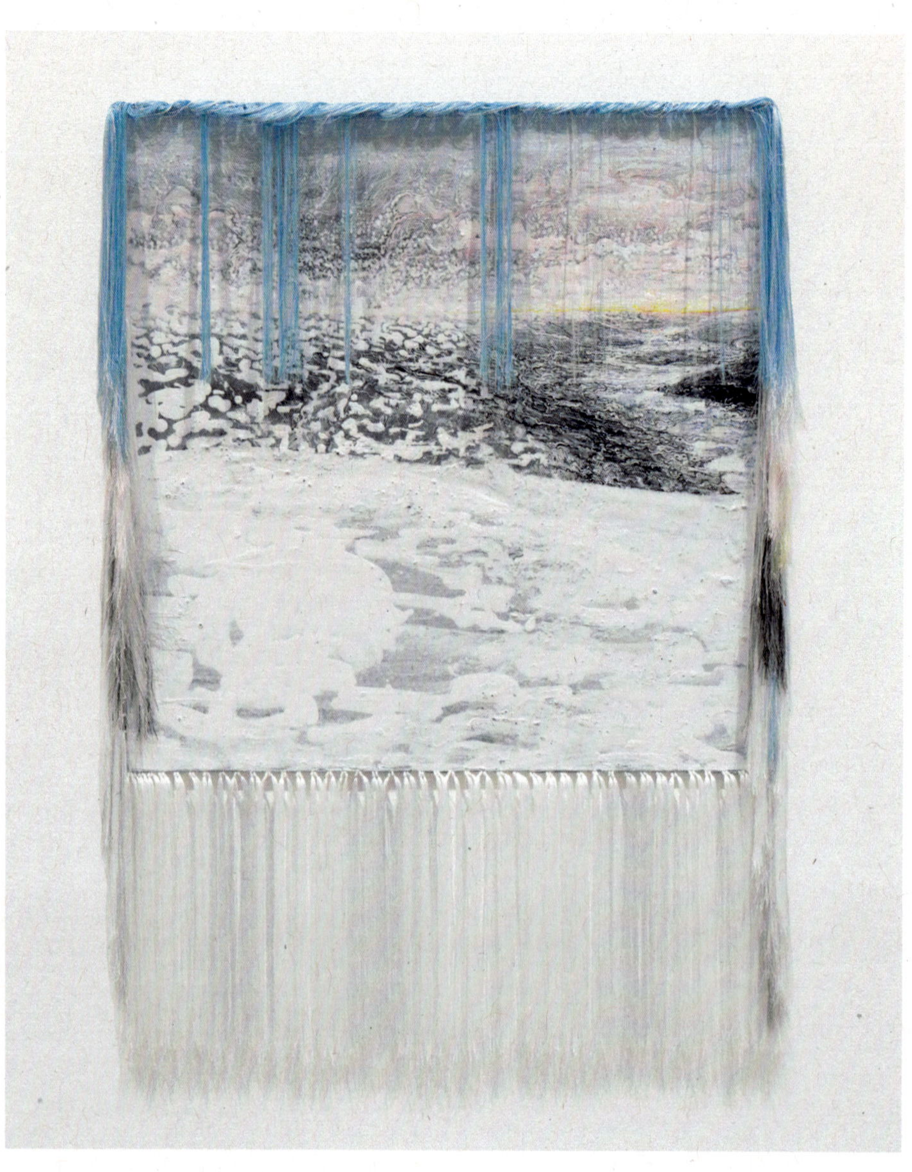

Nuvvos Áilegasa oaivvis
Top of the Nuvvos Áilegas
2013

Nuvvos Áilegas, dulvi
Nuvvos Áilegas, flood
2011

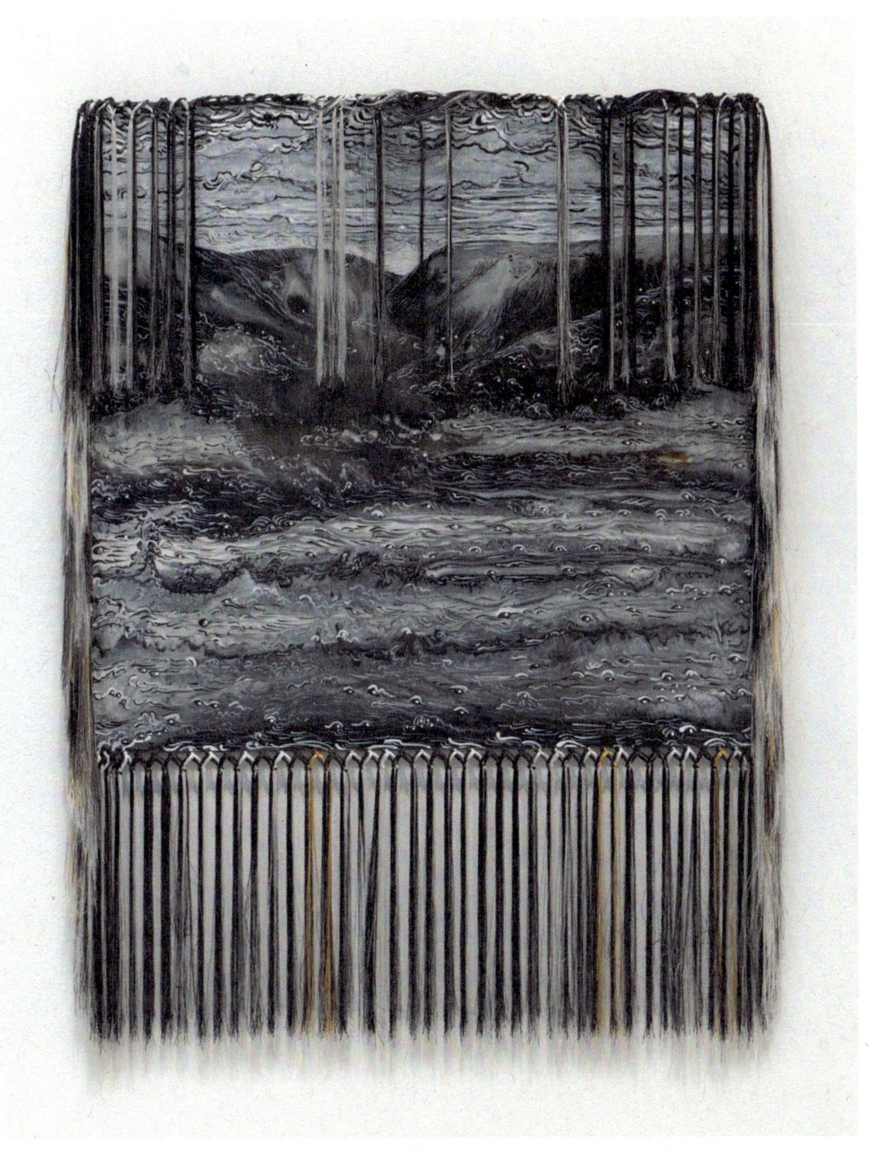

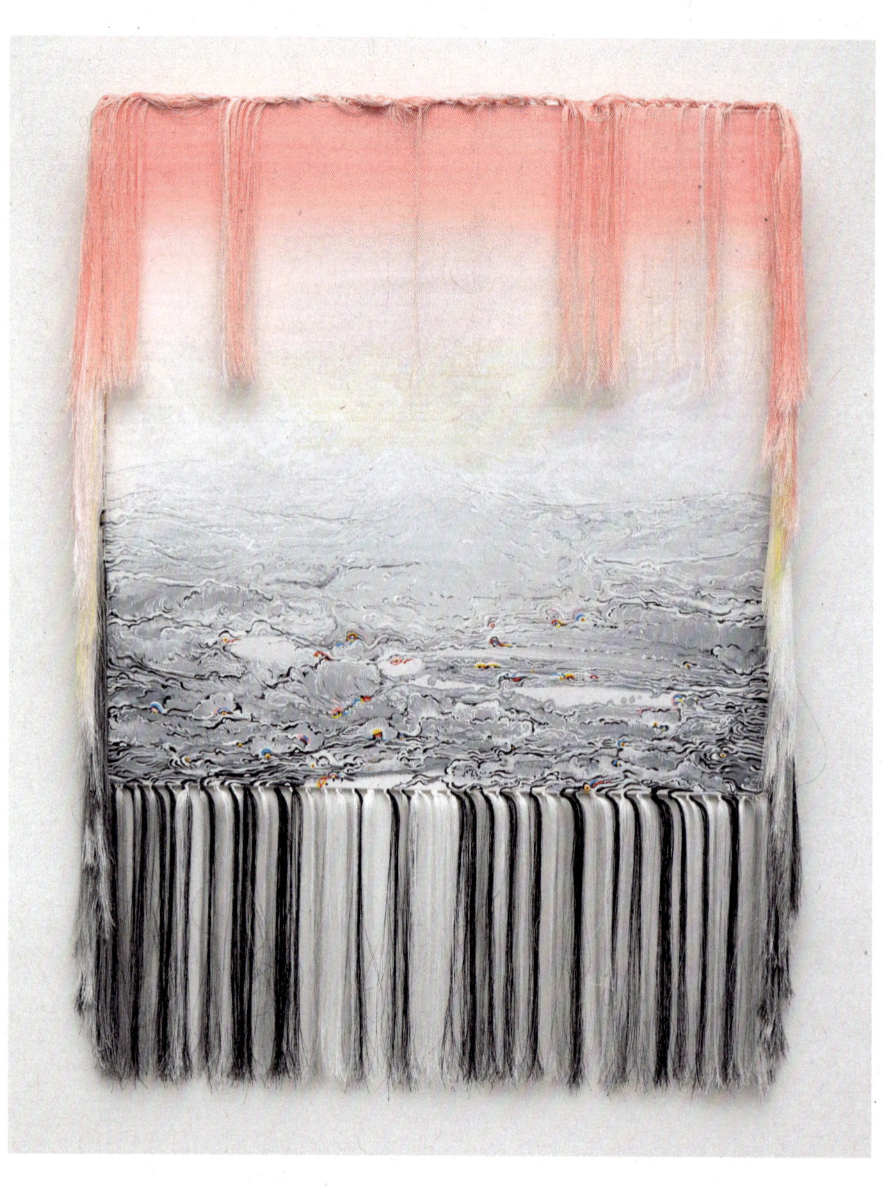

Nuvvos Áilegas, oaidnemeahttun
Nuvvos Áilegas, Fell Unseen
2013

Nuvvos Áilegas, českes
Fell Nuvvos Áilegas in White
2011

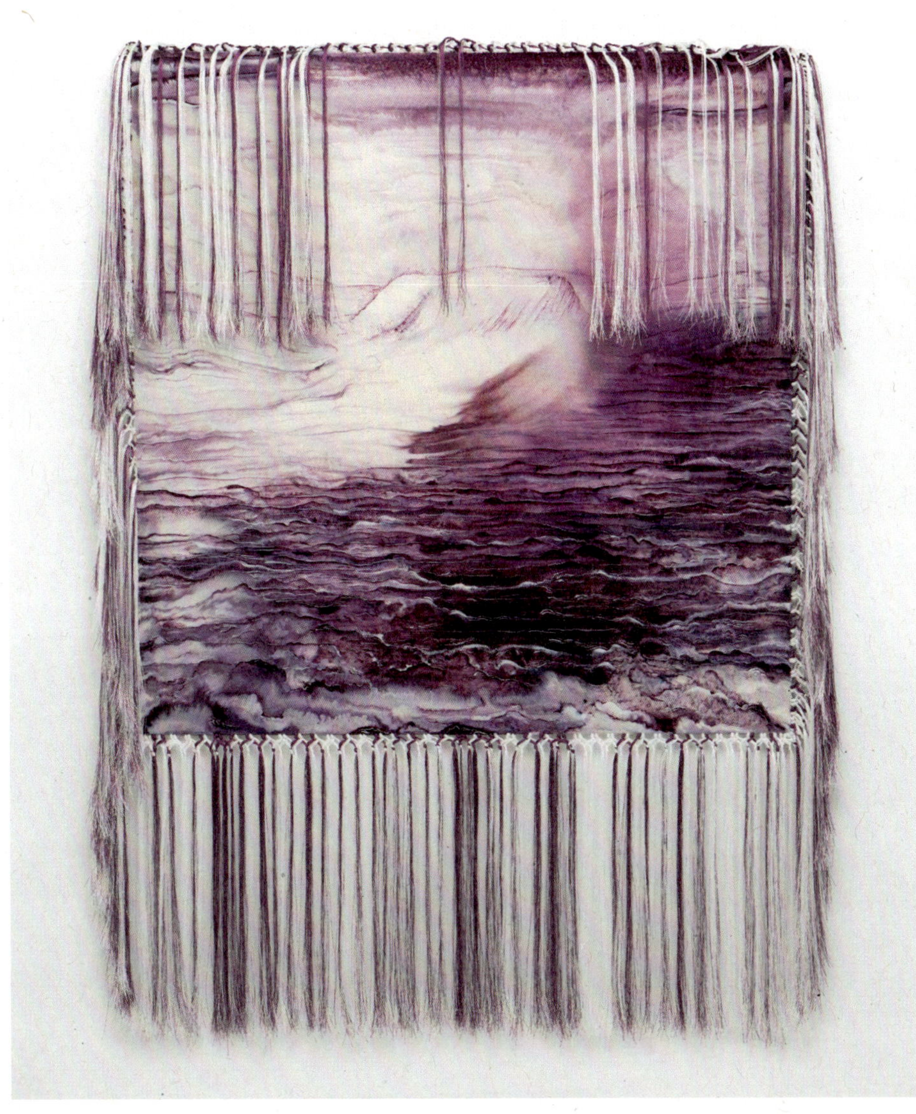

15   Outi Pieski

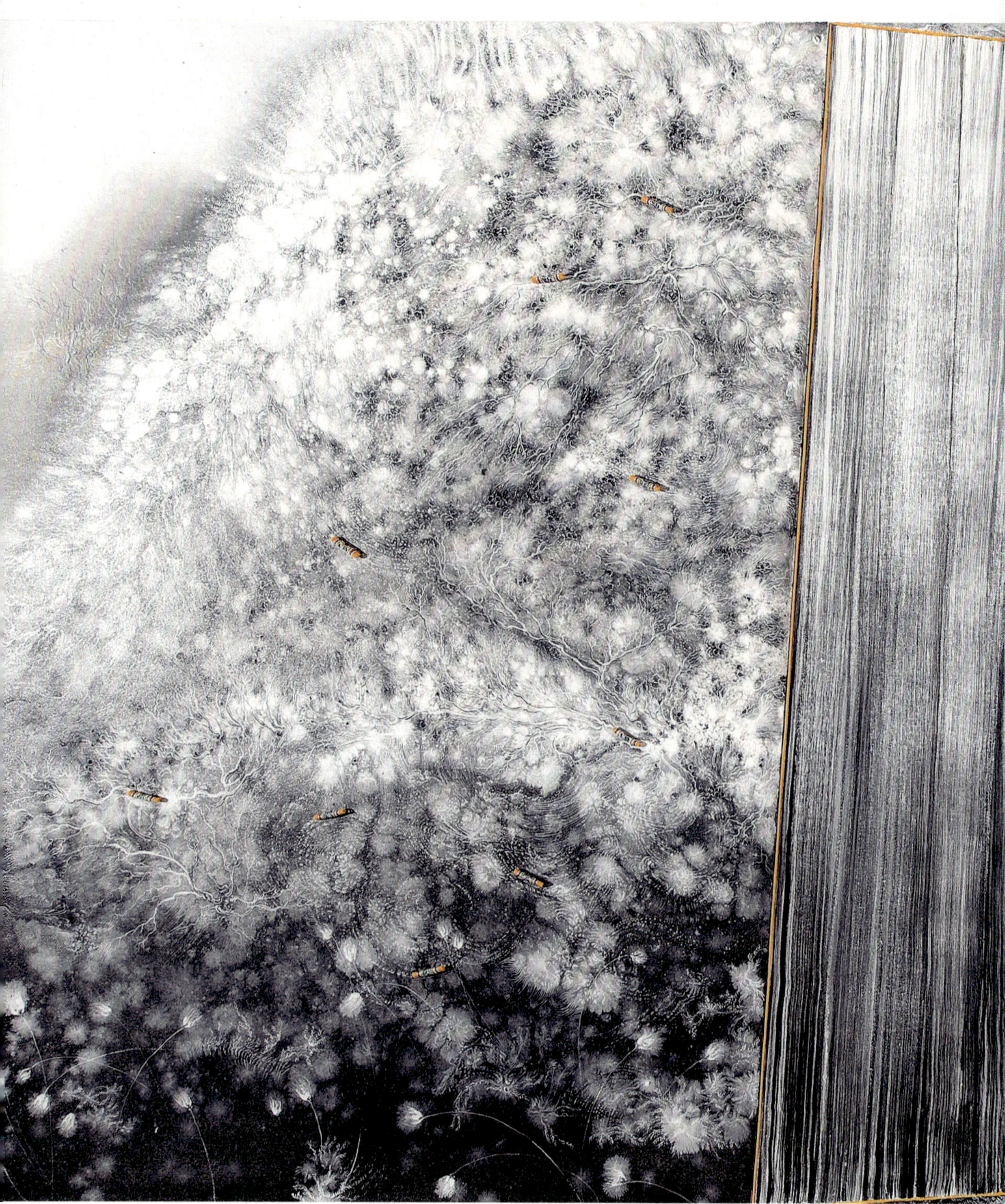

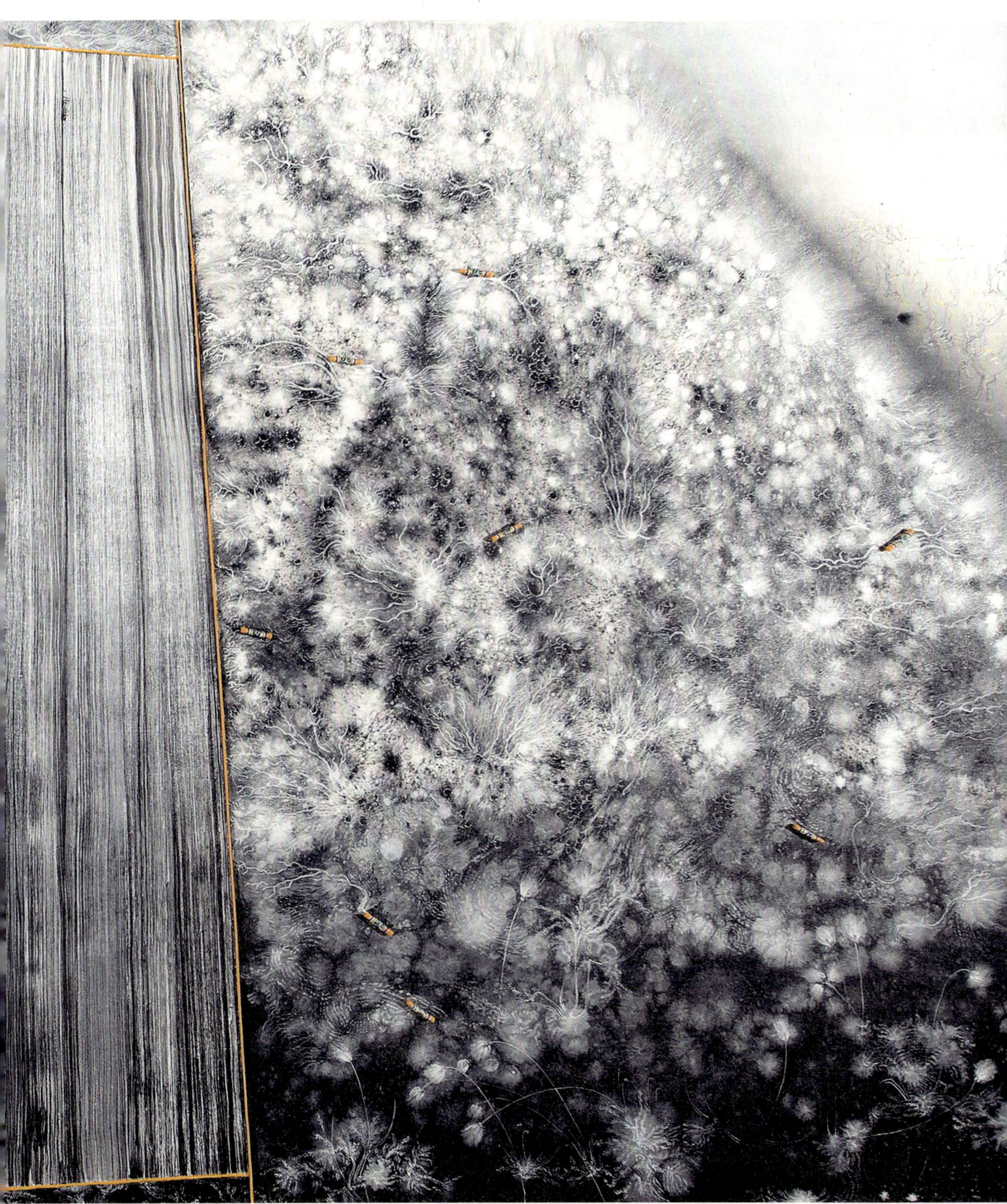

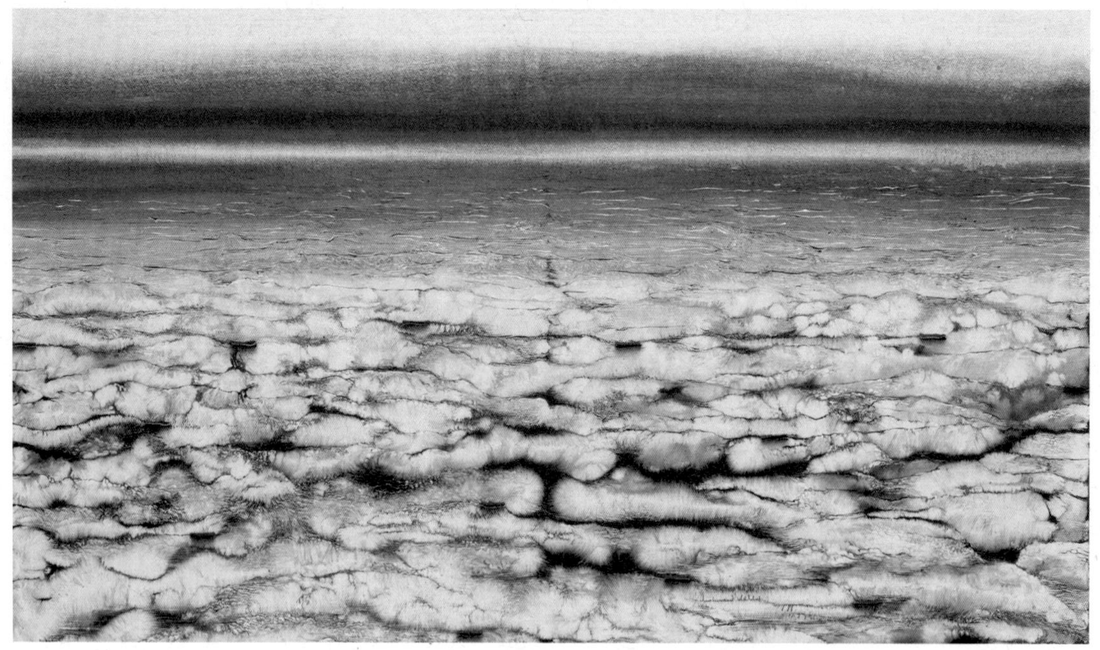

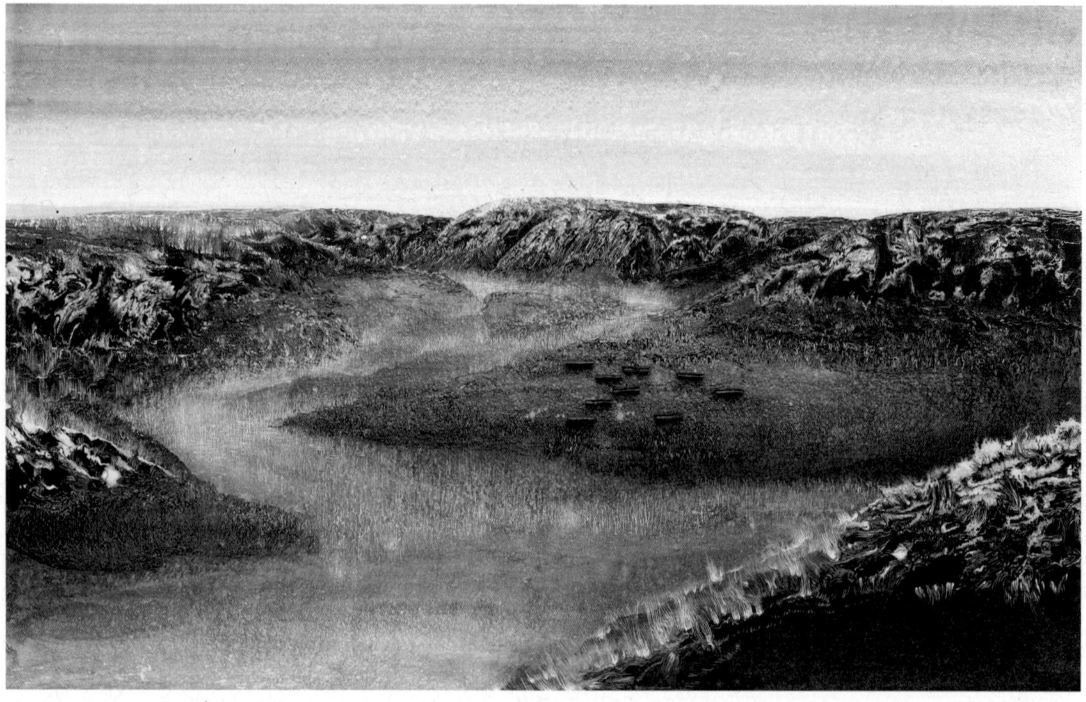

Rádjajohtin I
Pacing the Borders I
2014

Rádjajohtin III
Pacing the Borders III
2014

Iehčanas vuoigatvuohta leat ja lieđđut
Independent Right to Exist and Flourish
2018

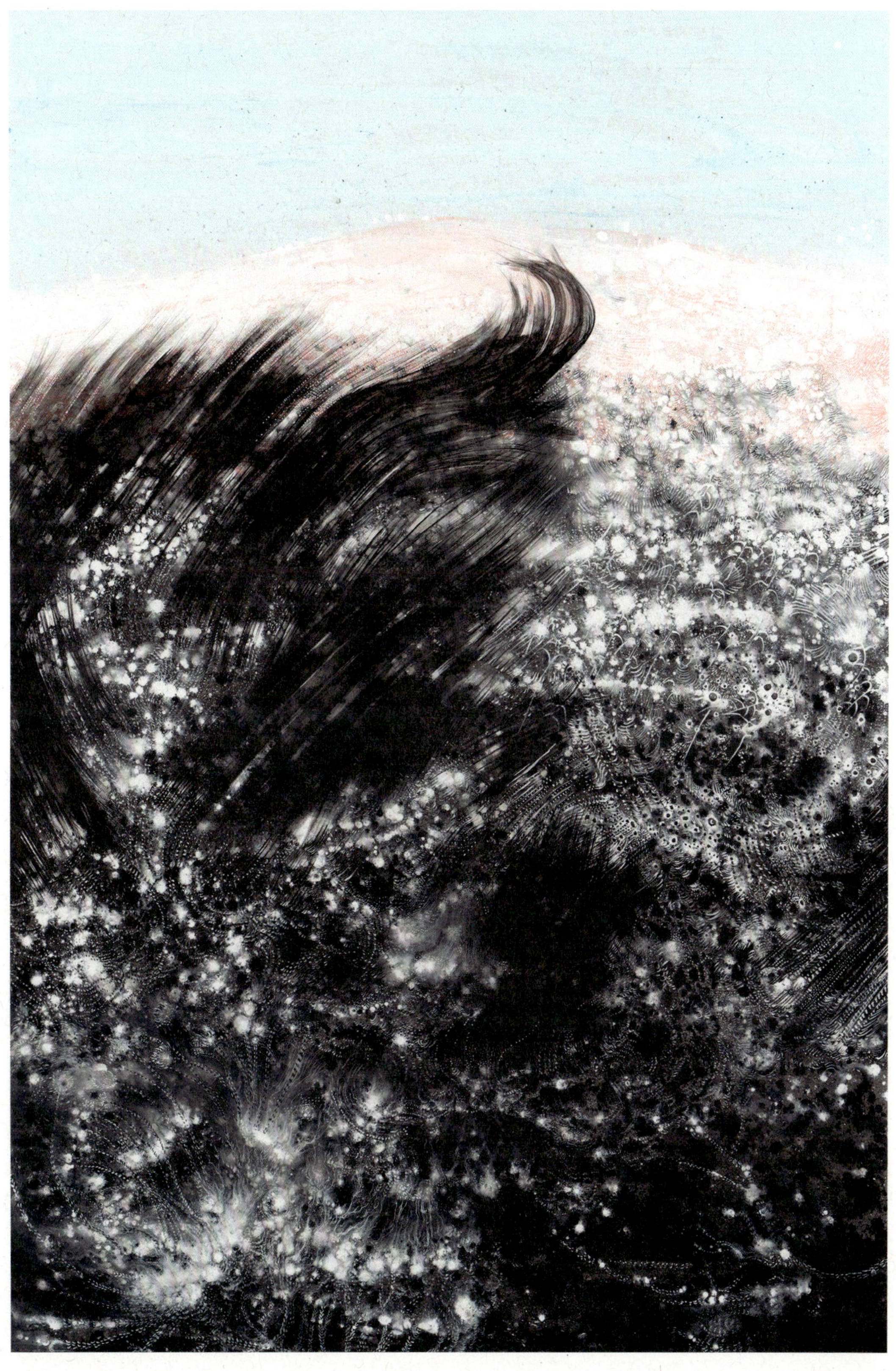

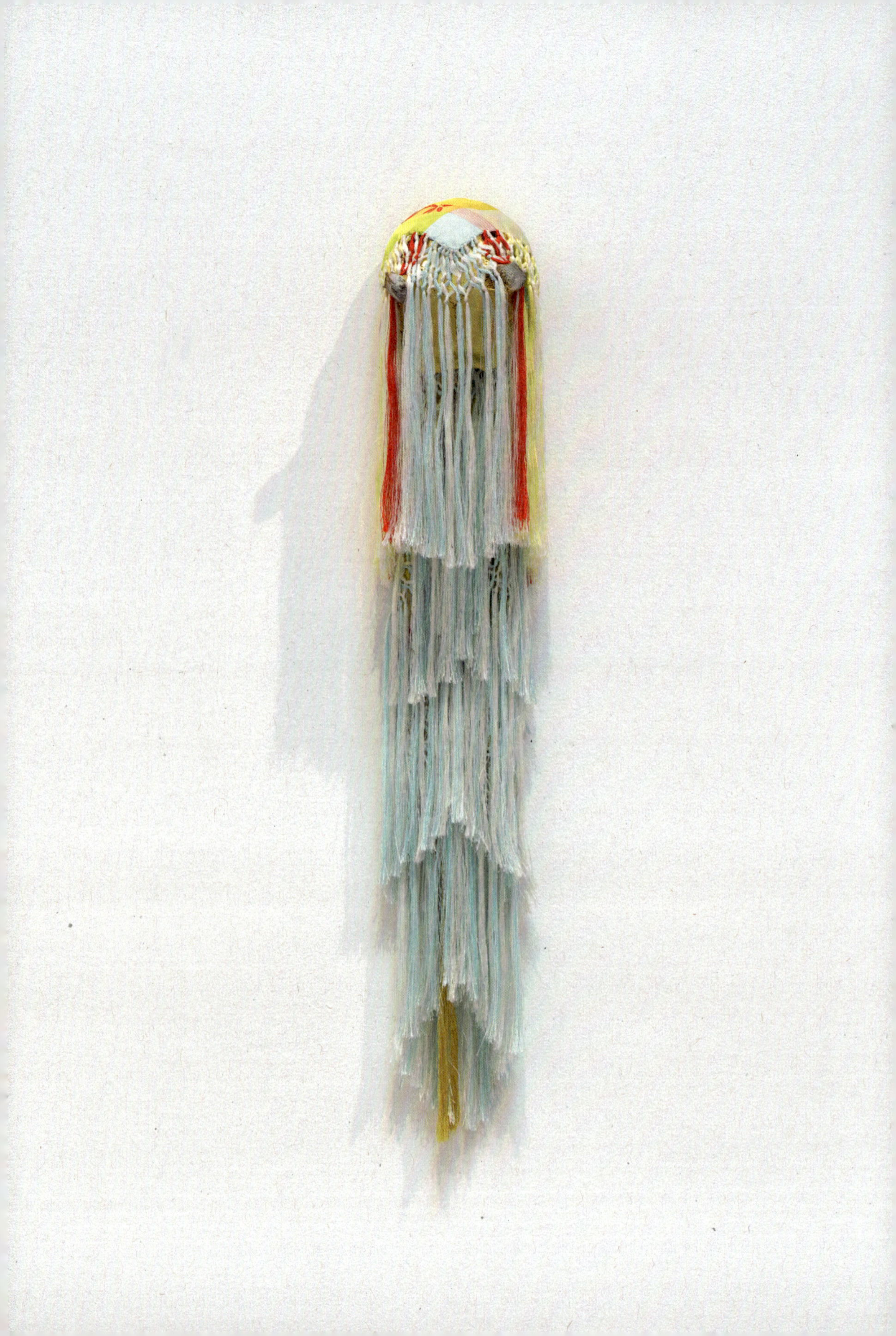

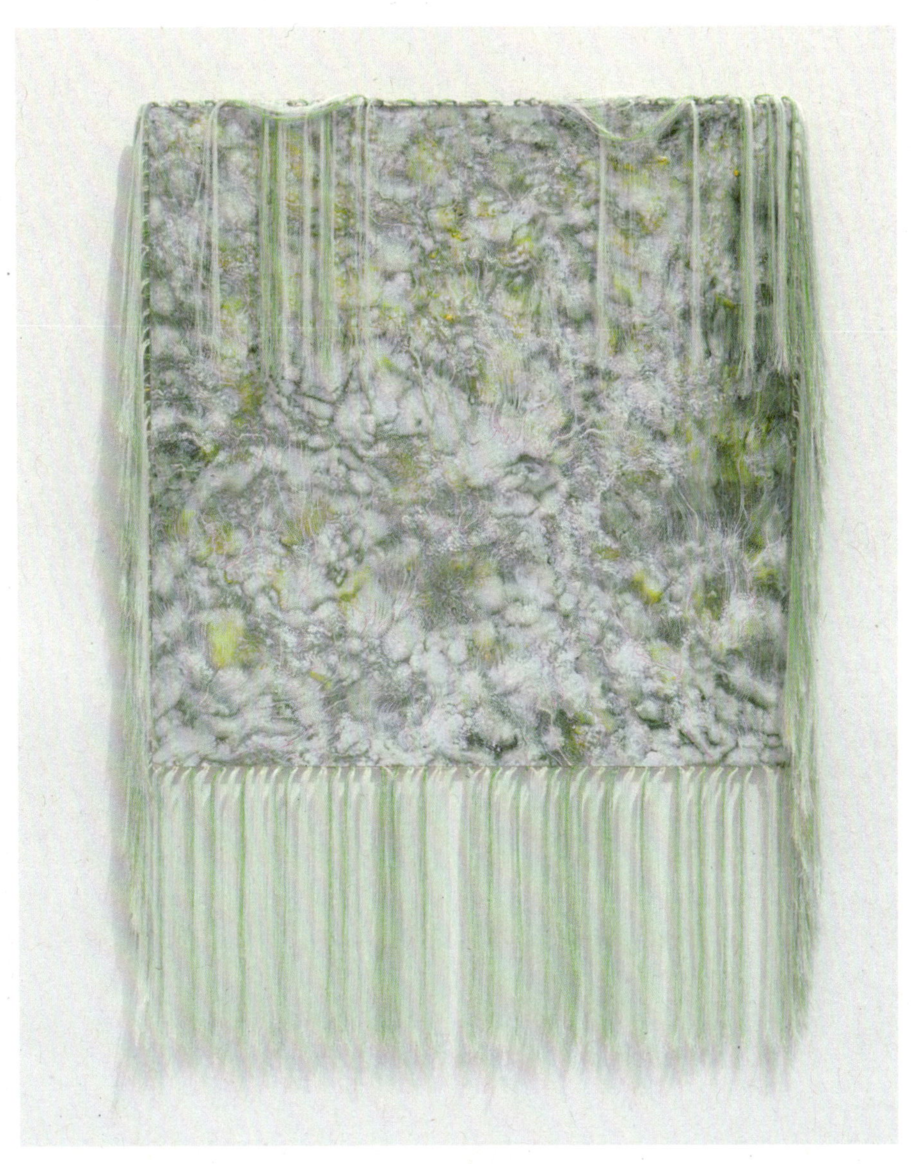

Gorži
Waterfall
2016

Bovdna
Tussock
2012

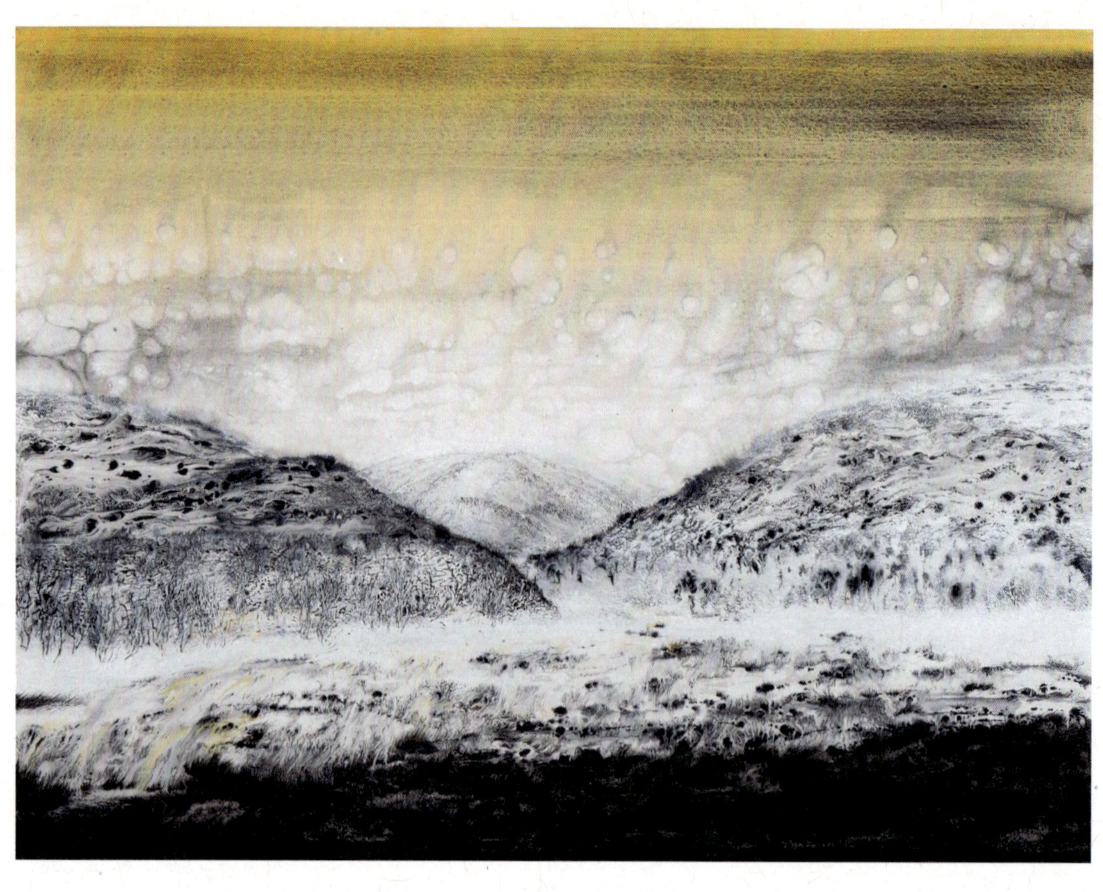

Oh, Gárdečohka
2014

Deatnu ijabealde
Deatnu River by the Night (detail)
2013

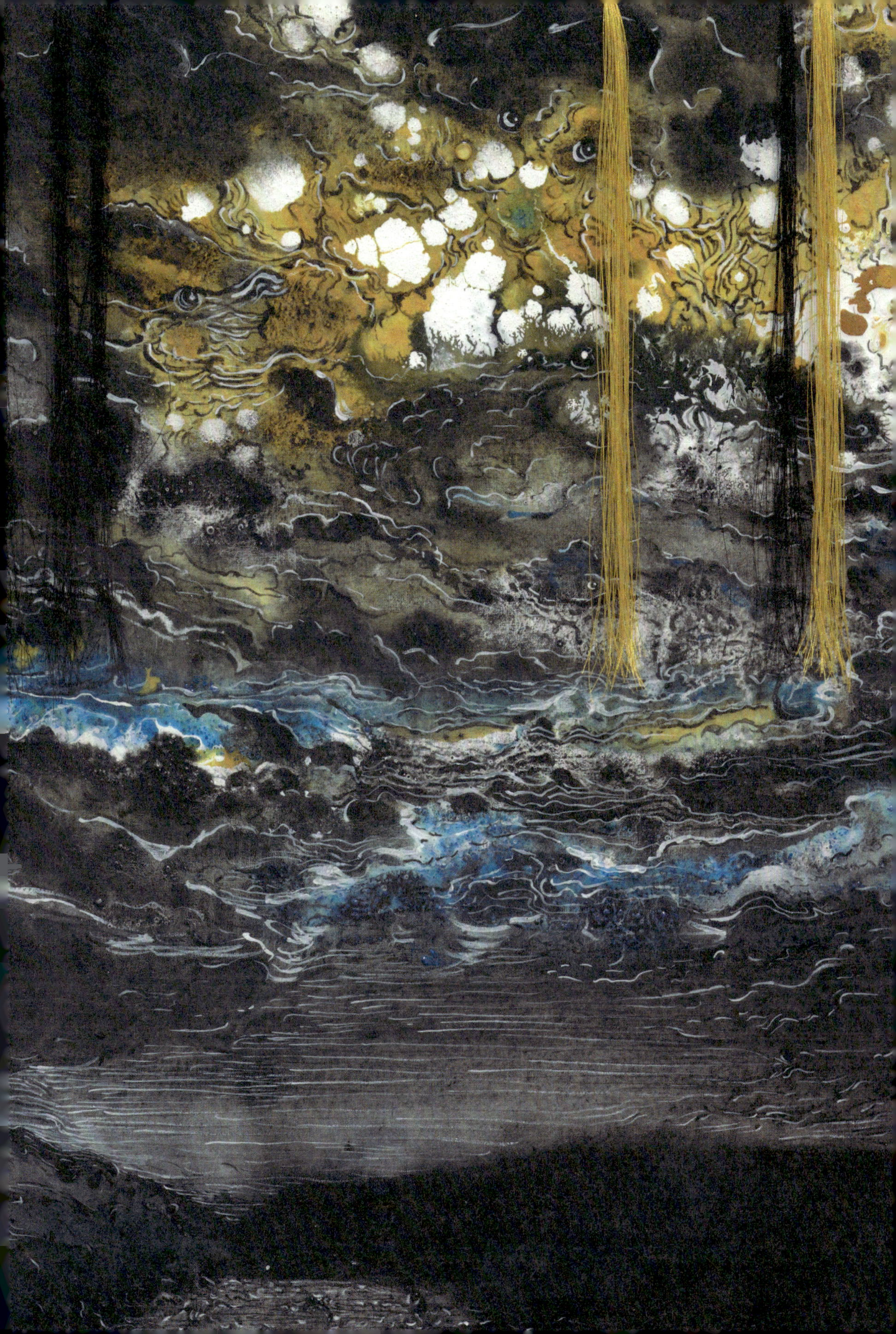

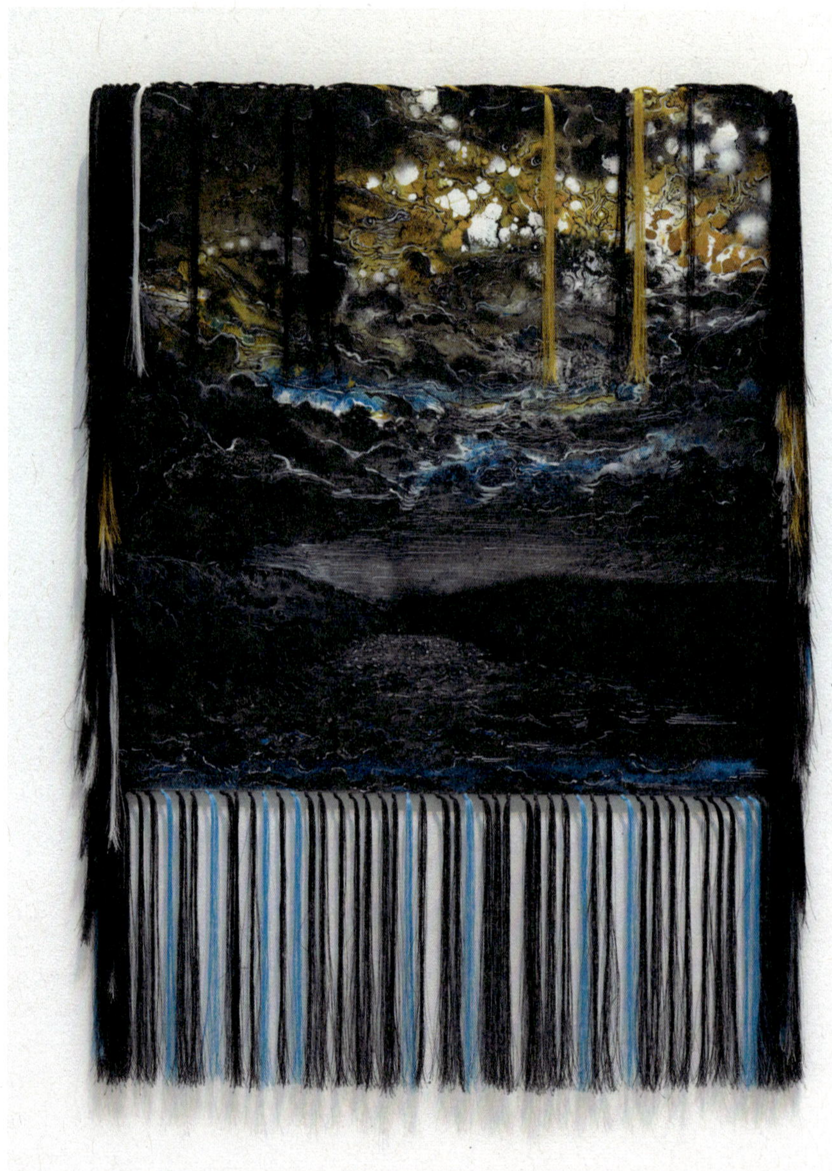

Deatnu ijabealde
Deatnu River by the Night
2013

Gollejohka
River of Gold
2014

24   Outi Pieski

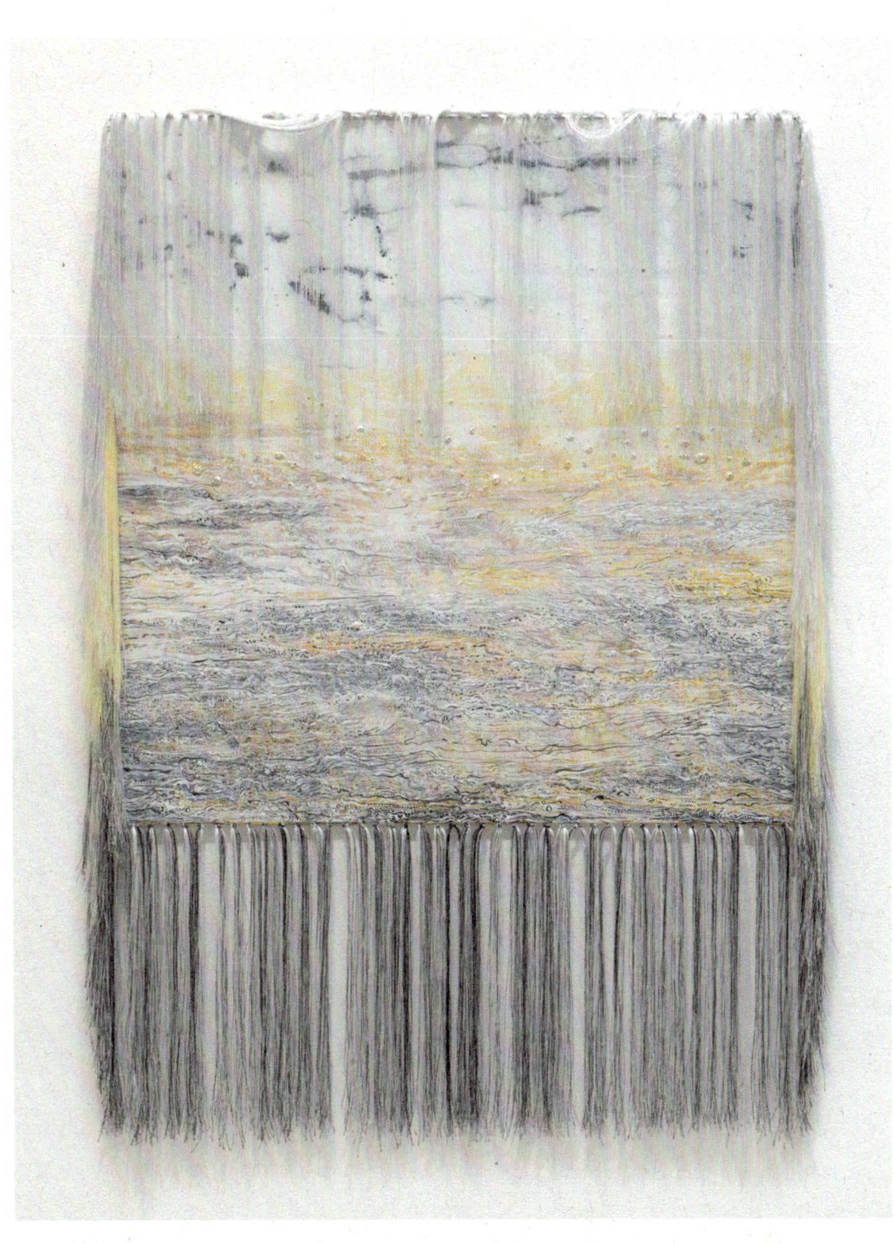

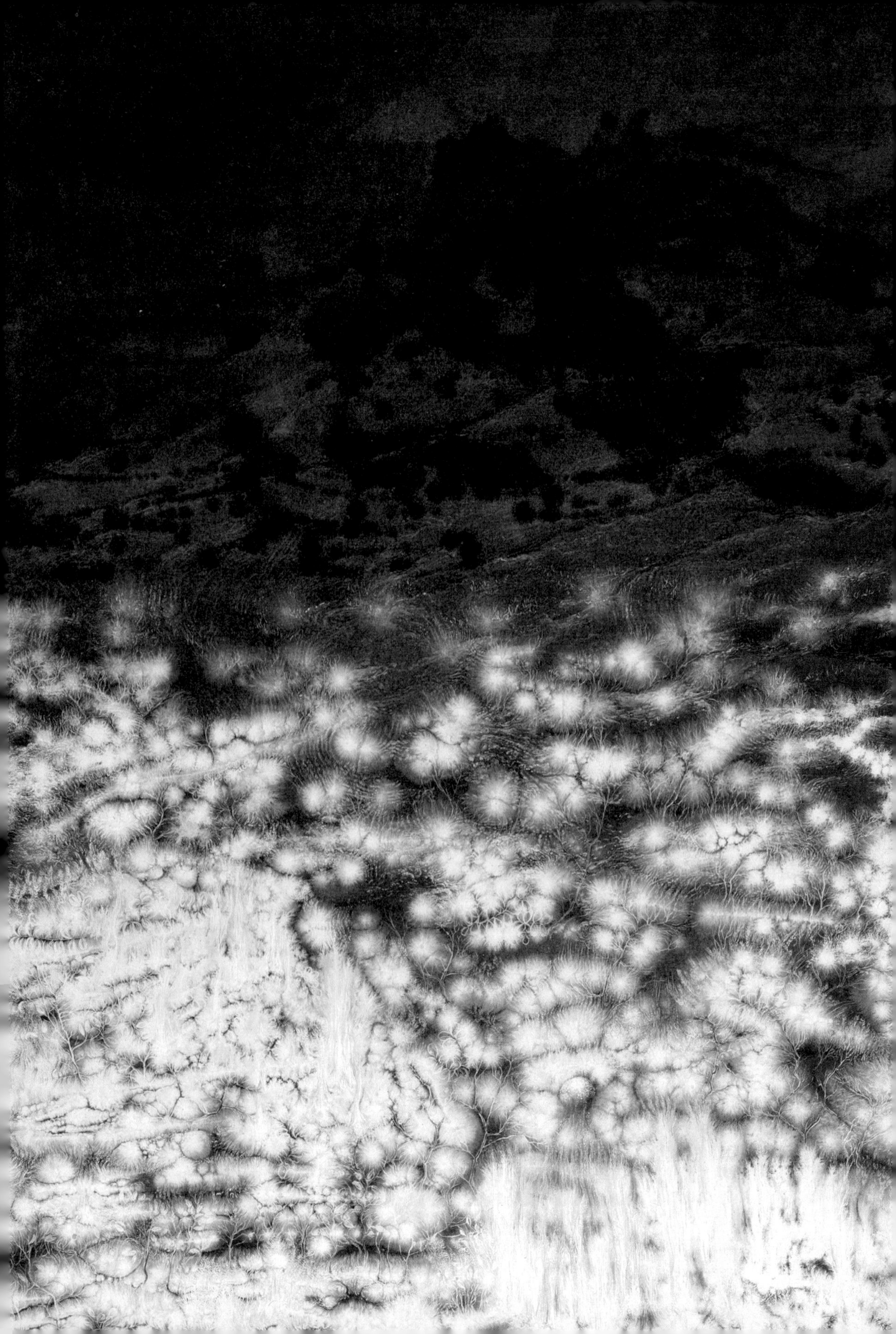

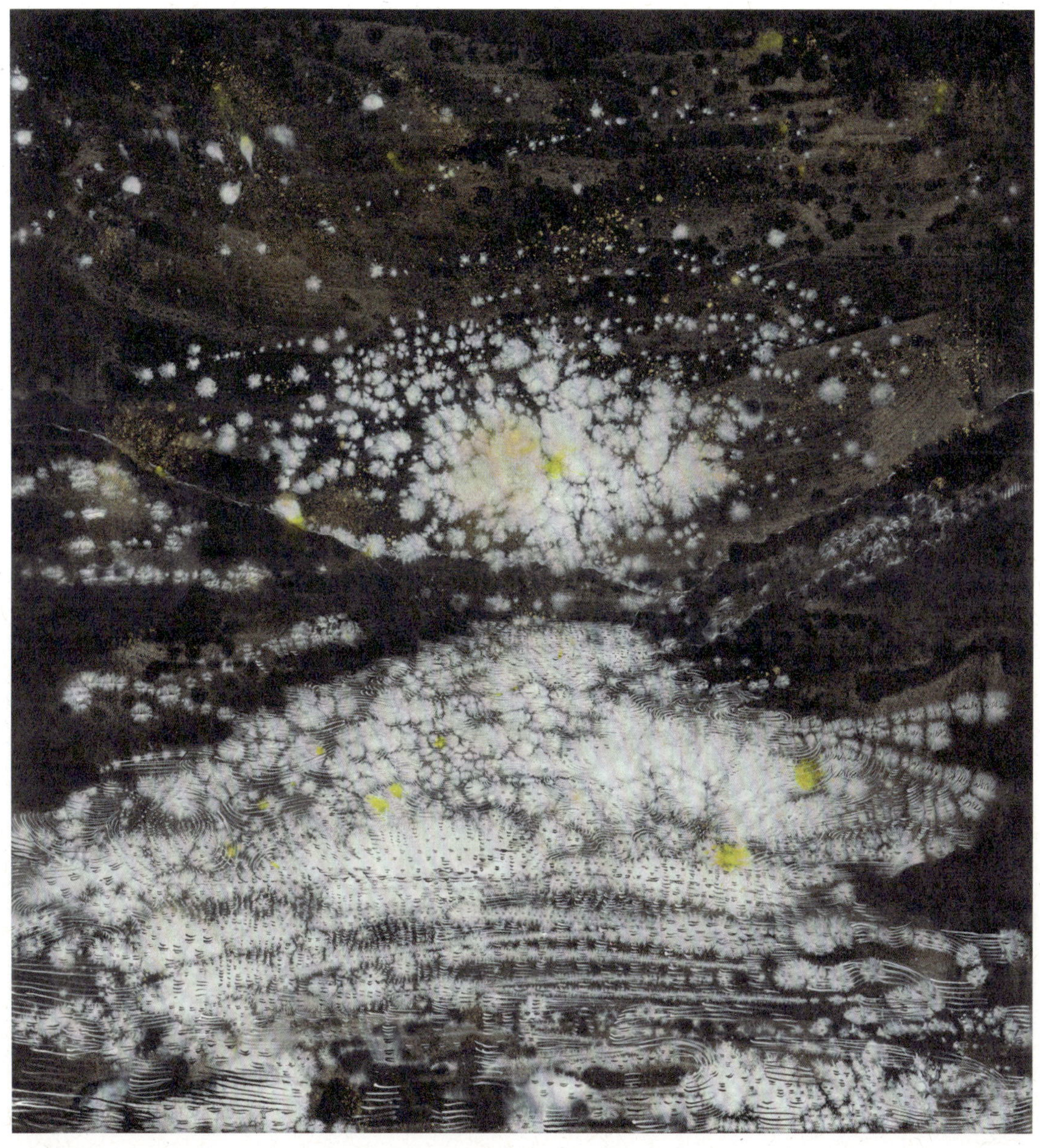

Opposite:
*Gurra
Gorge*
2014

Above and next spread:
*Deatnu, máttožan
Deatnu River, Our
Ancestor*
2018

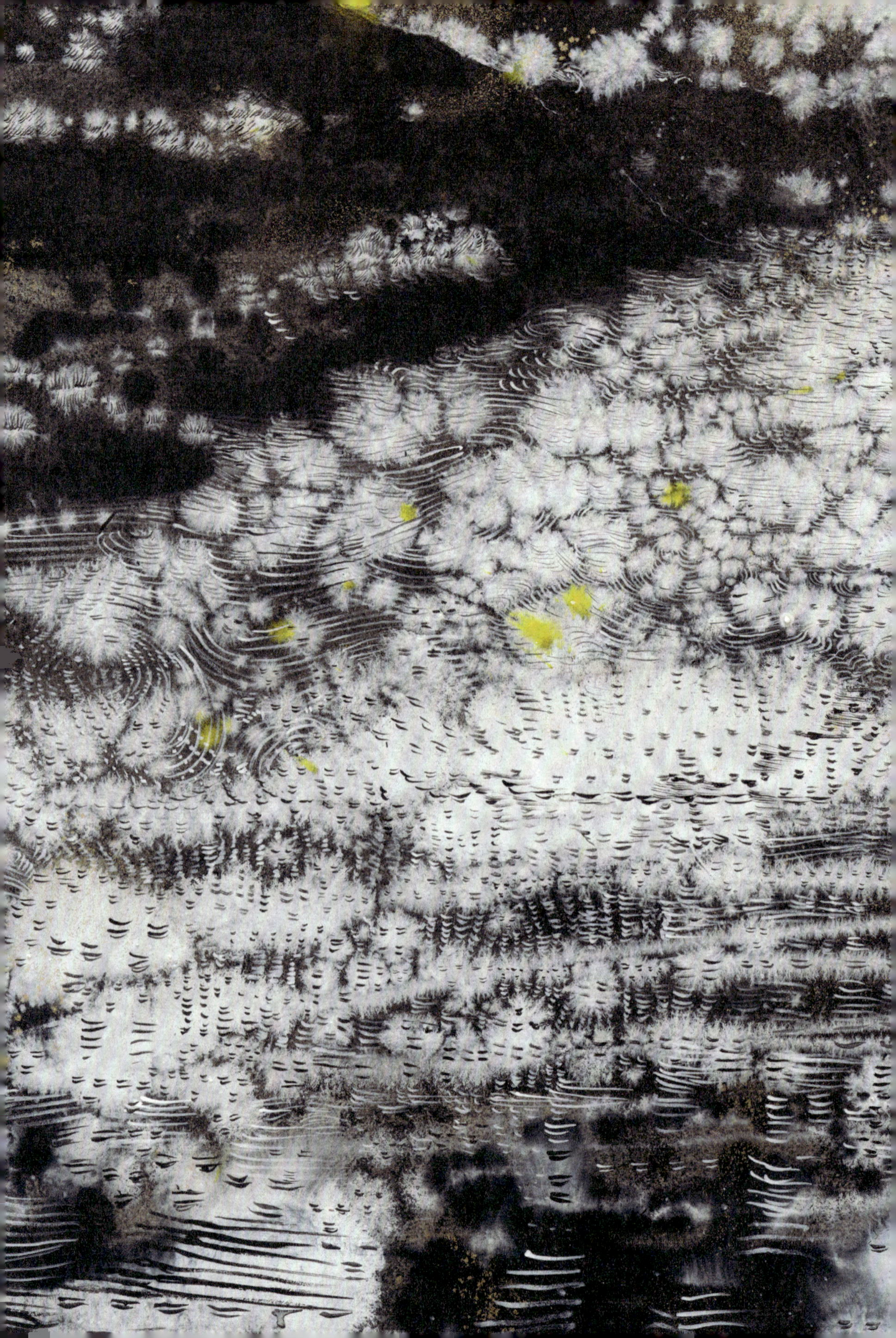

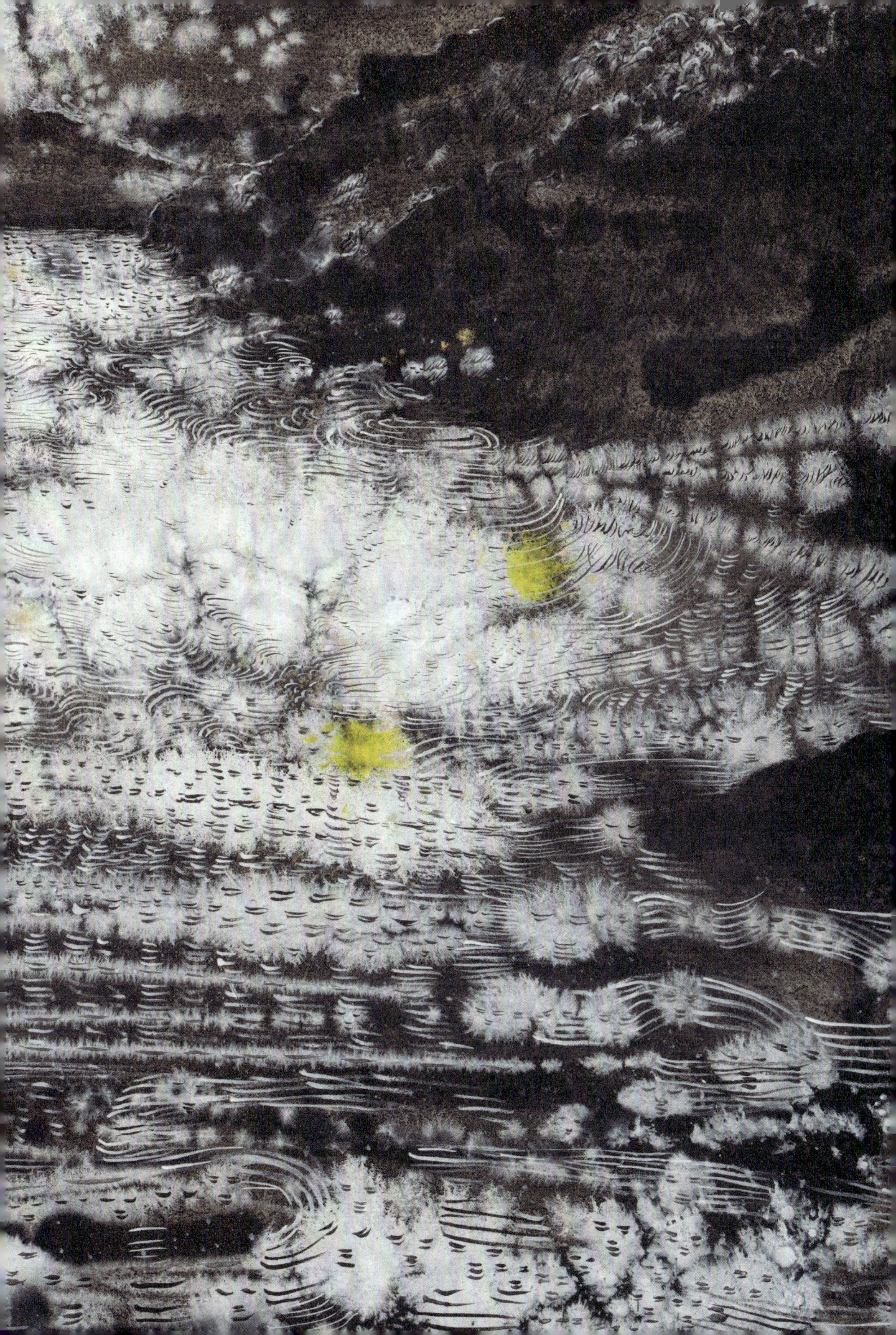

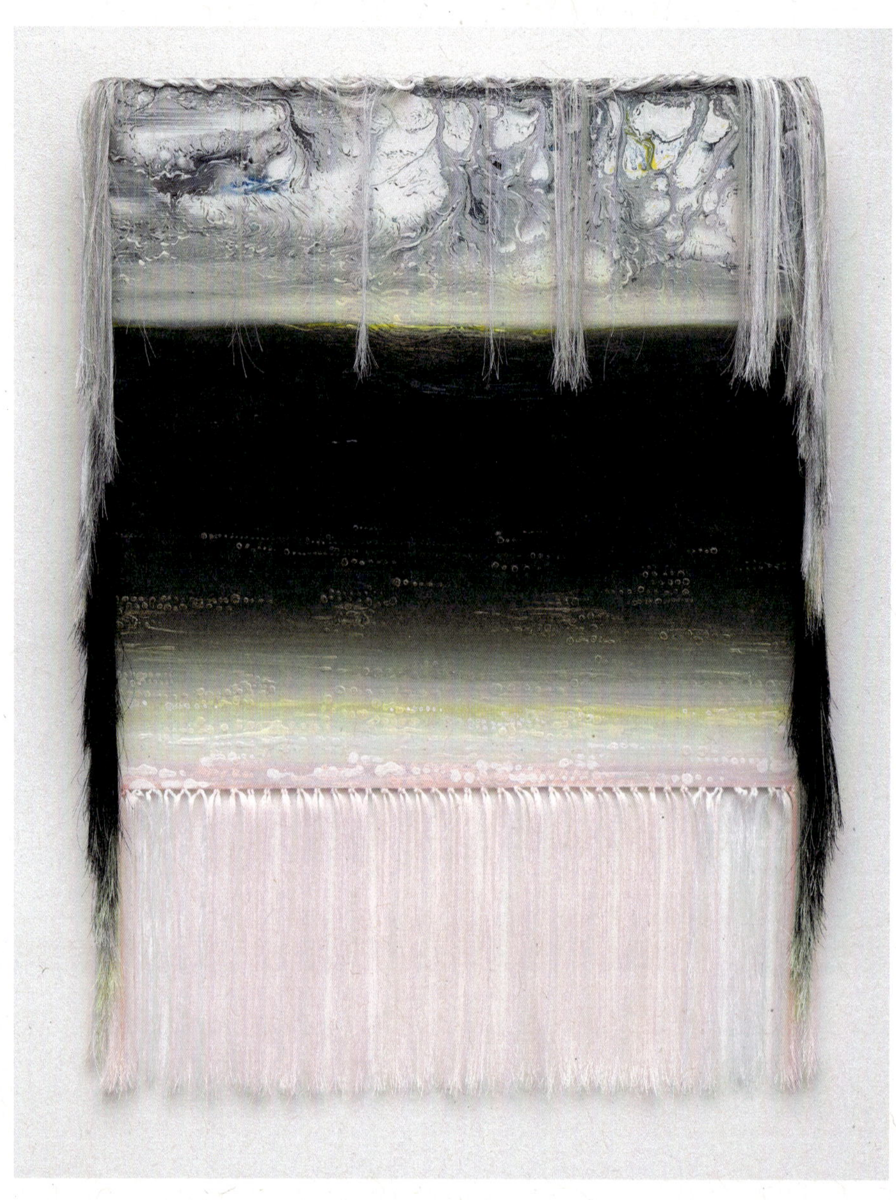

Gulul golgá Deatnu
Slowly Flows the Deatnu River
2013

Gámasvárri
Gámasvárri Fell
2014

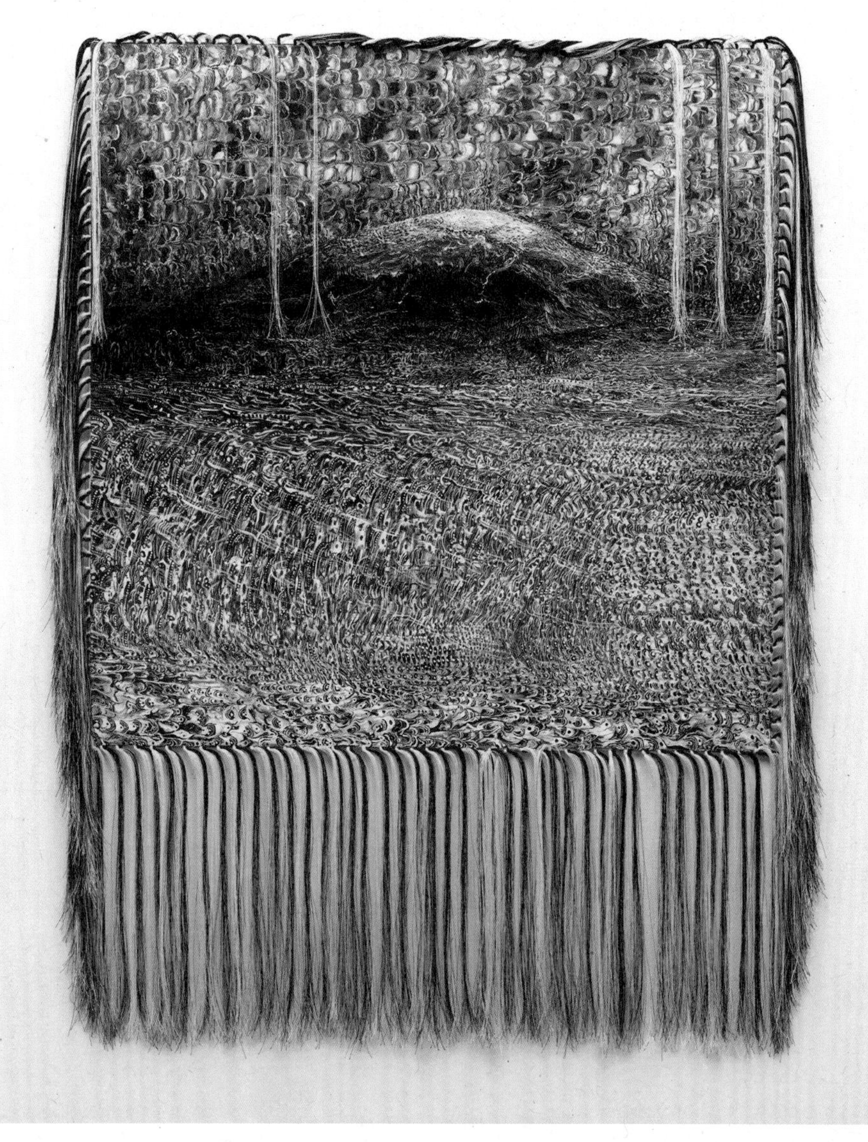

31 Outi Pieski

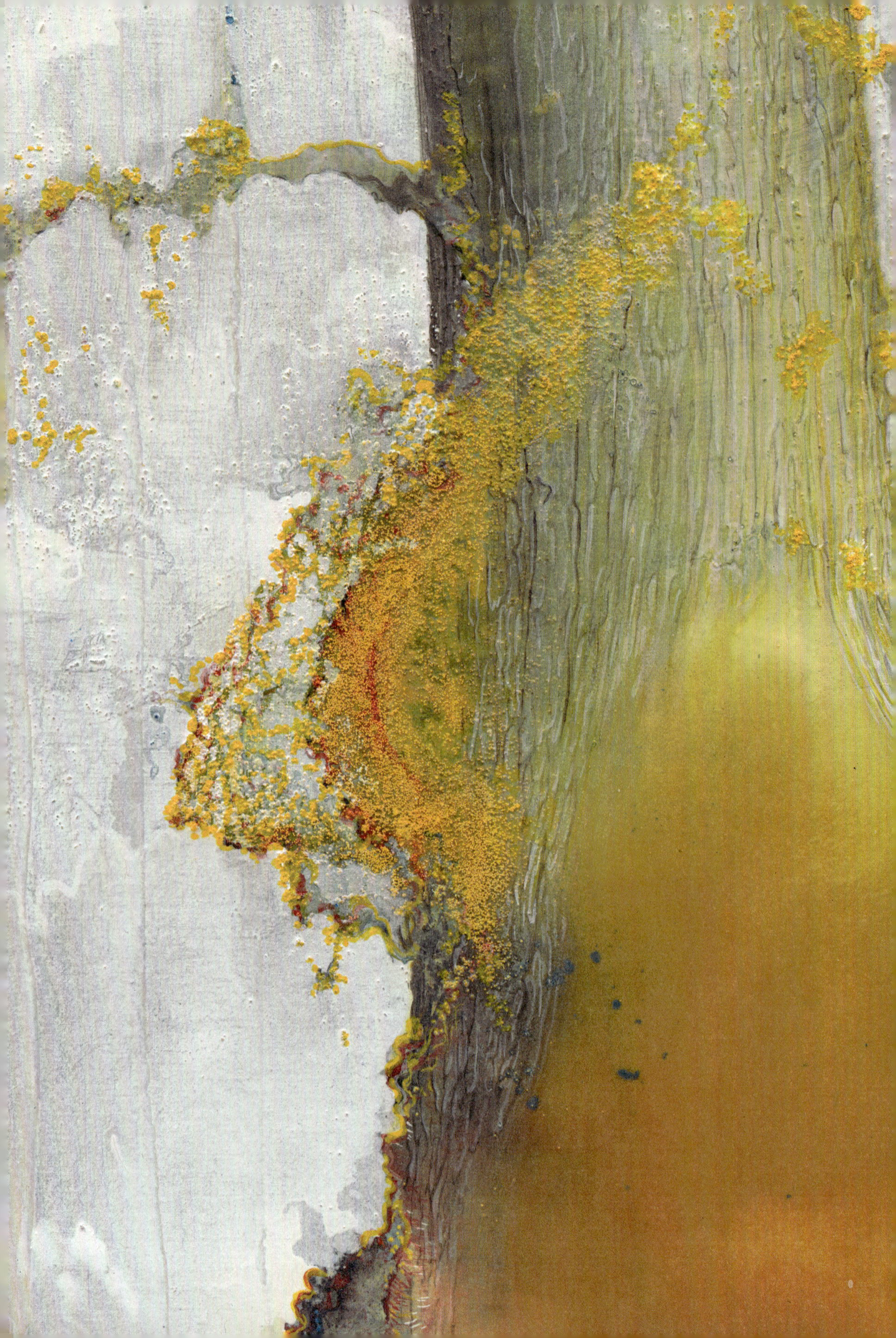

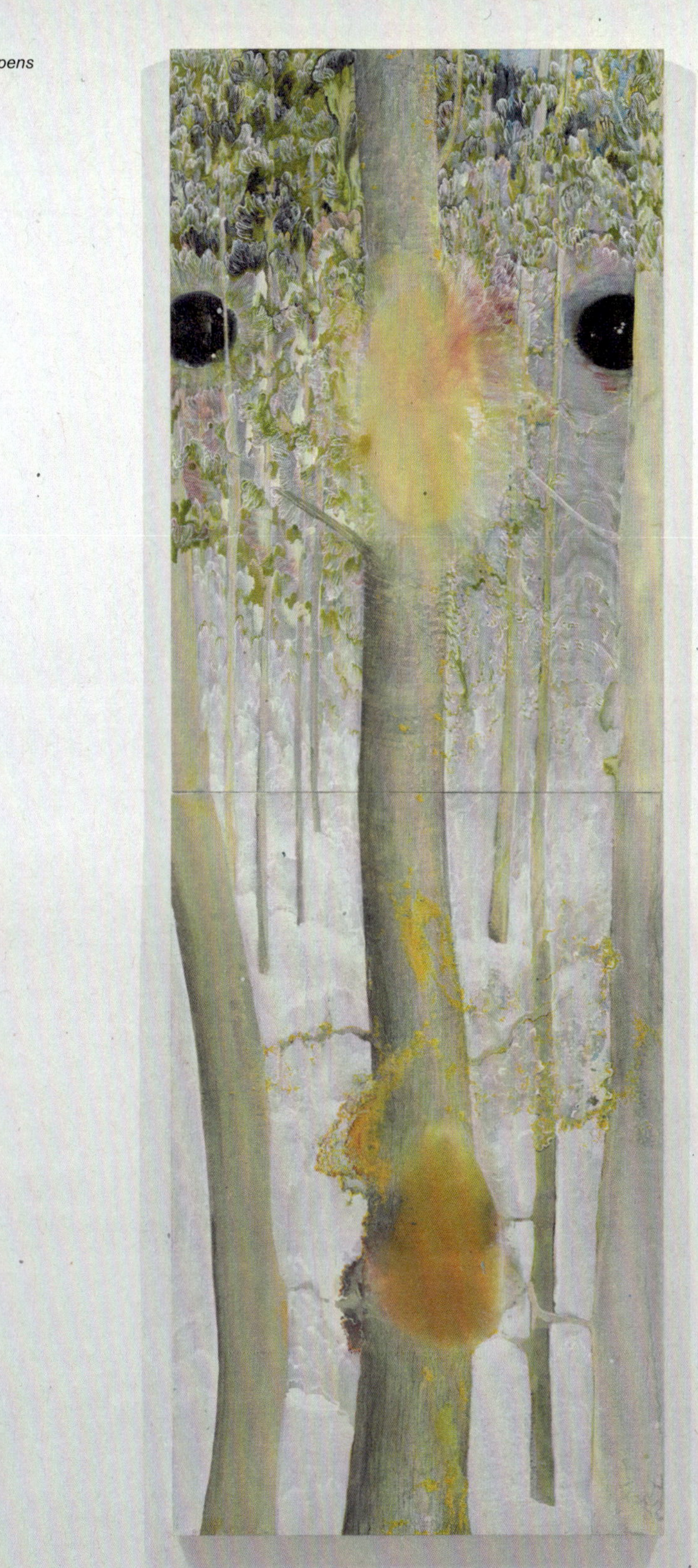

Suhpiid luhtte
Close by the Aspens
2009

Below:
Čáhppes Giisavárri
Black Fell Giisavárri
2009

Next spread:
Rematriašuvdna – Máhccat eatni lusa
Rematriation – Return to Mother
2018

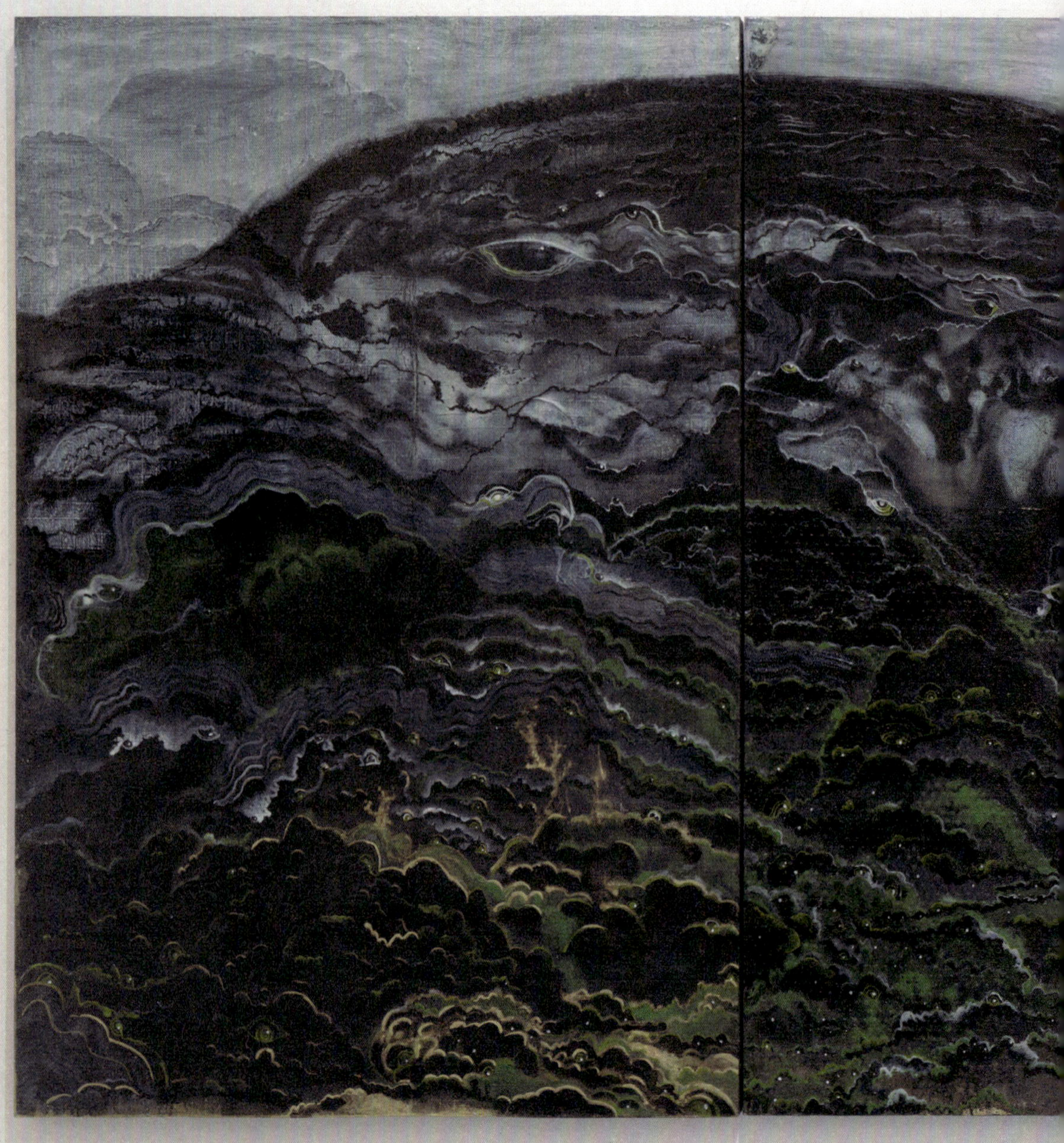

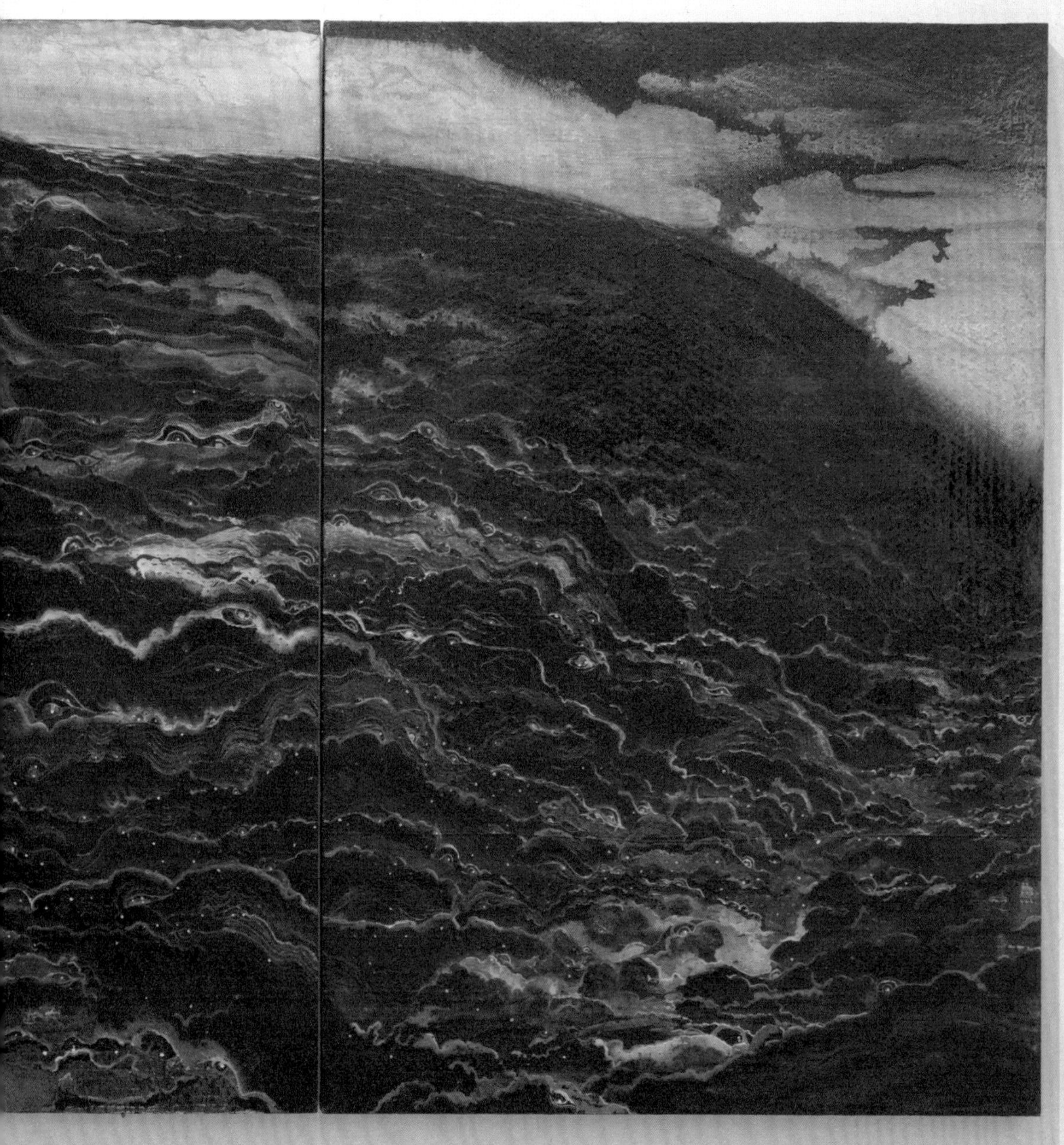

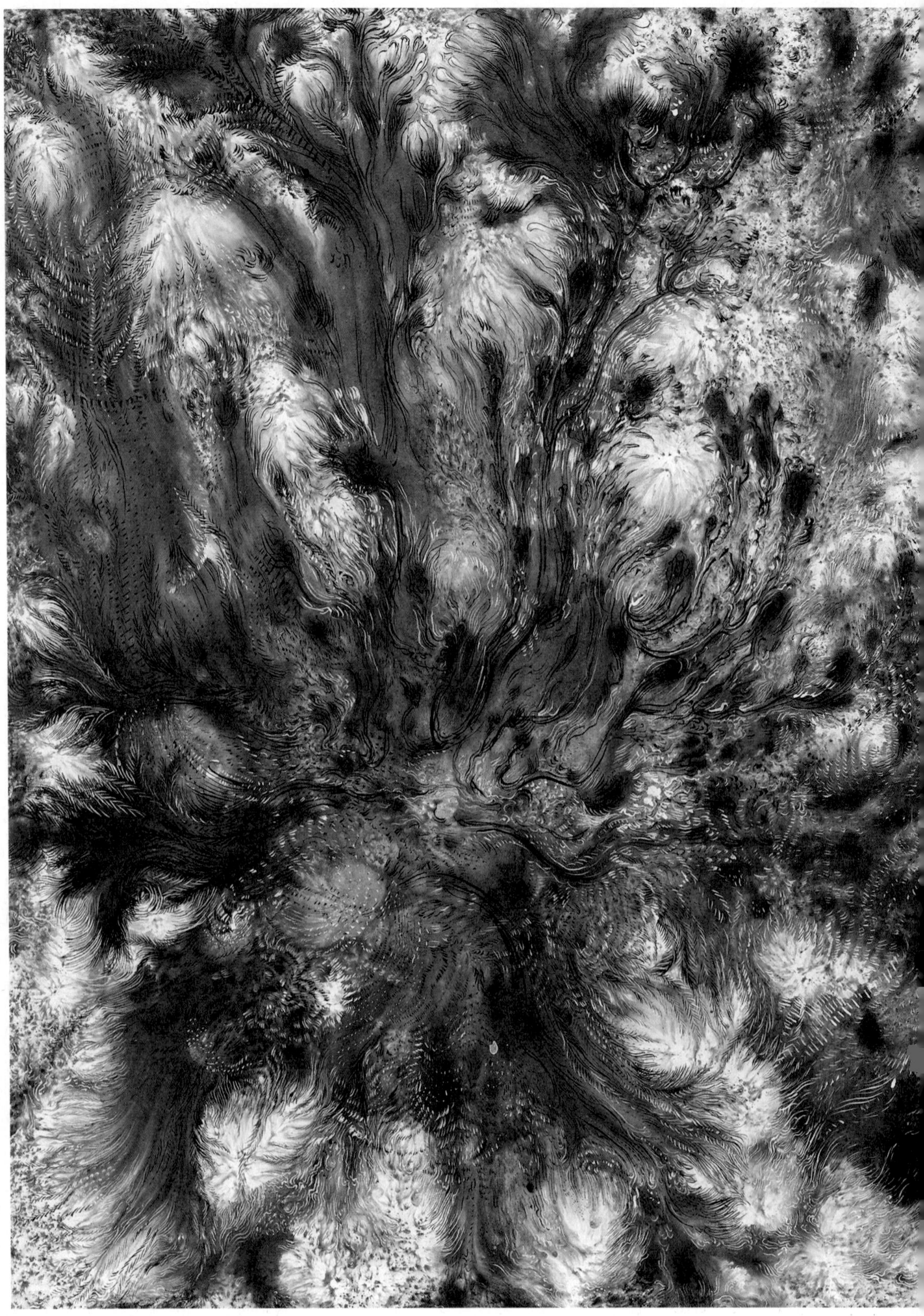

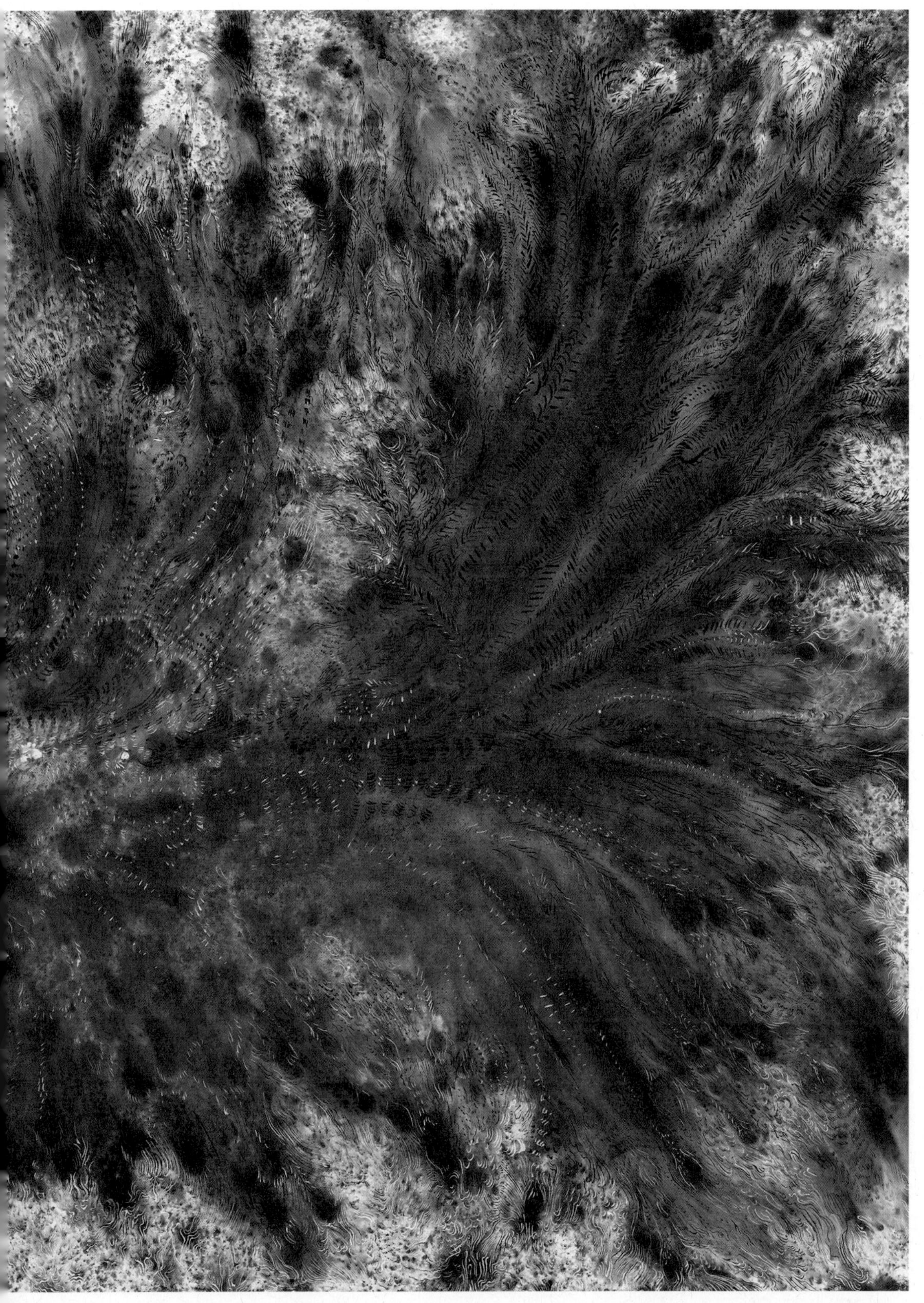

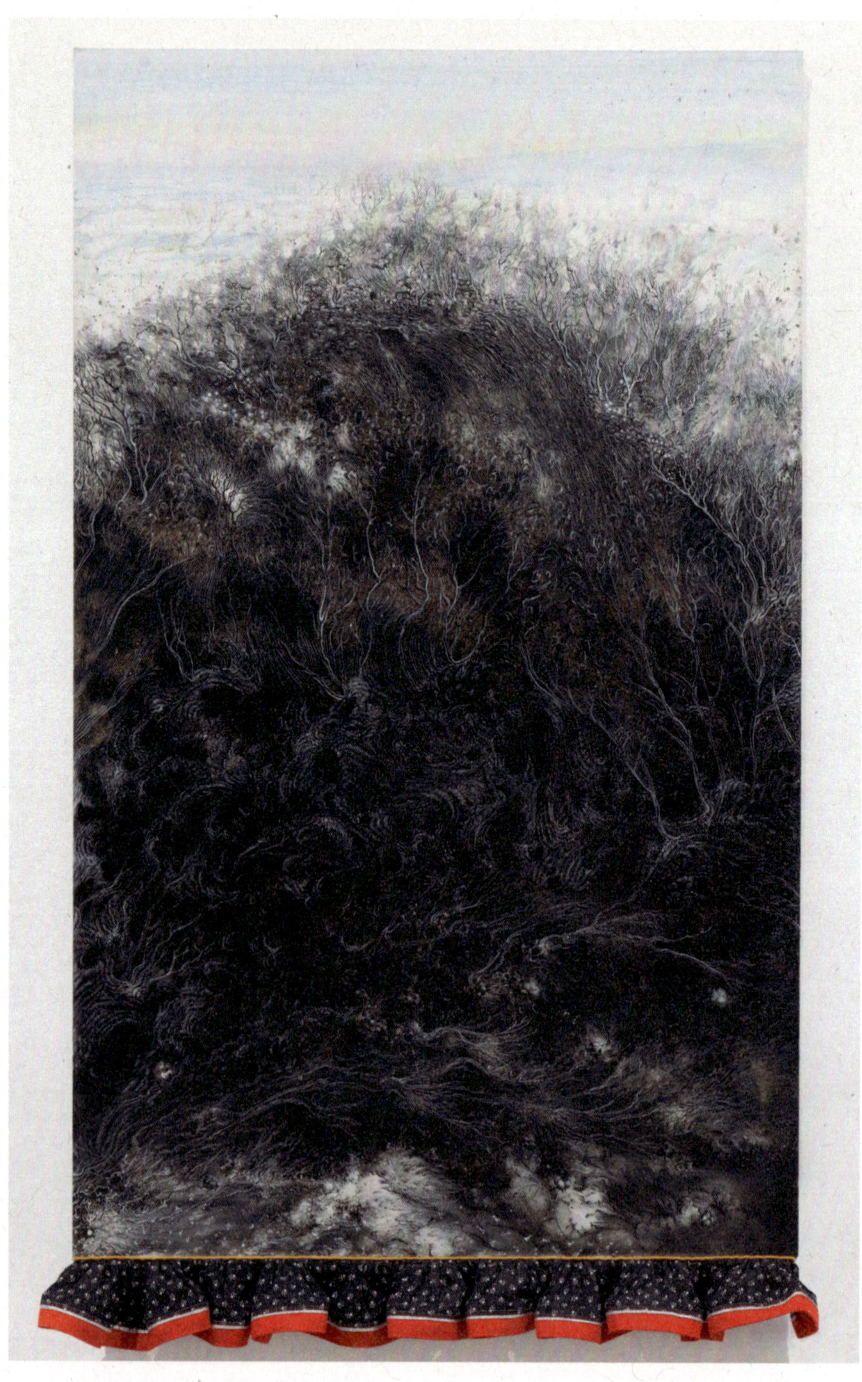

Juoksáhkká Liŋkinjeakkis
Goddess Juoksáhkká at
Liŋkinjeaggi Marsh
2014

Sáráhkká Liŋkinjeakkis
Goddess Sáráhkká at
Liŋkinjeaggi Marsh
2014

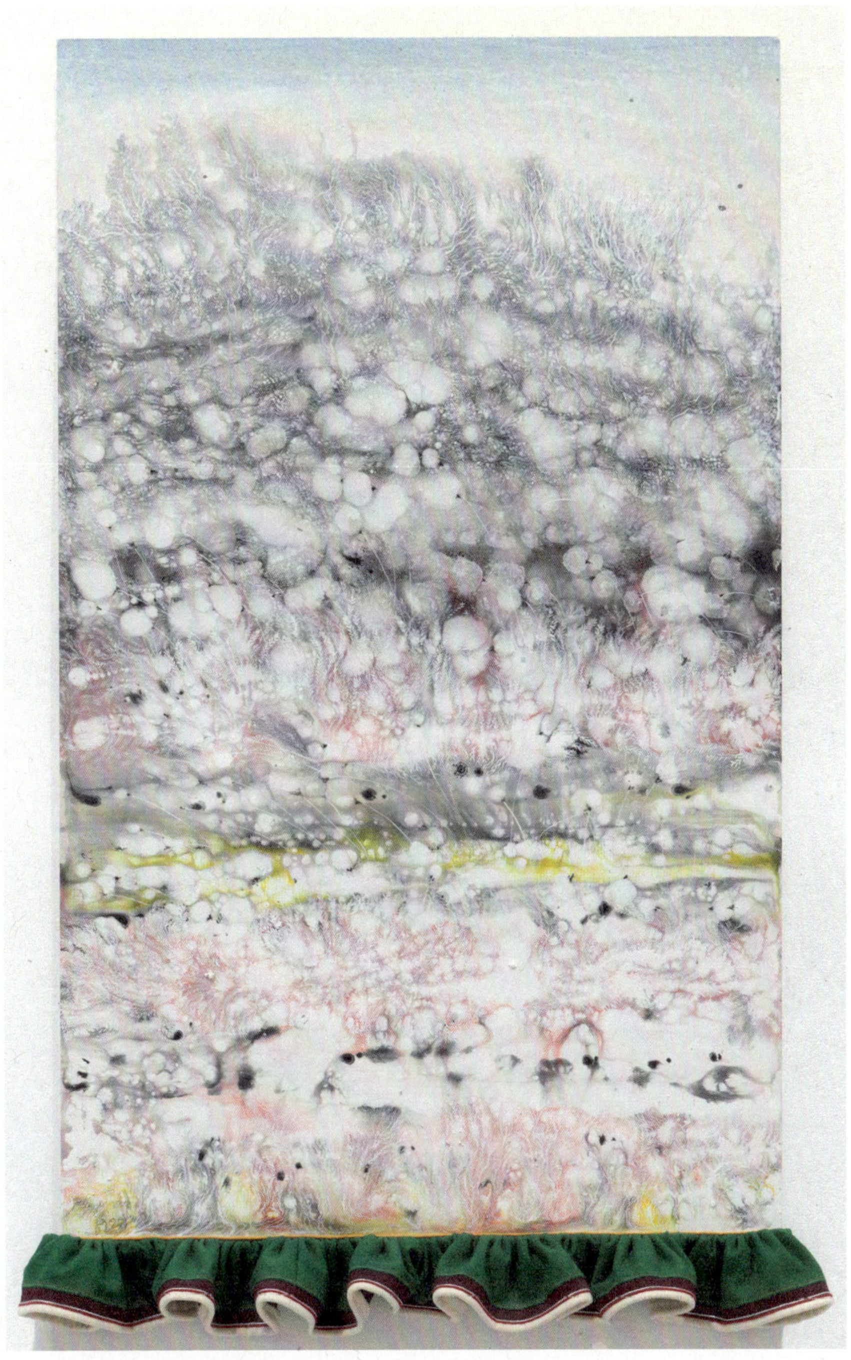

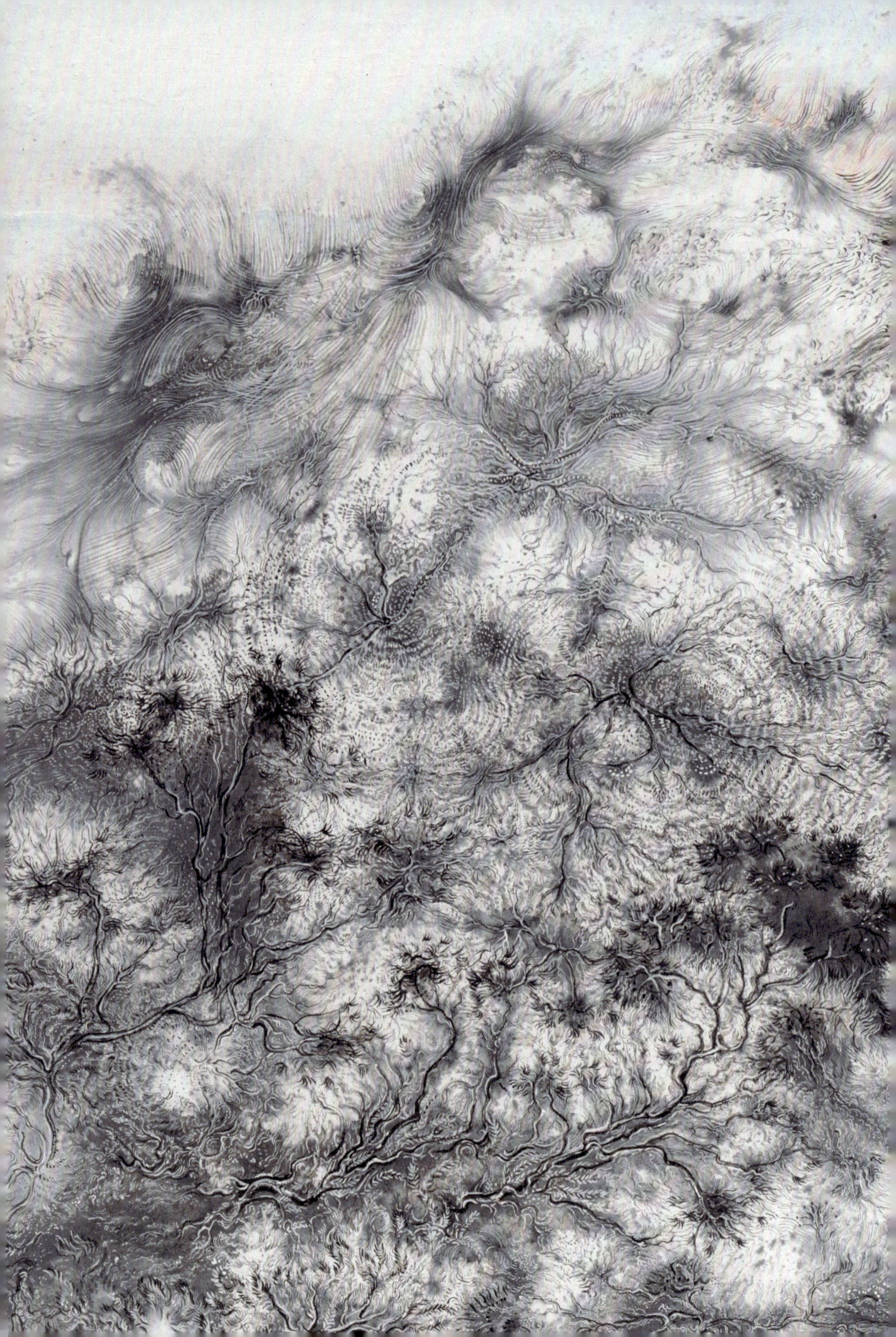

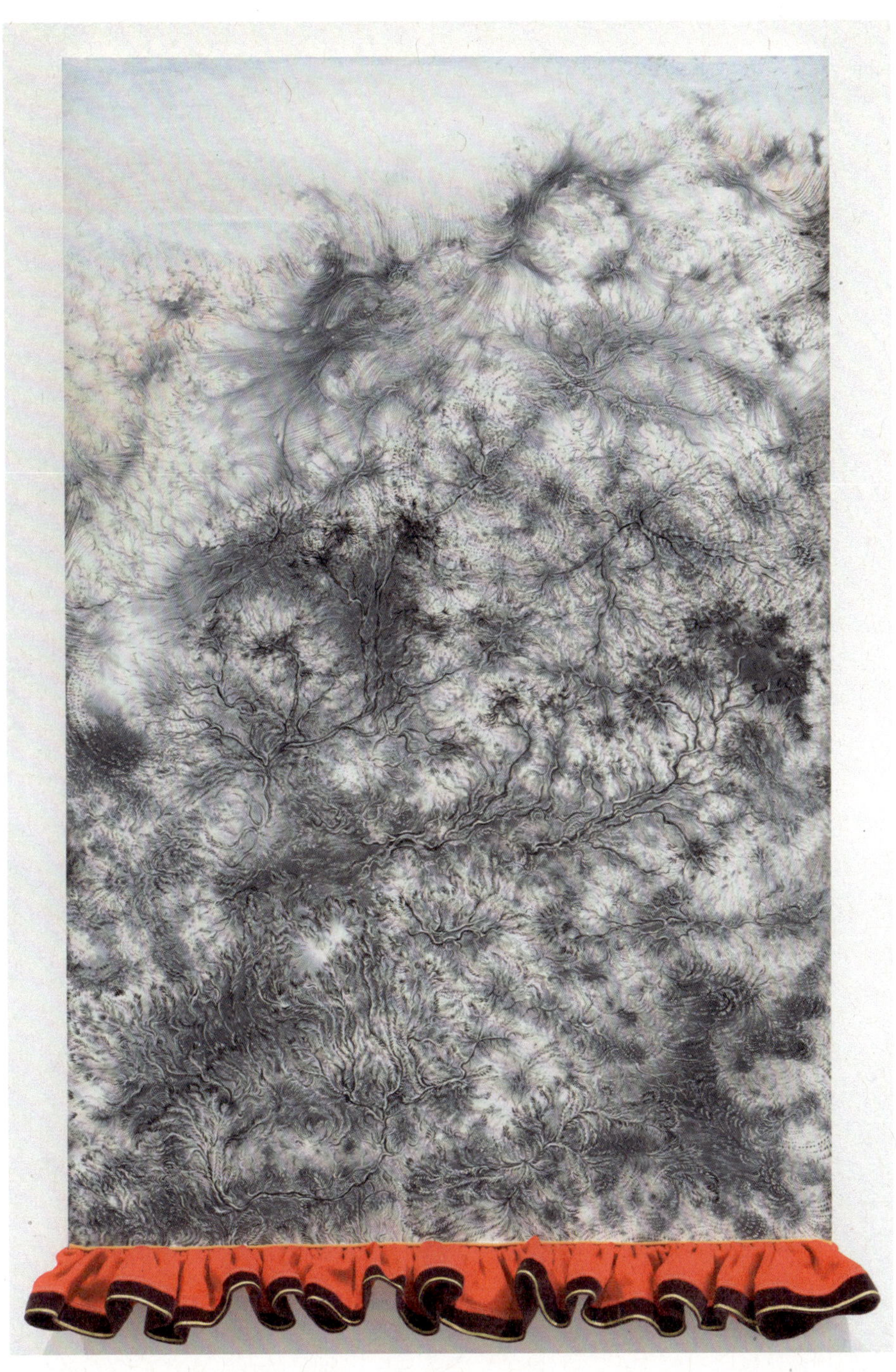

Uksáhkká Bissočuollanjeakkis
Goddess Uksáhkká at
Bissočuollanjeaggi Marsh
2017

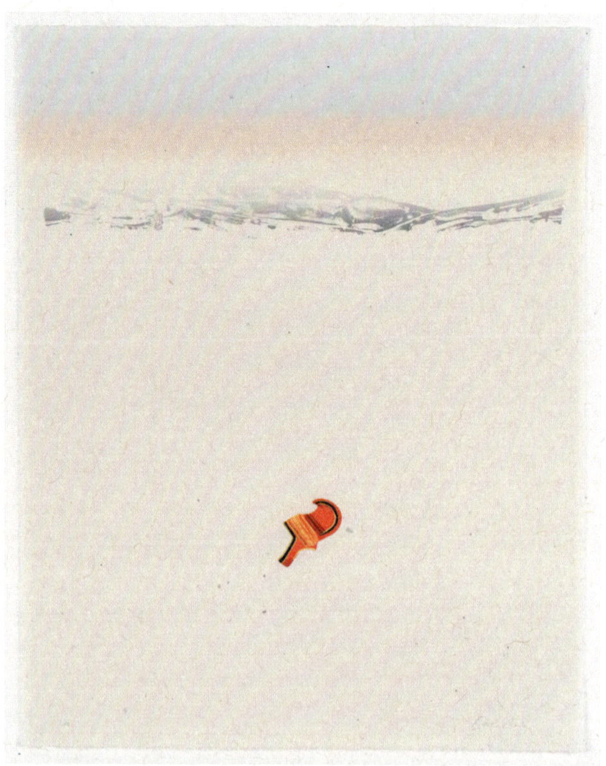

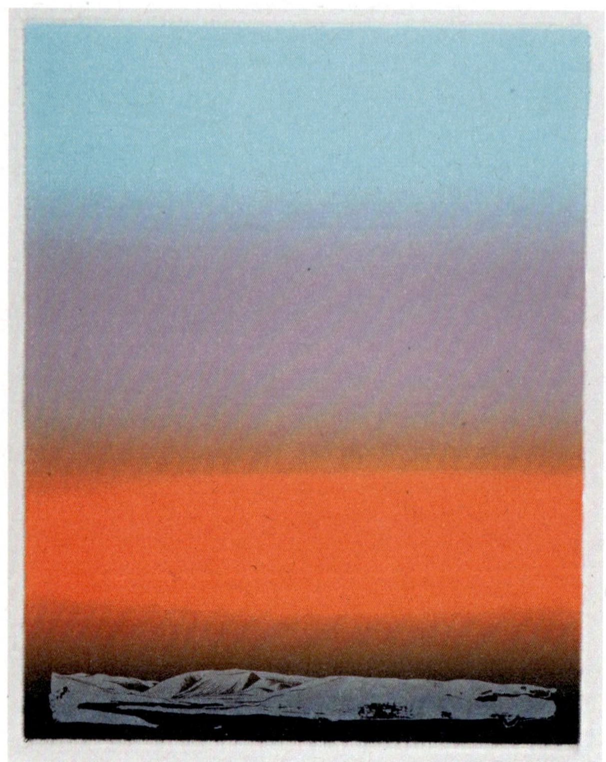

Gahpiraš
Sweet Hat Mountain
2018

Čáppa muđot Áilegas
Sweet-faced Mountain
Nuvvos Áilegas
2018

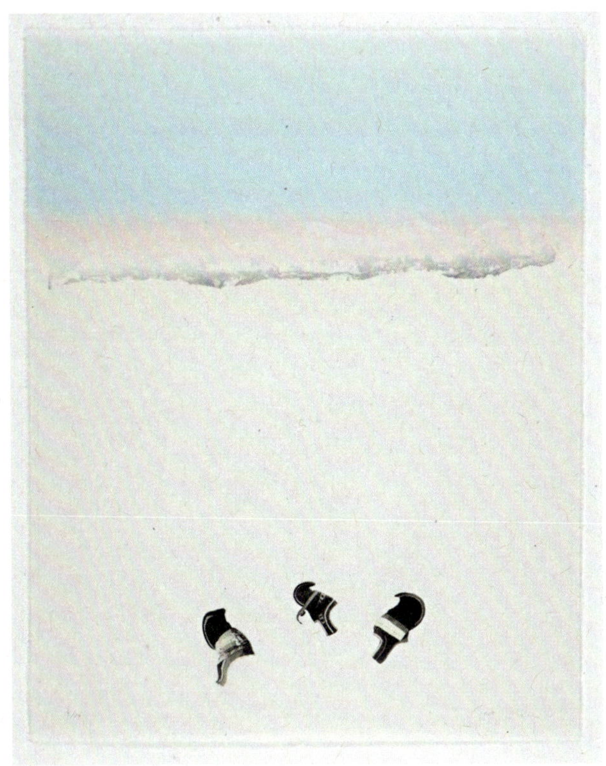

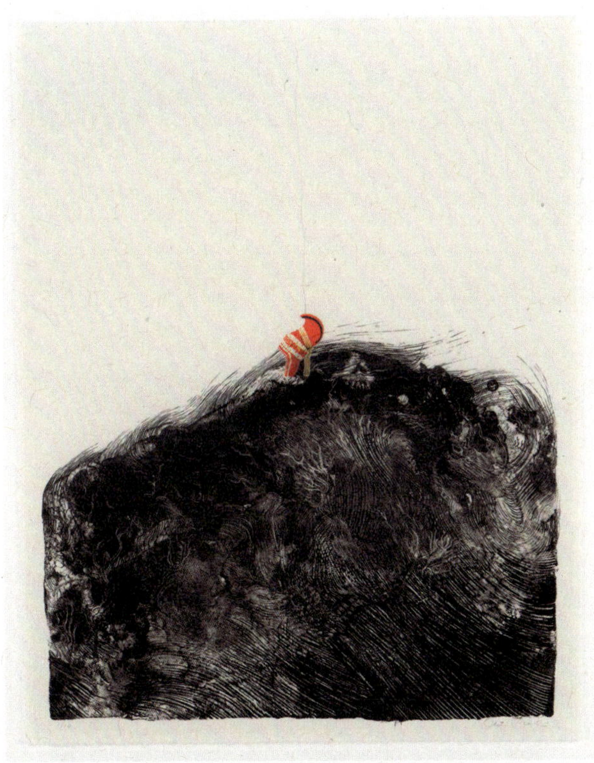

Golbma oabbaža
Three Sisters
2018

Alážis
At the Top
2018

43   Outi Pieski

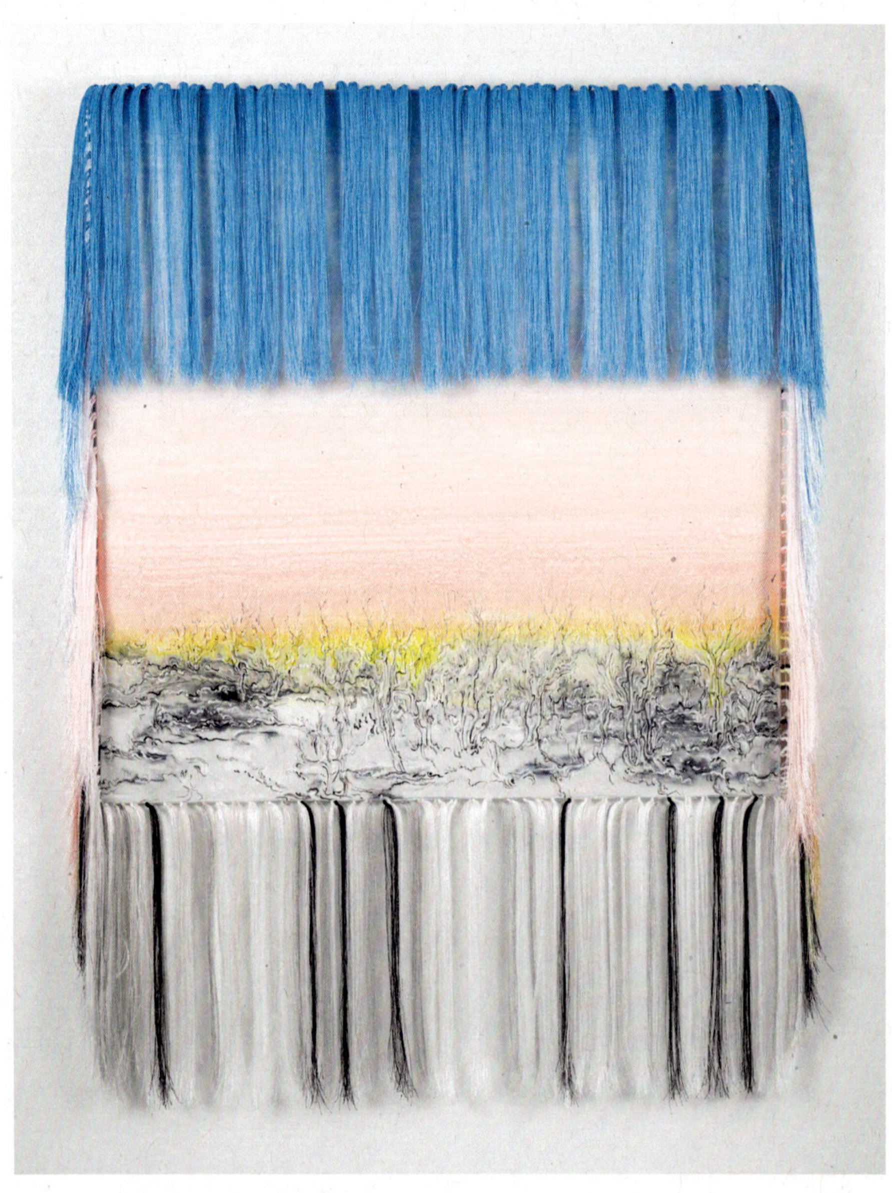

44   Outi Pieski

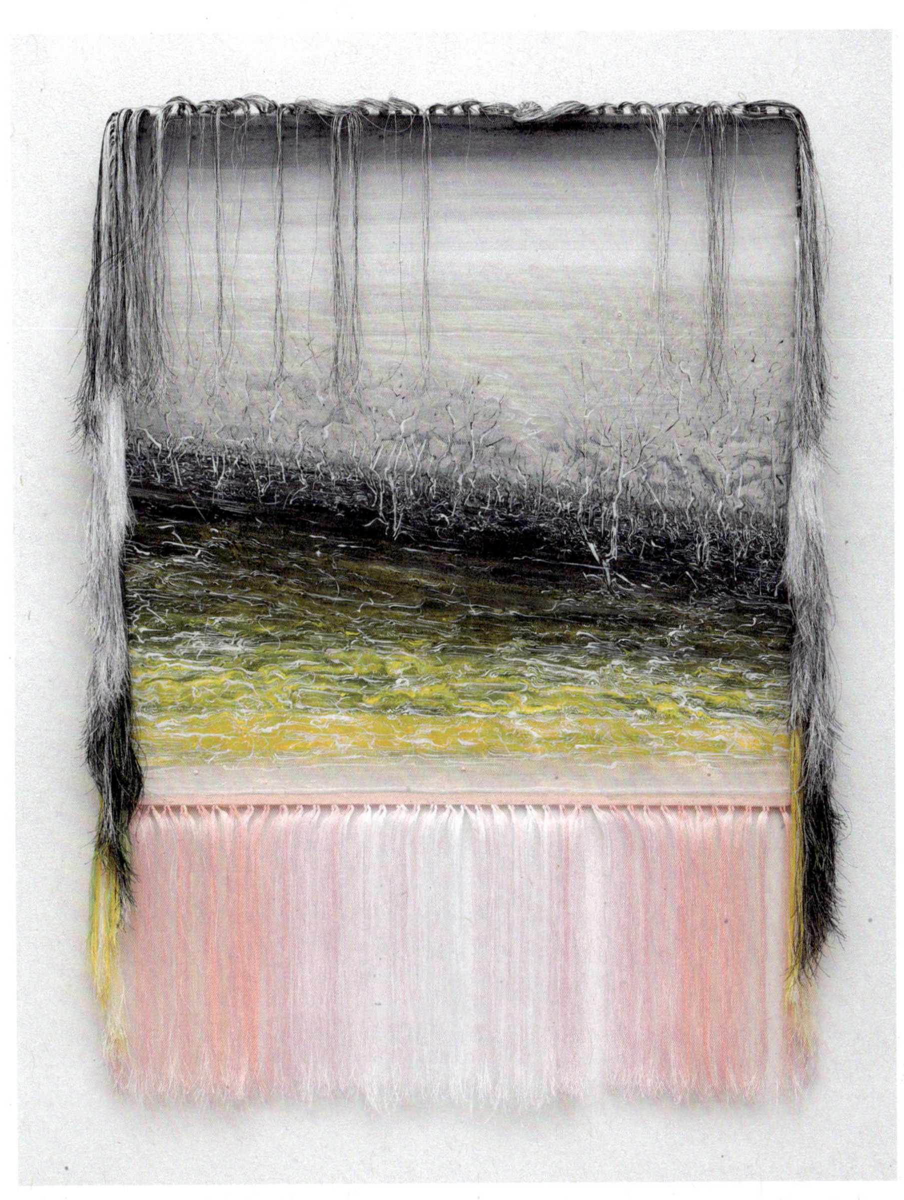

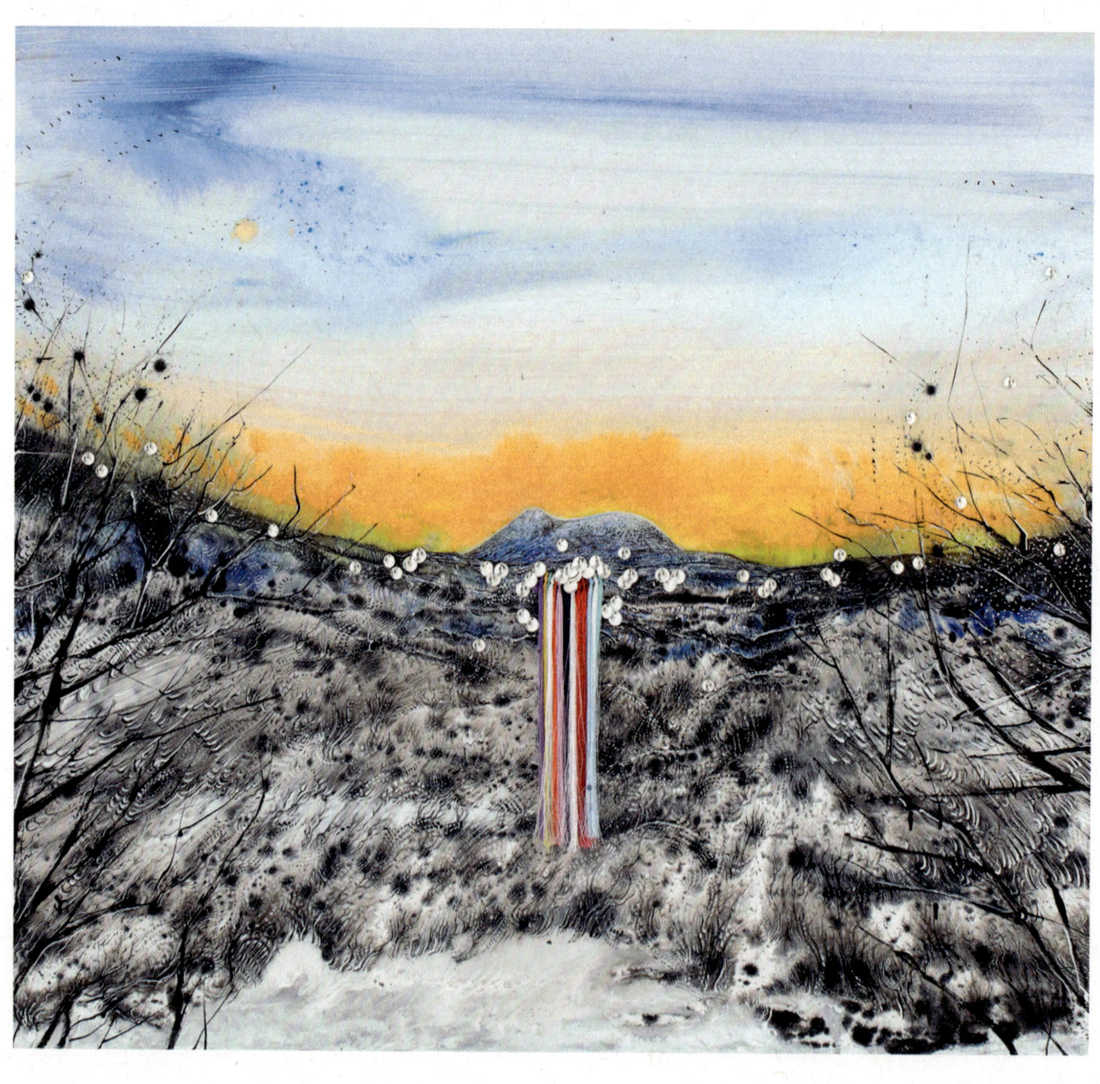

Rástegáisá lágalaš riektesubjeaktan II
Sacred Mountain Rástegáisá as a
Legal Person II
2018

Nuvvos Áilegas lágalaš riektesubjeaktan
Sacred Mountain as a Legal Person
2018

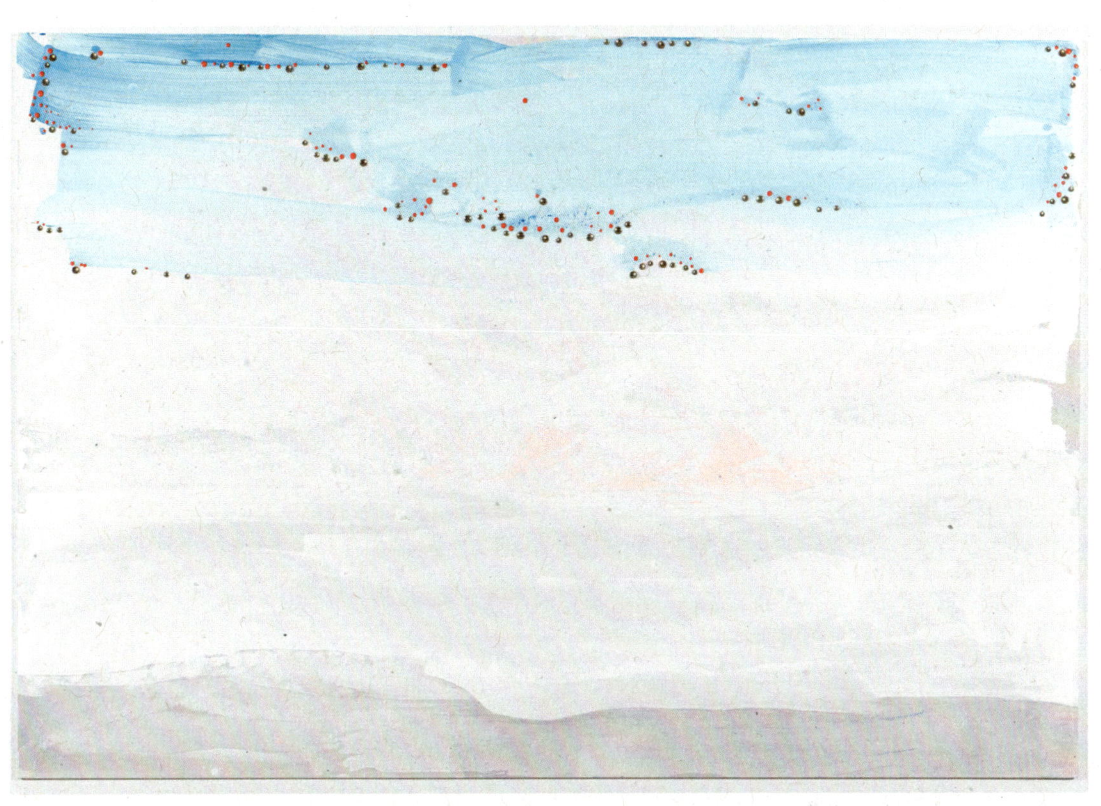

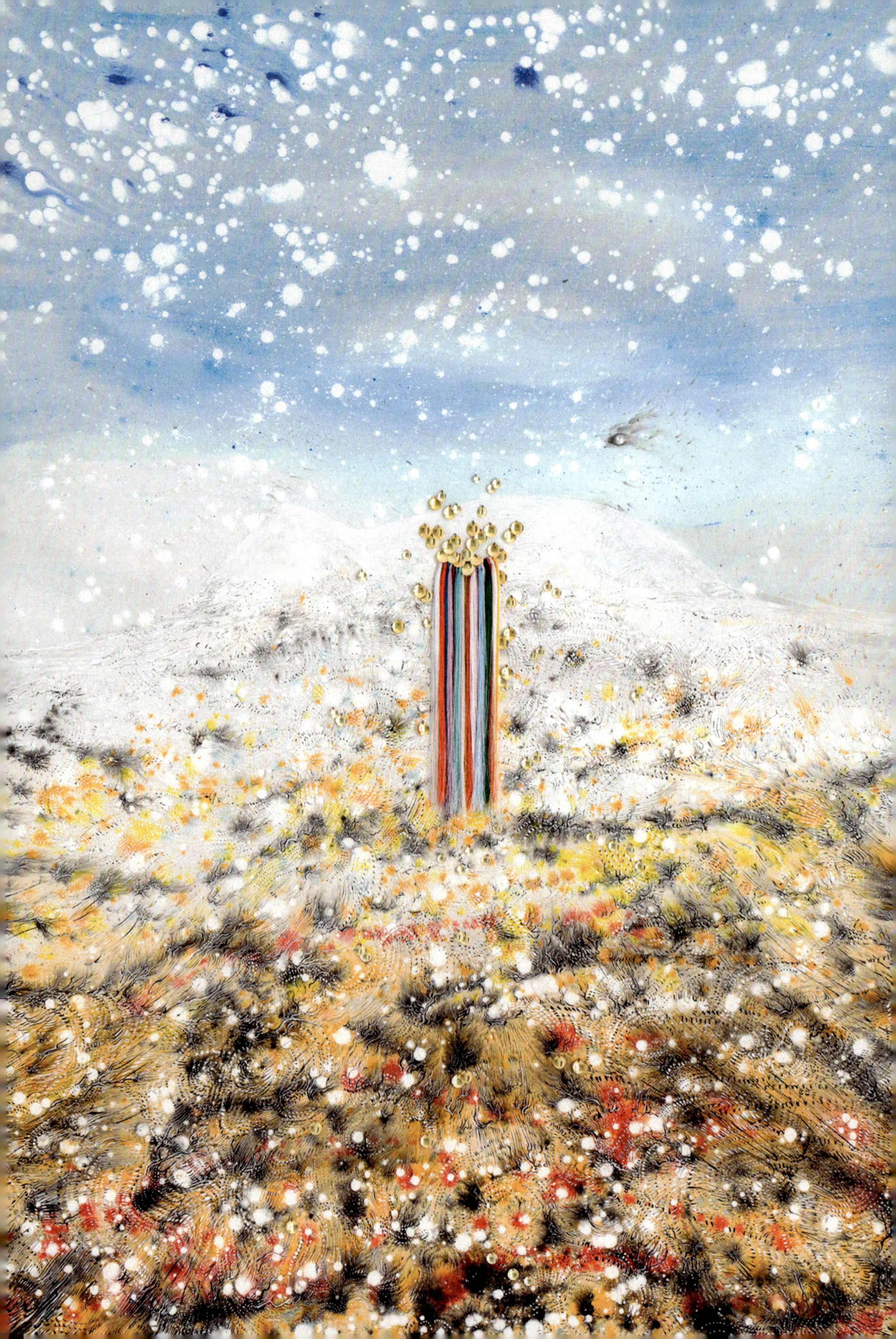

Outi Pieski

Tate St Ives

Contents

*Rástegáisá lágalaš riektesubjeaktan I
Sacred Mountain Rástegáisá as a
Legal Person I
2018*

Radical Softness

Anne Barlow

The Sámi tradition is based on reciprocity, respect and equal status for nature and people. Our land is often pictured as wilderness or no-man's land. I want to show it is a cultural environment that has evolved in coexistence with all living entities, including humans. I use the term 'radical softness' when describing my work because I find it is radical to love, to wish well, to help and heal.

Outi Pieski, 2024

This is the first large-scale museum exhibition of Outi Pieski's work in the UK, bringing together early and rarely exhibited works, recent paintings and installations, and a new installation created during her artist residency at Porthmeor Studios, St Ives in January 2024.

Pieski is based in Ohcejohka (Utsjoki), Finland, in the region referred to as Sápmi, the traditional territory of the Sámi people that extends across northern Norway, Sweden, Finland and the Kola Peninsula in Russia. Through an artistic practice that encompasses painting, printmaking, photography, video and installation, Pieski explores the relationship between humans and their environment, raising questions around ancestral knowledge and Indigenous peoples' rights. Both the subject matter and making processes of Pieski's work are imbued with multiple meanings and associations which draw on the history of Sámi culture and philosophy as well as issues affecting Sámi people today.

Central to Sámi culture is a holistic worldview in which all entities – humans, animals, nature and deities – are regarded as living beings within a non-hierarchical structure. In her catalogue essay 'Sámi: The Daughters of the Moon and Sons of the Sun', Asta Mitkijá Balto observes that this notion of co-existence and interdependency, in which 'the universe is composed of everything that lives and exists' and humans are 'inextricably connected to nature', entails certain values and ethics, such as humans not taking more from the land than they need. Outi Pieski's practice relates to this by embodying the Sámi philosophy of *soabadit* (positive reciprocity), which balances life with the environment by uniting spiritual, ancestral, elemental and practical knowledge.[1]

Balto also emphasises the importance of storytelling in Sámi culture as a way of preserving and passing on ancestral knowledge across generations. In this publication, author, musician and activist Niillas Holmberg reflects on Sámi traditions, life and culture from the perspective of different generations, and the inevitable changes that the passing of time brings.

The notion that ancestors are always present and that current generations can be a conduit for past and future generations is significant. As Dr Eeva-Kristiina Nylander observes: 'The Sámi worldview holds that the past is in the present and in the future, proposing one's responsibility towards past and future generations.'[2]

Many of the landscapes Pieski refers to are close to her home in Ohcejohka (Utsjoki), among them the Deatnu River, Giisavárri Fell, Nuvvos Áilegas and Rástegáisá (one of the most sacred places for the Sámi people). Rather than simply 'representing' or depicting these environments, Pieski conveys an active sensation of a place of which she is intrinsically part. As curator and writer Jan-Erik Lundström notes: 'In the work of Outi Pieski, nature is not an Other, nature is not that which exists in opposition to the human world of culture … Likewise, landscape is not a noun, an object, a thing, but always a verb, an activity, an event.'[3]

Experienced as a whole, the exhibition reveals a profound sense of 'interconnectedness' in its formal and thematic concerns. In *Geasi vuordin / Waiting for Summer* 2007, the oil paint is thickly applied in broad directional strokes that give the impression of movement and light. Several 'figures' made of reindeer bone and pieces of cloth stand on a ledge which is covered in fur, whereas in *Lottelávlunmuórra / A Bird's Singing Tree I* 2008 a found reindeer skull acts as the host, or transmitter, of the *yoik*, a form of traditional Sámi song that uses tonal chanting and sounds to evoke a person, animal or place, or to mimic noises of nature such as rivers or the wind.

After 2009, Pieski's approach to the painted surface of the canvas shifts. *Suhpiid luhtte / Close by the Aspens* 2009 combines a granular application of paint with areas that are

almost luminescent, resembling the golden hue of resin. In
other paintings, vast landscapes contain an extraordinary level
of detail, as in *Čáhppes Giisavárri / Black Fell Giisavárri* 2009,
whose rolling black and green hills are populated by myriad
eyelet-like shapes.[4] For Pieski, these forms represent the
underground guardian spirits of nature who protect a hidden
treasure in a wooden chest that has never been found. As
Pauliina Feodoroff writes in her texts for this exhibition: 'In the
Sámi worldview, the entire world is animated with life ... Deities
appear in placenames, and goddesses and mythological
creatures are understood to inhabit the landscape – living
entities, just as the mountains, fells and rivers are.'[5]

In *Giisavárri / Giisavárri Fell* 2009 the directional brushstrokes
are finer and more abundant. Pieces of marrowbone and
woollen cloth are embedded in its surface, while an element of
gákti (Sámi traditional clothing) is attached to the canvas's
lower edge; similarly, in versions I and III of *Rádjajohtin /
Pacing the Borders* 2014, pieces of *diehppi* – used for many
kinds of textile decoration, including in a fur hat for women –
are set into landscapes that Pieski has described as
resembling reindeer fur. For Pieski, these make the borders
within the land visible, and bring out its femininity.

In a number of later paintings, Pieski primarily uses shades of
black and white, with occasional elements of colour. The
viewer may feel they are simultaneously perceiving different
'layers' in the landscape, as in *Gurra / Gorge* 2014, in the dark
depths of whose hills glisten areas of white suggestive of
plant life within. Similarly, in *Deatnu, máttožan / Deatnu River,
Our Ancestor* 2018 – which relates to the belief that a river
could be an ancestor – are bright reflections of light,
suggestive of multiple spirits or beings, and sparks of yellow
often associated with the sun. The 'frond-like' swirling forms in
*Rematriašuvdna – Máhccat eatni lusa / Rematriation – Return
to Mother* 2018 are interspersed with areas of soft green,
symbolic of the earth, while a multitude of directional lines and
brushstrokes create sensations of intense life and energy.

The importance of the female – and the idea of the Earth as
sacred and feminine – flows through and across Pieski's
work. The three 'Goddess' paintings in this exhibition directly
refer to the three daughters of Máttaráhkká (Mother Earth),

Sáráhkká, Uksáhkká, and Juoksáhkká.[6] Here, Pieski has attached parts of *gákti* (specifically the hems of traditional Sámi dress) to the bottom edge of each canvas, an act described by Nylander as 'inserting the female guardian spirits into her art'.[7] Such elements relate to and are expressive of *duodji*, a practice of making which was marginalised in the wake of the colonisation of Sápmi.[8]

Duodji, 'the philosophy from which Sámi material culture and creative practices emerge',[9] is integral to Pieski's work. As she states:

> *Duodji* is a holistic concept that preserves the Sámi philosophy, values and spirituality, and connects them with practical and traditional skills. *Duodji* is doing and making, crafting and creating ... In Sámi culture material items hold energy and power. The energy comes from the material itself, from the maker who has transformed skills, care and love into the item, and from the user who has used and lived with the item and its power. Material is seen not as passive, but as an active author.[10]

Distinct from 'craft', which carries associations relating to Western art histories, 'crafting' here relates to 'a specifically Sámi and complex worldview, combining spiritual, material and environmental knowledge, concepts of beauty and utility, and manual work, that converge in the processes of making objects and in the objects themselves.'[11] As Pieski and Nylander note, in more recent times, *duodji* has become politicised and the *gákti* 'one of its strongest symbols [as] a visual political statement, a sign of belonging and expressing the vitality of the Sámi culture, in opposition to colonialism'.[12] Accordingly, in Pieski's work this 'craftivism' has been seen as 'a form of activism centred on the practice of "domestic crafts" and associated with anti-capitalism, feminism and environmentalism'.[13]

Interspersed throughout the Tate St Ives exhibition are a number of the 'shawl paintings' that Pieski has been creating since 2008. In these works, Pieski incorporates tassels from traditional shawls on all sides of the canvas. Each work varies in colour, tone and texture and has a distinct presence, from the rich and dark hues of *Deatnu ijabealde / Deatnu River by the Night* 2013 to *Golle-eana / Land of Gold* 2013's luminous turquoises, pinks and yellows.

Like the durational process of her painting, Pieski sees the tying of knots – in which concept and making go hand in hand – as fundamental to her work, creating a living connection across generations and acting as 'ritual, sacrifice, atonement, and renunciation'[14] and a 'matriarchal counterforce to a competitive, individual-centred society'.[15] The tassels themselves are suggestive, as Emma Lilja notes, of a human presence in ways both spiritual and political: 'The landscape depicted by Pieski is part of the Sámi homeland that has been coloured [by] past, present and future generations living there. In the work, human presence is both symbolically and materially part of the landscape in which one lives.'[16] Monica Grini sees Pieski as making a comment on the land itself, reminding us 'that these landscapes are indeed populated … in contradiction to certain conceptions about the area as so called terra nullius or "no man's land"'[17] – conceptions that often lead non-Sámi people to picture Sápmi as a wilderness freely available for industrial land use.

For her large-scale installations, Pieski initially attached tassels to tree branches. Since 2015, she has mostly employed V-shaped pieces of steel that create inherent structures or geometries according to their number and dimensions. The exhibition presents three such installations. *Beavvit / Rising Together II* 2021 derives its name from the Northern Sámi term for 'many good friends', which is similar to the word *beaivi* (the sun); as such, it is suggestive of a gathering of friends dressed in the vibrant colours of *gákti*, and also of solidarity and collective action. *Guržot ja guovssat / Spell on You!* 2020 and Pieski's new work *Skábmavuoddu / Spell on Me!* 2024 are presented in tandem, inviting viewers to move through and around their forms. The latter's title merges the words *skábma* – the polar night when the sun does not rise above the horizon – and *vuoddu,* meaning the bottom or base, and Pieski refers to this new work as having good spirits around after a period of depression. *Guržot ja guovssat,* meanwhile, references both *Guoržžu*, a bad luck bird or evil spirit, and *Guovssat*, a Siberian jay known to bring good luck.

Pieski views these two installations as 'counter-images', creating 'a spiritual forest that carries wisdom and a variety of contradictory forces; fears, wishes and desires'.[18]

*

Much of Pieski's work addresses the historical suppression and intentional erasure of Sámi customs, languages and rights through colonisation and assimilation policies. As an artist and activist, she brings attention to these histories, connecting them with issues affecting Sámi people today.

For the interdisciplinary project *Máttaráhku ládjogahpir / Foremother's Hat of Pride* 2017–21 Pieski collaborated with Finnish archaeologist Eeva-Kristiina Nylander to explore the complex legacy of the *ládjogahpir*, the headdress traditionally worn by Sámi women between the 1750s and the turn of the twentieth century. The *fierra* – a curved, horn-like wooden shape inserted into and covered by the fabric of the hat – gives the *ládjogahpir* its distinctive look. Following the arrival in the mid-nineteenth century of the Christian Pietistic movement called Laestadianism, these hats were banned, as the Laestadian preachers claimed that the devil lived in the *fierra*.

In this publication, Nylander notes that the rise of patriarchy through colonisation was a suppression not only of Sámi beliefs but also of women's rights. For many Sámi artists the *ládjogahpir* 'symbolises the empowerment of Sámi women and the flourishing of Sámi culture and values',[19] as can be seen in Pieski's series of portraits of women wearing the headdress.

As part of their research, Pieski and Nylander created an inventory of all surviving *ládjogahpir* in archives, collections and libraries across Europe. They found that museums generally present these as 'objects' in the context of ethnographic displays, and that many lack provenance information due to the way in which they were collected as examples of people's way of life or culture – not as *duodji* with histories and symbolism of their own. This is addressed in a new video work, *Ceagganaddat / Listening with Foremother* 2023, a collaboration between Outi and Biret Haarla Pieski, which shows two *ládjogahpir* hats (one in the collection of the Museum am Rothenbaum – Kulturen und Künste der Welt in

Hamburg) meeting each other across generations and foremothers, as 'subjects' rather than 'objects'.

Pieski and Nylander also note that as a consequence of such collecting practices, Sámi communities do not have access to their own ancestral cultural heritage – a situation they wish to see rectified through a process of 'rematriation' to Sápmi. (Importantly, they use the term 'rematriation' instead of 'repatriation' due to the latter word's associations with the patriarchy and colonialism.)

Their research resulted in a publication and in artworks by Pieski in various media, collectively presented under the title *Ládjogahpir rematriašuvdna – Máhccat eatni lusa / Rematriation of a Ládjogahpir – Return to Máttaráhkká.*[20] This installation includes prints and wallpaper works featuring repeated images of the artist's daughters Biret and Gáddjá Haarla Pieski, and a grid of brightly coloured photographs, *47 eanemus ohccojuvvon máttaráhkut / The 47 Most Wanted Foremothers* 2019, which refers to forty-seven of the known sixty original *ládjogahpir* in museum collections. In alluding to Andy Warhol's *13 Most Wanted Men* 1964, in which Warhol controversially reproduced police mugshots, Pieski and Nylander suggest that these *ládjogahpir* are akin to 'prisoners' held against their will.

Notions of self-determination and self-governance are evident in much of Pieski's work. Versions I and III of *Rádjajohtin / Pacing the Borders* 2014 draw attention to the differences between land boundaries defined by the Sámi and later designated by the nation-states of Finland, Norway, Sweden and Russia; other works allude to the extractive industries and invasive development that threaten Sámi ways of life including reindeer herding and the rights to Arctic salmon fishing.[21] Such concerns around the role of nation-states connect with wider debates around Indigenous rights and land issues.[22] In Pieski's words: 'The problems of minority cultures are intertwined with each other, and on a global level, they are ultimately also linked to nature conservation issues. When we open our ears to the marginalised and side-lined minority representatives in our society, we may increase our awareness on issues that are topical and meaningful for everyone.'[23]

An emerging field of law, Earth Jurispridence, 'seeks to develop a philosophy and practice of law that gives greater consideration to nature, by recognizing the interconnectedness of Earth's natural systems, the inherent rights and value of nature, and the dependence of humanity and all living beings on a healthy Earth'.[24] Pieski addresses this matter perhaps most explicitly in four 2018 paintings, *Nuvvos Áilegas lágalaš riektesubjeaktan / Sacred Mountain as a Legal Person*, *Rástegáisá lágalaš riektesubjeaktan / Sacred Mountain Rástegáisá as a Legal Person I* and *II* and *lehčanas vuoigatvuohta leat ja lieđđut / Independent Right to Exist and Flourish*, saying of the mountain in the latter works that it 'has an inherent right to be Rástegáisá without being subjected to the extraction of resources, such as "green" wind electricity or for tourism'.[25] The title relates to the historic moment in 2008 when Ecuador became the first country to recognise Rights of Nature in its national constitution. While similar rights have since been granted in other parts of the world, the topic remains a pressing issue for many communities.[26]

Both *Rástegáisá lágalaš riektesubjeaktan / Sacred Mountain Rástegáisá as a Legal Person I* and *II* are resplendent with vivid colours, whereas *Nuvvos Áilegas lágalaš riektesubjeaktan / Sacred Mountain as a Legal Person* almost seems to emit light from its distant pink landscape. In such works, what Pieski calls her 'radical softness' is not a sentimental gaze but an expression of strength and complexity. In the words of Pauliina Feodoroff, Pieski is 'an extreme realist … dedicated to what is about to arrive or to emerge and which cannot be commanded, imagined, envisioned or decided in advance.'[27]

NOTES

1. Statements by Outi Pieski, 2024.
2. Eeva Kristiina-Harlin et al, *The Ládjogahpir: The Foremothers' Hat of Pride* (Ládjogahpir: Máttaráhkuid gábagahpir), Karasjok 2020, p.79.
3. Exhibition text by Jan-Erik Lundström for *Outi Pieski: Ássojuvvon báiki / Inhabited Land*, Gallery Korjaamo, Helsinki 2014.
4. As curator Trude Schjelderup Iversen observes, Pieski has also used montages of Sámi symbols in other works, often in the lower part of her paintings. See Trude Schjelderup Iversen (ed.), *Stortinget: Materialets Tale* (Parliament: The Materials Speak), Oslo 2019, pp.141–2.
5. Quoted from exhibition wall text by Pauliina Feodoroff.
6. *Juoksáhkká Liŋkinjeakkis / Goddess Juoksáhkká at Liŋkinjeaggi Marsh* 2014, *Sáráhkká Liŋkinjeakkis / Goddess Sáráhkká at Liŋkinjeaggi Marsh* 2014 and *Uksáhkká Bissočuollanjeakkis / Goddess Uksáhkká at Bissočuollanjeaggi Marsh* 2017, all acrylic paint and textile on canvas.
7. See Eeva-Kristiina Nylander, 'Rematriation in the art and research project *Foremother's Hat of Pride*' in this volume, pp.71–5.
8. For a wide range of texts on *duodji*, see Harald Gaski and Gunvor Guttorm (eds.), *Duodji Reader: A selection of twelve essays on duodji by Sámi duojárat and writers from the past 60 years*, Kárášjohka 2022.
9. From 'A Sámi Perspective', The Sámi Pavilion press kit, 59th International Art Exhibition of La Biennale di Venezia (2022), https://oca.no/thesamipavilion, accessed 5 Jan. 2024.
10. Outi Pieski, artist statement, 23rd Biennale of Sydney (2022), https://www.biennaleofsydney.art/participants/outi-pieski, accessed 18 Nov. 2023.
11. See 'A Sámi Perspective' (2022), https://oca.no/thesamipavilion, accessed 5 Jan. 2024.
12. Kristiina-Harlin et al 2020, p.69.
13. Schjelderup Iversen (ed.) 2019, p.142
14. Quoted in 'Profile: How Outi Pieski Incorporates Elements of Sámi Clothing in her Activist Art', *Inuit Art Quarterly*, 3 Oct. 2023, https://www.inuitartfoundation.org/iaq-online/how-outi-pieski-incorporates-elements-of-s%c3%a1mi-clothing-in-her-activist-art, accessed 9 Feb. 2024.
15. Quoted from exhibition wall text by Outi Pieski.
16. Emma Lilja, 'Hand-Knotted Landscape: Reflections on Outi Pieski's "Our Land, Our Running Colours"', *FNG Research*, no.4, 2019, https://research.fng.fi/category/issues/2019-no-4, accessed 16 Apr. 2022.
17. Monica Grini, 'Contemporary Sámi Art in the Making of Sámi Art History: The Work of Geir Tore Holm, Outi Pieski and Lena Stenberg', in Svein Aamold, Elin Haughdal and Ulla Angkjær Jørgensen (eds.), *Sámi Art and Aesthetics: Contemporary Perspectives*, Aarhus 2017, p.307.
18. Outi Pieski to the author, 2024.
19. See Eeva-Kristiina Nylander, 'Rematriation in the art and research project *Foremother's Hat of Pride*' in this volume, pp.71–5.
20. Kristiina-Harlin et al 2020.
21. See the environmental community art and activist project *Rájácummá / Kiss from the Border* 2017–19, dealing with issues concerning self-government and the use of land and waterways, in which Pieski, Niillas Holmberg and Jenni Laiti collaborated with the Ellos Deatnu! group.
22. See Ánde Somby's essay on sovereignty in relation to nation-states and Indigenous peoples: Ánde Somby, 'Where the Hard Meets the Soft', in Katya García-Antón (ed.), *Sovereign Words: Indigenous Art, Curation and Criticism*, Oslo and Amsterdam 2018, pp.176–82.
23. 'Outi Pieski: Art is always the result of certain circumstances', *UniArts Helsinki*, 2 Feb. 2021, https://www.uniarts.fi/en/articles/interviews/outi-pieski-art-is-always-the-result-of-certain-circumstances, accessed 9 Feb. 2024.
24. For a definition of Earth Jurisprudence, see 'Earth Jurisprudence' (2015), Intergovernmental Science-Policy Platform on Biodiversity and Ecosystem Services, https://www.ipbes.net/glossary-tag/earth-jurisprudence, accessed 9 Feb. 2024.
25. Quoted from exhibition wall text by Outi Pieski.
26. As outlined in sources including the Rights of Nature timeline by the Community Environmental Legal Defense Fund (CELDF), https://celdf.org/rights-of-nature/timeline, accessed 19 Jan. 2024.
27. See Pauliina Feodoroff, 'OUTI PIESKI (Free)', trans. Aleksi Koponen, in this publication, pp.67–70.

Sámi: The Daughters of the Moon and Sons of the Sun

Asta Mitkijá Balto

Sámi people love to gather around a bonfire. It's a way of being together and sharing stories, talks and laughter in an outdoor activity surrounded by Mother Earth. Other peoples might also gather around a fire, but we Sámi feel that *dolastallan* (bonfire practice) is our way of carrying and bringing forth a precious tradition from long ago, from our ancestral heritage – one that honours the land and at the same time confirms our relationality as people. We are all relatives – the fire, the earth, the sky and ourselves as human beings. The story that follows honours Outi Pieski's way of carrying out such traditions, by relating her creative art to people, land, rivers, mountains, and to urgent historical and current situations.

In his books, *yoiks* (sung poems) and building art, Nils-Aslak Valkeapää (Áillohaš) includes many examples of humans behaving with respect and a unique reciprocity toward the environment and animals. For instance, his poem about the moving of reindeer from winter grazing land to summer grazing land touches upon cultural practices: when herdsmen arrived with their reindeer at their summer settlement, they dressed up in red *gáktis* (traditional outfits), poured out a splash of coffee for the beautiful area, thanked it for embracing them and then asked it for protection.

The act of spilling a little coffee on a bonfire to connect the earth to the spiritual world is still regularly practiced, even if most doing so have 'forgotten' its meaning. For many Sámi today it is just a habit, but others witnessing this gesture may wonder about the meaning behind it. The reason is that helpers for fertility, birth, and upbringing live in the ground – more specifically, under the *árran* (hearth) in a *goahti* (turf hut) or a *lávvu* (Sámi tent). This is where the female helping spirits Sáráhkká, Uksáhkká and Juoksáhkká lived. These *áhkás* were important for everything related to fertility and childbirth, protection and the safe upbringing of children. Some use the term 'goddesses' to describe these figures, which isn't surprising considering that it was mainly missionaries and priests who wrote about them, and it was natural to use terms they themselves were familiar with. In Sámi, however, they are our *áhkás*, which personally I think is the more fitting term for our female helpers. When we pour some coffee on the fire, then, it is to ask for the protection of the *áhkás*, and to express our wish for our children to stay healthy, grow strong and continue where we left off.

Sámi are great storytellers. Our traditional stories inspire and vitalise performers, musicians, writers and artists engaging in all kinds of of creative expressions. Researchers and teachers can also benefit from storytelling as a source of ancestral knowledge: stories carry and transfer our history, beliefs, struggles, victories, values, wisdom, ethics, humour, myths and spirituality. These stories can be valuable in building and maintaining pride in our traditions, and to adjust them to make these traditions and their messages relevant for today's society.

One of these stories is the Sámi creation myth, the story of how our people came to be. It is nearly two hundred years since the Sámi priest Anders Fjellner presented this story as an epic poem, 'The Son of the Sun's Courting Journey to the Land of the Giants'. This elegant, beautiful *yoik* describes how, in his search for a wife, the Son of Beaivi must sail to the Giants' land – which is so far away that it is beyond the sun and the moon. The *áhkás* have made the Son of Beaivi strong for this journey: he has been given tough muscles and strength by Sáráhkká, and protection and understanding by Uksáhkká. Upon his arrival, the Son of Beaivi is seen by a Giant's daughter, who falls in love with him. He must then triumph over her father, a blind Giant, in a contest. The Giant loses, and the couple get married. As part of the ceremony, the Giant scratches the newlyweds' little fingers to mix their blood, and also ties some special knots. Following the traditions of the Giants' land, the couple spend their wedding night on a whaleskin on the coast. Just as the couple are about to sail away from the Giants' land, though, the Giant's sons return home and, missing their sister, launch their boat and set off in pursuit of the couple. When the bride sees that her brothers are catching up with them, she unties three of the knots the Giant has tied, and three times the Sámi female divinities – even Máttaráhkká, the mother of the other *áhkás* – increase the storm winds until finally the brothers are left behind. Next morning, at sunrise, the brothers mount a headland to look for their sister but are transformed into peaks of stone. On their return to his own land, the Son of Beaivi and the Giant's daughter are happily

married in a second ceremony. This time the wedding night
is spent on bear- and reindeer skin. The giant bride shrinks to
the size of a human being and is made a Sámi. Later, on their
deaths, the couple are transformed into stars in the sky called
Gállábártnit, and become the ancestors of the Sámi people.

Vuokko Hirvonen's analysis of this epic poem underlines how
it makes concrete the mental world of the Sámi people, and
the words of the *yoik – dajahusat –* become a valuable source
of study for understanding Sámi society's conventional roles.
As I have written elsewhere, the Sámi people have traditionally
understood life to be 'part of a whole, an understanding
based on how the universe is composed of everything that
lives and exists. This understanding is rooted in the fact that
nature is not just an object for human beings to use, but that
humans and everything that lives mutually depend on each
other. Our worldview (cosmology) considers humans to
be inextricably linked to nature, while my studies show that
ethical guidance in the form of *olmmožin eallit* (living like a
good human being, a responsible person) is essential in Sámi
upbringing. *Olmmožin eallit* ensures that future generations
learn to maintain balance in all life forms, allowing them to
live in peaceful and mutual coexistence with the environment,
nature, other people, and every form of life'.

Sámi spiritual practices are both poorly and seldom described
for several reasons, not least because people want to protect
them from outsiders. Nevertheless, these practices can be
glimpsed in gestures such as asking for permission to use
nature or natural resources when, for example, we light a
fire, set up a *lávvu* or catch fish in a river. This also applies
to the custom of returning something to the natural world to
thank it for its generosity, such as offering the leftover bones
from a meal of reindeer back to nature. The understanding
of such rituals can be seen in everyday practices, stories,
sayings, legends, poems, *yoiks*, reseach and various artistic
expressions.

The first Sámi to write about Sámi life was Johan Turi. In 1910
he described the close and reciprocal relationship between
humans and their surroundings. When humans are happy, Turi
suggests, the landscape smiles; when humans cry, so do the
mountains.

This way of understanding one's own dependence on nature stands in strong contrast to the Western way of thinking, in which man is master of nature. Indigenous peoples' close reciprocal relationship with nature has recently been the subject of much attention. Fikret Berkes, an ecologist working at the interface of nature and resources, notes that the wider world now seems to be recognising the value of such traditional ways of life and how they can lead to a more sustainable, environmentally conservative use of nature and resources.

The Sámi have long considered it important to maintain a sensitive relationship with nature – to listen to and communicate with animals, with the earth, with what grows, and even with the landscape, as Johan Turi describes. All of this was necessary to maintain a sustainable way of life and ensure the survival of animals and humans. Despite the fact that differing means of survival in Sámi communities over the last forty to fifty years have made people less dependent on nature, these traditional values, ways of thinking and practices continue to live on in the consciousness of the Sámi people.

Such ways of thinking are also present in the work of Outi Pieski, the Sámi contemporary artist who has gained a considerable international reputation in recent years. A 2019 article on Norwegian arts site *KORO* discussed Pieski's relationship with nature, based on four of her paintings that hang in the Norwegian Parliament, concluding that the conventional dualism between nature and culture is absent from Pieski's landscapes. These depiction of bogs and atmospheric, luminous expanses show that nature isn't a foreign being that stands in opposition to 'culture', but that the paintings themselves *are* nature – more than showing it, they practically breathe it.

According to Sámi philosopher Nils Oskal, human beings must be able to get along well with nature and the areas where they travel, as well as with other people. Both in his doctoral work on being a successful reindeer herder in 1995 and in a later article of 2000, Oskal points out that success does not arrive in a vacuum, but depends on how you live your life – on being a good person. From a reindeer husbandry perspective, for instance, you must be honest and honourable, and you must cooperate with others when it comes to grazing areas, migration routes, calving lands and settlements. 'Such places have protective spirits which you must also get along with somehow. An appropriate way is to ask for permission from the land and to make requests of the land.'

Humans are part of a circle of life, in which everyone is 'related' and mutually interdependent. A well known rule of thumb for living in such a world of kinship is that we should not take more than we need. Greed, which leads to overtaxing or depleting nature, breaks that rule. We are responsible for maintaining the balance of taking and giving back; if the circle is broken, access to the goods we need to survive will be lost. By asking for permission to take the benefits that nature, our homes, the Earth, the cloudberry bogs and animals offer us, and by expressing gratitude for them, continuity and sustainability can be ensured.

This story ends here, but Outi Pieski's voice for upholding Sámi unity through art and actions will never go silent.

Poems

Niillas Holmberg

In the old times our boats had two
prows. My generation has never seen
one. Some of us would like to build a
boat with two prows. The elders find
it suspicious, and we get offended by
that. It's not that the elders don't see
any value in it; it's just dangerous to
rework our watercraft so dramatically.

A boat with two prows, there wasn't
anything special about it in the old
times. It was respected in a calm
fashion. Nowadays, the head needs to
be distinct, and it has been like that for
a long while.

The first one to speed up

made the others feel

short of time

The first walker to obtain wings

made the others feel

immobile

Even though walking was like oxygen

it now feels naive

foolish

Dragons don't walk about.

(future)

Whose grandchildren

won't buy tickets to a museum exhibition

with old movie clips

of people actually walking?

Whose grandchildren

won't laugh themselves to death

seeing how people actually

used to take living things from water

and eat them?

Whose grandchildren

won't laugh themselves to death

seeing that people

actually used to eat?

Whose grandchildren

won't laugh?

The first one to obtain eagle eyes

made the others

give up their hearing too

But prior to that…

(past)

Whose ancestors

didn't leave for the bottomless lake

upon hearing the news

of all depths getting measured?

Whose ancestors

didn't leave for the bottomless lake

upon chewing the news

of everything being declared measurable?

Whose ancestors

didn't leave for the bottomless lake

upon swallowing the news

of the endangeredness of bottomlessness?

Whose ancestors

never left for the bottomlessness?

Whose ancestors

never left?

OUTI PIESKI (Free)

Pauliina Feodoroff

Translated by Aleksi Koponen

'Your gaze needs to move freely,' Outi Pieski whispered. It was one of the final nights of high summer, and we were standing some five feet away from her painting *Deatnu, máttožan / Deatnu River, Our Ancestor* 2018. For hours I had tried to put into words my time with the painting.

Freedom is the highest value of the Western world, and in this system, artists are the freest of them all. The birth of the nation-state that followed the Peace of Westphalia in 1648 gave rise to a pact: each nation was sovereign within its borders in any way it chose to be. Furthermore, laws of individual freedom protected any expression of the citizens' free will and must not be violated.

The environmental disaster through which we are living has accelerated the debate about natural law, the role that Indigenous people's knowledge of nature might play with regards to international decision-making and, above all, the question of whether we can continue to do what we want at the expense of the whole of humanity. Can the freedom of the few be allowed to destroy the whole world?

Whether Outi Pieski is painting *Rástegáisá lágalaš riektesubjeaktan / Sacred Mountain Rástegáisá as a Legal Person I* and *II* 2018, making the environmental community art work *Rájácummá / Kiss from the Border* 2017–19 (on which Niillas Holmberg, Jenni Laiti and Pieski collaborated with the Ellos Deatnu! group) or fashioning a forest out of Siberian jays in the corridor of the First Aid department of a new hospital in Rovaniemi, her gaze demands free movement beyond the didactic, beyond acquired knowledge. It is a gaze that calls into question ideas of land as territories or as a natural resource, of images as objects, and of art itself as a superhuman field where hermit-like toil, the automatic writing of geniuses and bohemian resistance alike become sidekicks to democracy and where the artist may act as a barking watchdog, a toppler of perspective or a calming magician using the opiates of aesthetics to lure the grown-up mind to a safe haven. Sometimes art stays on the sidelines, sometimes it thrusts itself forward – but always it is firmly tied to the economic surplus and to government grants. It might even try to bridge the hundred-odd-year gap between the people of Sámi communities and a kind of freedom. A century ago, these lands validated the gaze of their inhabitants and what was looked at. A gaze that was able to decipher what any region was communicating to it was a condition of existence, even if you were looking with your hands, your back, your guts.

Outi Pieski has been educated in the Finnish system to the highest degree and has lived with Teuri Haarla, another uncompromising artist. She also collaborates with her daughters, who are professional dancers, and her own steps are continuously moving from sweetgrass meadows to the world's most acclaimed artistic arenas. She may move from setting up an exhibition to observing a halo of light above a fell. This world sways, and though we may feel flung from one extreme to another by this movement, it cradles Pieski. She is building a bridge bit by bit, by a miraculous force, through a total emptying or filling up. The bridge is built between the responsibilities already disappeared from the mind of free gaze, in a way that is not a metaphor, a manifest or a description of a subject. It is a space where the gaze is free to roam, to enter into the precise, nearly microscopic manifestations of her land that she brings in front of our eyes.

I am convinced that the land shows its will through people, by making us sensitive to the ways or skills by which we can bring out something that needs to be communicated in order to be understood.

Outi Pieski is not sentimental or romantic with regards to her own work or the land her bloodlines stem from. Rather, she is an extreme realist, alert and subtle, profound, dedicated to what is about to arrive or to emerge and which cannot be commanded, imagined, envisioned or decided in advance. The mental fortitude she requires is an intrinsic quality as well as a skill that must be constantly honed, a channel that needs to be maintained and kept clean.

She is a harbinger of a new age: the first visual artist of her kind in a region that only became familiar with the word *art* in the decade of her birth. As if born with that familiarity, Pieski has always had the ability to transmit images, always had art as an inner solution. The swiftness with which times have changed has given her voice the opportunity to emerge on a scale that would not have existed even a decade ago, and it is becoming the strongest voice of her generation. Once a whisper, it now speaks without words, giving us a measure against which to compare the depth of our own personal ethics, morals and ability to work. It wills us to slow down, to become sensitive to the ways the internal and external can exist as one, to understand that the vital knowledge contained in land and landscape finds its form with the tools and in the shapes our time both offers us and understands.

To me, the knowledge in Outi Pieski's art is the knowledge of a woman who has far outgrown the paths of learning given to her, and has moved towards a freedom of gaze that instinctively warrants respect, appreciation, listening. She possesses not only knowledge of herself, her own life and history, but knowledge that spans generations and that she shares with the land – knowledge that must emerge in order to strengthen the forces that maintain life. She is not finished, she is on her way, she is in transit, going to a place with no temporal equivalent, doing something that others have not yet done. And as her journey continues, she leaves behind artistic actions, signs, hints, secrets from which anyone's gaze is free to pick up what it can.

I cannot say what her work communicates to me. It is too intimate – and I am still far too possessive of my reaction to share it. More, I like to think that keeping the reception of her work personal prolongs its effect on me. What I saw there has become internal to me, an inner talisman that I can turn to for advice, strength, confirmation whenever I need it.

There is no shortcut to achieving an equilibrium between technology, sense of form, knowledge of the land and being human in such a remarkable way that it resonates with other people. But in the presence of Outi Pieski and her work, I become activated, opening up and rearranging myself, finding layers in myself that are inaccessible at other times. It is an intoxicating, intense, sometimes frightening experience, because our culture has lost any protocol for breaking away safely from this circle. One has to operate like two artists would: one work at a time, one conversation at a time.

We are not free from the forces of nature, nor have we ever
been. At this moment especially, we see that we are not free
from the consequences of the last centuries of our human
freedom. My greatest experiences of freedom are related to
the feeling of communicating: those times when I do not
raise my voice to be heard or try to drown out others, but
when I truly get to participate in dialogue, the exchange with
the land and the people who live on it. This communication
has to move freely in order for us to survive as a species.
Outi Pieski, the guardian and promoter of this sort of
communication, shares with you, people not from the Deatnu
river, directions on how to use your freedom.

Rematriation in the art and research project

Foremother's Hat of Pride

Dr Eeva-Kristiina Nylander

The Sámi handicraft form named *duodji* carries within it the whole ontology, worldview and philosophy of the Sámi people. My work with the artist Outi Pieski introduced the term 'rematriation' to the study of Sámi crafts and therefore to that of *duodji*. In 2017, we started a project in which we combined art, research and craftivism to study an iconic piece of *duodji*: the *ládjogahpir* hat. The *ládjogahpir* was worn by Sámi women between the 1750s and the turn of the twentieth century, and in studying the hat we studied not only the history of *duodji*, but also of Sámi women.

Although the *ládjogahpir* was no longer worn by Sámi women by the time we made our studies, it had not disappeared from oral histories and folklore. The practical uses of the *ládjogahpir*, as well as its symbolic meanings, remain a mystery, but there is a strong narrative connected to the end of the use of the headwear. This tells us that Christian priests prohibited the wearing of the *ládjogahpir* as they thought the devil lived in the *fierra*, the wooden support inside the hat. This led to the burning of the hats. This narrative has since inspired many Sámi artists, and the *ládjogahpir* has become a subject of numerous artworks, in which it often symbolises the empowerment of Sámi women and the flourishing of Sámi culture and values. The *ládjogahpir* represents ancient cosmology and a solid social and equal relation between the genders. It represents, too, a society that prospered before colonial gender violence brought heteropatriarchy and Western epistemologies to Sápmi (the land of the Sámi). Relatedly, the narrative of the *fierra* as the devil's horn can be interpreted as a metaphor for demonising the Sámi female guardian spirits that are the foundation of Sámi cosmology and society. When European patriarchy was established in Sápmi, Sámi women were displaced from their original positions of respect. Patriarchalism brought a new world order and hierarchies, which generated the development towards an unbalanced society. The burning of the hats resembles the earlier confiscation and burning of sacred Sámi drums, and reflects the philosophy of the Christian church that fire cleanses. Such acts represent the heteropatriarchy's violence towards the Indigenous worldview, philosophy, ontology and being.

In our project, Outi Pieski and I used *duodji* such as *ládjogahpir* as a form of Sámi feminist activism or craftivism. We interwove

historical and archaeological research with community art
and craftivism, because of which the use of the hat has now
been revived in Sámi communities. Our project progressed
in dialogue with Sámi women as we developed forms of
cooperation and combined our skills. We made visits to
inspect many of these hats and undertook traditional 'object
studies' in the Nordic countries and Europe, alongside
studying archive materials. We decided to revive the making
of the hats in workshops: under Pieski's tuition, craftswomen
learned how to make *ládjogahpir* with new materials but
old patterns. I was able to return the research data I had
collected, sharing it with the Sámi women, and to participate
in the workshops as they revived the cultural heritage of
their foremothers. I also had the opportunity to interview the
women, which resulted in the many stirring, informative and
even moving conversations that became the centre of our
study. This was our way to make the Sámi women's voices
heard. Our collaboration culminated in the publication in
2020 of the art and science book *The Ládjogahpir: The
Foremothers' Hat of Pride* (Ládjogahpir: Máttaráhkuid
gábagahpir). The project served as an inspiration for many
of Outi Pieski's works of art, which she has displayed in
exhibitions around the world.

We use the term 'rematriation' to describe the process which
the *ládjogahpir* has undergone in our project. Rematriation
– referring to Earth as a mother, the sacred feminine that
enables life for all beings – is a relatively new concept that
is used in Indigenous feminist thinking and activism. Lately it
has been used also in the field of cultural heritage studies.
It applies well to Indigenous peoples like the Sámi for whom
the sun is father and the Earth is mother. Rematriation refers
to reclaiming ancestral spirituality, culture, knowledge and
resources, to going back to Mother Earth, and to reciprocal
ways of being that existed before the patriarchal destruction
and colonialism brought by Christianity. It also emphasises
equality between all genders and all living beings (including
those we cannot see) and collectivism.

Like many other Indigenous peoples, the Sámi consider the
Earth to be sacred and feminine, their mother. In the North
Sámi language, mother is *eadni* and Earth is *eana*, and the
two words share etymologies and semantics. Sámi folklore

contains narratives of ancestors who have hidden treasures
in nature: in the Sámi spirituality, the female guardian spirits
Sáráhkká, Uksáhkká and Juoksáhkká dwell in the earth
underneath the *goahti*, the Sámi hut, and beneath the *árran*,
the fireplace of the *goahti*, suggesting that the treasure is
the earth itself. Knowledge and wisdom reside in our Mother
Earth and it is our obligation to listen to her: if we do, she
will tell us how to walk our paths, as she told our ancestors
before us. When we embrace gender equality and the larger
biocultural reality, we also understand that Earth as a female
being must be respected. Sacredness is in all genders, but
we live in a world where the balance between them has been
disturbed. Violence towards women is synonymous with
violence towards – and the plundering of – the Earth. We
need to restore the balance between genders and achieve
reciprocity with all beings.

In her art, Pieski is in constant discussion with the land
of Sápmi and the Sámi culture, especially femininity. By
combining elements from women's clothing with landscape
painting, she inserts the female guardian spirits into her
art, reminding the viewer of the sacredness of the Earth
and the reciprocity between all beings that we find in Sámi
philosophy and ontology. We have to listen to the Earth and
nurture her; without Mother Nature, we have nothing. In this
way, Pieski's art embodies the very meaning of rematriation:
listening to and having an emotional connection with the
ancestors. We understand rematriation as a process that
starts where repatriation ends – both the repatriation of
objects and of their related knowledge. It is something that
happens within an Indigenous community when its members
study, discuss and use bodily movements to remake their
artifacts (such as *duodji*). Rematriation therefore includes
the restoration of learning, action and the knowledge of
materials. In addition to exploring archive data, such as
material that describes how the piece of *duodji* was banned,
the process of rematriating an object includes sharing
the Sámi expertise, philosophy and worldview related to
it, as well as the restoration of proverbs, narratives and
terminology.

Although oral traditions such as the *diiddat* – spells related
to objects – have been forgotten, an object such as the

ládjogahpir may today gain new meanings which are as
important as those that existed before. Our project with
the *ládjogahpir* is not only the rematriation of the hat itself,
but of the part of Sámi women's history related to *duodji*
and the *ládjogahpir*. When pieces of *duodji* are returned to
Sápmi and the knowledge related to them is restored, they
can be transformed into part of their society's living culture.
It remains to be seen whether the collective memory will
be revived, but what is already clear is that the discussions
opened with the help of the *ládjogahpir*, for example, have
deeply influenced people and enabled discourse on even
such difficult matters as gender violence, issues of equality
and the healing of the wounds of colonialism.

These debates are also empowering, as rematriation
expressly entails the creation of a new emotional connection
with the *duodji* of the past. This is how we bring about the
resocialisation – the return to Mother Earth, to their own
societies – of collections which have previously remained
mute. *Duodji* is a holistic concept, representing the
connection to Sámi ancestors, the *árbevierru* (Sámi way)
passed down by them and, ultimately, the basic values of
the Sámi identity. Integrating archive data, *árbevierru* and
árbediehtu (oral tradition) into the community's work with the
objects is what gives rise to rematriation, or genuine return.
It springs from deep connections with one's own culture and
ancestors, and from collective working and the repetition
of ancient movements in terms of *duodji*. *Árbediehtu* is the
collective wisdom and skills of the Sámi people and has
been used to enhance their livelihood for centuries. It has
been passed down from generation to generation, both orally
and through work and practical experience. Through this
continuity, *árbediehtu* binds the past, present and future.

Today, something utterly special and powerful occurs when
Sámi women wear the *ládjogahpir*. Although much of the
original meaning of the *ládjogahpir* is lost, as are large
parts of the overall history of Sámi women, now that the
hat is being made and worn again it will invite and house
new meanings. In addition, Gunvor Guttorm suggests in
her writings that the body remembers movements and that
when you move while gathering or working with materials,
those memories are reawakened. What if the mind and the

body remember intergenerationally? The *ládjogahpir*, like other Sámi artifacts, carries the traditional knowledge of the ancestors with it, forwarding messages across generations. For those who can read their language, the artifacts hold encoded knowledge about their own cultural heritage.
In addition, they may be regarded as a symbol of a new decolonial feminism: *duodji*, rematriation and working with repatriated artifacts are sensible means by which to initiate decolonial practices in Sámi society. These may also be productive concepts in further developing research regarding Sámi artifacts and historical processes.

List of Works

Geasi vuordin
Waiting for Summer
2007
Oil paint on canvas, bones, mixed media
Kalleinen & Kochta-Kalleinen Collection

Lottelávlunmuorra I
A Bird's Singing Tree I
2008
Reindeer skull, Sámi shawl
Sámi Museum Siida

Murku II
Fog II
2008
Oil on canvas, bones, mixed media
Private collection

Áhku Dálkkasbeahci
Áhkku's Medicine-pine
2009
Acrylic paint on canvas, Sámi-crafted *duodji*
Rovaniemi Art Museum / Jenny and Antti
Wihuri Foundation Collection

Čáhppes Giisavárri
Black Fell Giisavárri
2009
Acrylic paint on canvas
RiddoDuottarMuseat

Giisavárri
Giisavárri Fell
2009
Acrylic paint on canvas, Sámi-crafted *duodji*
RiddoDuottarMuseat

Suhpiid luhtte
Close by the Aspens
2009
Acrylic paint on canvas
Courtesy of the artist

Nuvvos Áilegas, českes
Fell Nuvvos Áilegas in White
2011
Acrylic paint on canvas, thread
Private collection

Nuvvos Áilegas, dulvi
Nuvvos Áilegas, flood
2011
Acrylic paint on canvas, thread
Private collection

Bovdna
Tussock
2012
Acrylic paint on canvas, thread
Stortinget / The Norwegian Parliament

Deatnu ijabealde
Deatnu River by the Night
2013
Acrylic paint on canvas, thread
Private collection

Golle-eana
Land of Gold
2013
Acrylic paint on canvas, thread
Yle Sápmi

Gulul golgá Deatnu
Slowly Flows the Deatnu River
2013
Acrylic paint on canvas, thread
Rovaniemi Art Museum / Rovaniemi City
Collection

Nuvvos Áilegas, oaidnemeahttun
Nuvvos Áilegas, Fell Unseen
2013
Acrylic paint on canvas, thread
Stortinget / The Norwegian Parliament

Nuvvos Áilegas feaskkir
The Corridor of Nuvvos Áilegas
2013
Acrylic paint on canvas, thread
Private collection

Nuvvos Áilegasa oaivvis
Top of the Nuvvos Áilegas
2013
Acrylic paint on canvas, thread
Yle Sápmi

Gámasvárri
Gámasvárri Fell
2014
Acrylic paint on canvas, thread
The Finnish National Gallery, State Art
Deposit Collection

Juoksáhkká Liŋkinjeakkis
Goddess Juoksáhkká at Liŋkinjeaggi Marsh
2014
Acrylic paint on canvas, textile
Courtesy of the artist

Sáráhkká Liŋkinjeakkis
Goddess Sáráhkká at Liŋkinjeaggi Marsh
2014
Acrylic paint on canvas, textile
Private collection

Gollejohka
River of Gold
2014
Acrylic paint on canvas, thread
Stortinget / The Norwegian Parliament

Gurra
Gorge
2014
Acrylic paint on canvas
Courtesy of the artist

Oh, Gárdečohka
2014
Acrylic paint on canvas
RiddoDuottarMuseat

Rádjajohtin I
Pacing the Borders I
2014
Acrylic paint and baize on canvas
RiddoDuottarMuseat

Rádjajohtin III
Pacing the Borders III
2014
Acrylic paint and baize on canvas
Private collection

Silbajohka
Silver River
2014
Acrylic paint on canvas, thread
Stortinget / The Norwegian Parliament

Lavdnegoahti I
Turf Hut I
2015
Acrylic paint on canvas, textile
Courtesy of the artist

Gorži
Waterfall
2016
Gilded reindeer skull, Sámi shawl
Davvi Álbmogiid Guovddáš | Senter for
Nordlige Folk | Centre of Northern Peoples

Uksáhkká Bissočuollanjeakkis
Goddess Uksáhkká at
Bissočuollanjeaggi Marsh
2017
Acrylic paint on canvas, textile
The Finnish National Gallery, State Art
Deposit Collection

Alážis
At the Top
2018
Lithograph print on paper
Courtesy of the artist.
Printed at Tamarind Institute

Čáppa muđot Áilegas
Sweet-faced Mountain Nuvvos Áilegas
2018
Lithograph print on paper
Courtesy of the artist.
Printed at Tamarind Institute

Deatnu, máttožan
Deatnu River, Our Ancestor
2018
Acrylic paint on canvas
Courtesy of the artist

Gahpiraš
Sweet Hat Mountain
2018
Lithograph print on paper
Courtesy of the artist.
Printed at Tamarind Institute

Golbma oabbaža
Three Sisters
2018
Lithograph print on paper
Courtesy of the artist.
Printed at Tamarind Institute

Iehčanas vuoigatvuohta leat ja lieđđut
Independent Right to Exist and Flourish
2018
Acrylic paint on canvas
Rovaniemi Art Museum / Jenny and Antti
Wihuri Foundation Collection

Nuvvos Áilegas lágalaš riektesubjeaktan
Sacred Mountain as a Legal Person
2018
Acrylic paint on canvas, gilt metal
Courtesy of the artist

Rástegáisá lágalaš riektesubjeaktan I
Sacred Mountain Rástegáisá as a Legal
Person I
2018
Acrylic paint on canvas, gilt metal, thread
Private collection

Rástegáisá lágalaš riektesubjeaktan II
Sacred Mountain Rástegáisá as a Legal
Person II
2018
Acrylic paint on canvas, gilt metal, thread
Private collection

Rematriašuvdna – Máhccat eatni lusa
Rematriation – Return to Mother
2018
Acrylic paint on canvas
Courtesy of the artist

Ládjogahpir rematriašuvdna
– Máhccat eatni lusa
Rematriation of a Ládjogahpir
– Return to Mother
2018–23
An installation comprising:
    Kolonialisttalaš metamorfosa 1852
    Colonialist Metamorphosis 1852
    2018
    Sámi-crafted *duodji*, mixed media
    Courtesy of the artist

Outi Pieski and Eeva-Kristiina Nylander
47 eanemus ohccojuvvon máttaráhkut
The 47 Most Wanted Foremothers
2019
Pigment prints on paper
Courtesy of the artist

Outi Pieski, Biret and Gáddjá Haarla Pieski
Ládjogahpir rematriašuvdna
– Máhccat eatni lusa
Rematriation of a Ládjogahpir
– Return to Máttaráhkká
2019
Inkjet print on vinyl wallpaper, pigment
prints on paper
Courtesy of the artist

Portraits of Anni Koivisto,
Anna Näkkäläjärvi-Länsman and
Elle Valkeapää
2019
Pigment prints on paper
Courtesy of the artist

Subjeavttat dutkamuša vuolde
Subjects of Research
2019
Pigment print on paper
Courtesy of the artist

Máhccat eatni lusa
Return to Máttaráhkká
2020
Sámi-crafted *duodji*, reindeer moss
Courtesy of the artist

Litna máttaráhkku
The Light Weight of the Foremother
2021
Sámi-crafted *duodji*, reindeer moss,
hat holder
Courtesy of the artist

Lossa máttaráhkku
The Heavy Weight of the Foremother
2021
Sámi-crafted *duodji*, tussock cottongrass,
hair, stone
Courtesy of the artist

Odđa ja eallilan
Empty and Filled
2021
Sámi-crafted *duodji*, mixed media
The National Museum of Art, Architecture
and Design, Norway

Outi Pieski and Biret Haarla Pieski
Ceagganaddat
Listening with Foremother
2023
Video, high definition, monitor, colour,
13 min 45 sec
Courtesy of the artist

Guržot ja guovssat
Spell on You!
2020
Thread, steel, wood
Courtesy of the artist

Beavvit
Rising Together II
2021
Thread, steel, wood
Moderna Museet, Stockholm. Purchase 2021
(Swedish Acquisitions 2021)

Skábmavuođđu
Spell on Me!
2024
Thread, steel, wood
Courtesy of the artist

All works © Outi Pieski

Photography credits:

Cover, pp.14, 18, 22, 26, 30, 45–6, 48:
© Jussi Tiainen

pp.1, 4–9, 11–13, 20–1, 23–5, 27–9, 32–5,
38–41, 81–111, 116–125, 128
© Tate (Sam Day) 2024

pp.2–3: © Sami Museum Siida

pp.10, 112–15, 126–7:
© Outi Pieski

pp.15, 19, 31, 36–7, 42 (top), 43 (bottom), 47:
© Ari Karttunen / EMMA
– Espoo Museum of Modern Art

pp.16–17:
© Petter Martiskainen

pp.42 (bottom), 43 (top):
© The Oulu Museum of Art

p.44:
© Ella Tommila / EMMA
– Espoo Museum of Modern Art

Colophon

First published 2024 by order of the Tate Trustees by Tate St Ives in association with Tate Publishing, a division of Tate Enterprises Ltd, Millbank, London SW1P 4RG, www.tate.org.uk/publishing, to support the development of the exhibition:

Outi Pieski
Tate St Ives, 10 February – 6 May 2024

Curated by Anne Barlow, Director, Tate St Ives, with Giles Jackson, Assistant Curator

Supported by

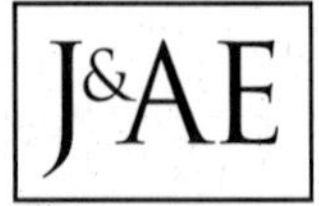

JANE AND AATOS
ERKKO FOUNDATION

With additional support from the
Outi Pieski Exhibition
Supporters Circle:
Barbro Osher Pro Suecia Foundation
Saastamoinen Foundation
Frame Contemporary Art Finland
Finnish Institute in the UK and Ireland
Embassy of Finland in London
Saami Council

Tate Americas Foundation
and Tate Members

Publication edited by Anne Barlow
and Giles Jackson
Texts by Asta Mitkijá Balto, Anne Barlow,
Pauliina Feodoroff, Niillas Holmberg,
and Dr Eeva-Kristiina Nylander
Copy-edited by Neil Stewart
Designed by SecMoCo
Printed by Die Keure

Thank you to all of the institutions and private lenders that have loaned works to this exhibition. With thanks also to Helen Bent, Louise Connell, Arielle Etheridge, Sally Noall, Ross Peakall, and Tate's conservation, design and technical teams.

Tate would also like to thank HM Government for providing Government Indemnity for the exhibition at Tate St Ives, and the Department for Digital, Culture, Media and Sport and Arts Council England for arranging the indemnity.

Outi Pieski would like to thank Biret Haarla Pieski, Gáddjá Haarla Pieski, Dr Eeva-Kristiina Nylander, Rita Nurmenrinta, Eveliina Guttorm and Laura Annika Pieski, Máret Johanna Huuva, Jenni Laiti, Ulla Magga, Leena Karoliina Mattanen, Sunnamaarit Sara-Tornensis, Kaarin West, Anni Koivisto, Anna Näkkäläjärvi-Länsman, Elle Valkeapää, Tamarind Institute, Govus / Erno Karjalainen, Frame Contemporary Art Finland, Arts Promotion Center Finland, Saami Council, and all others who have supported her practice.

Giitu Rástegáisá, Deatnu, Nuvvos Áilegas ja eara ruoktoguovllu duovdagat.
(Thanks to the Fell Rástegáisá, the Fell Nuvvos Áilegas, the Deatnu River and other places in the home land.)

A catalogue record for this book is available from the British Library.

ISBN: 978-1-84976-917-4

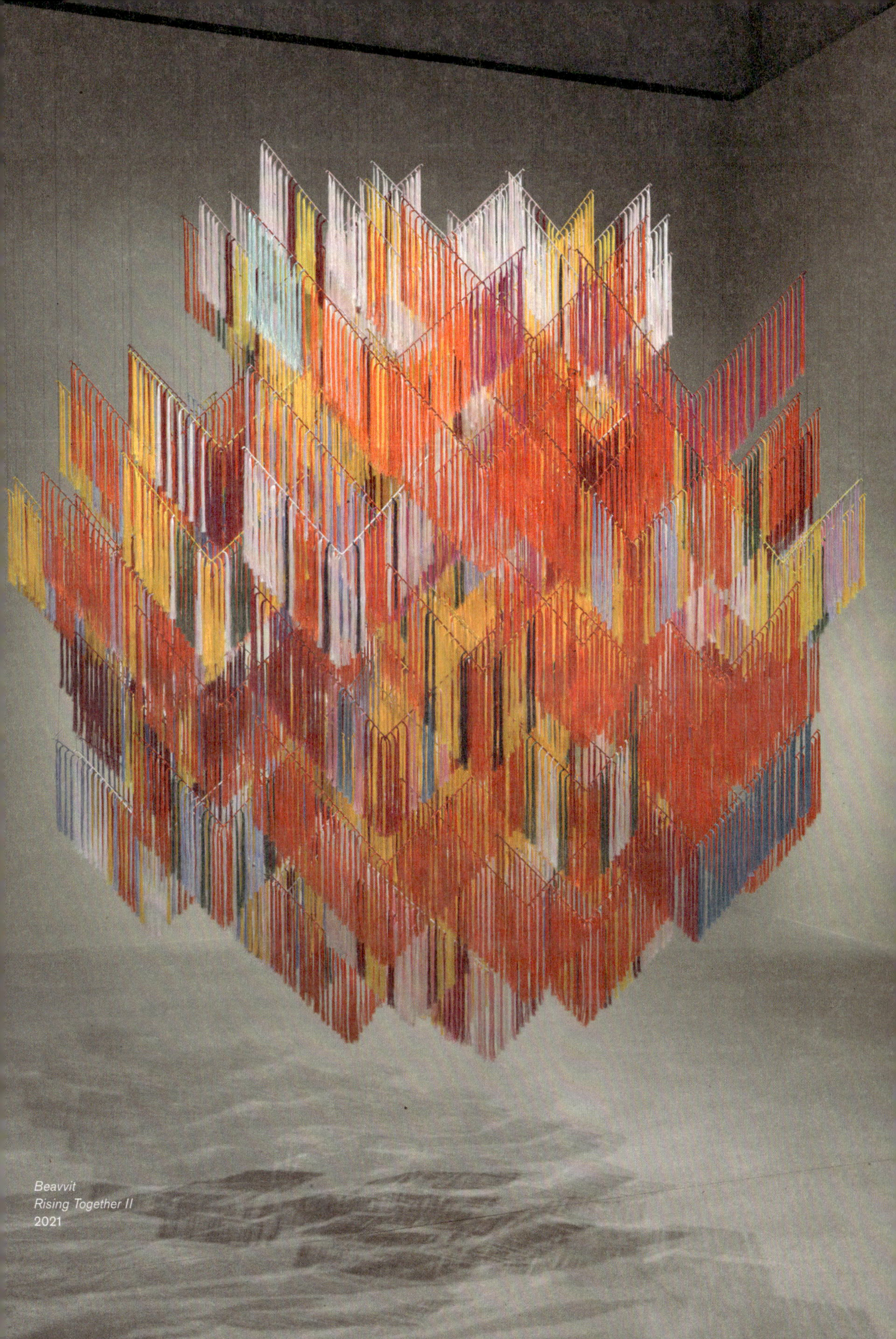

Beavvit
Rising Together II
2021

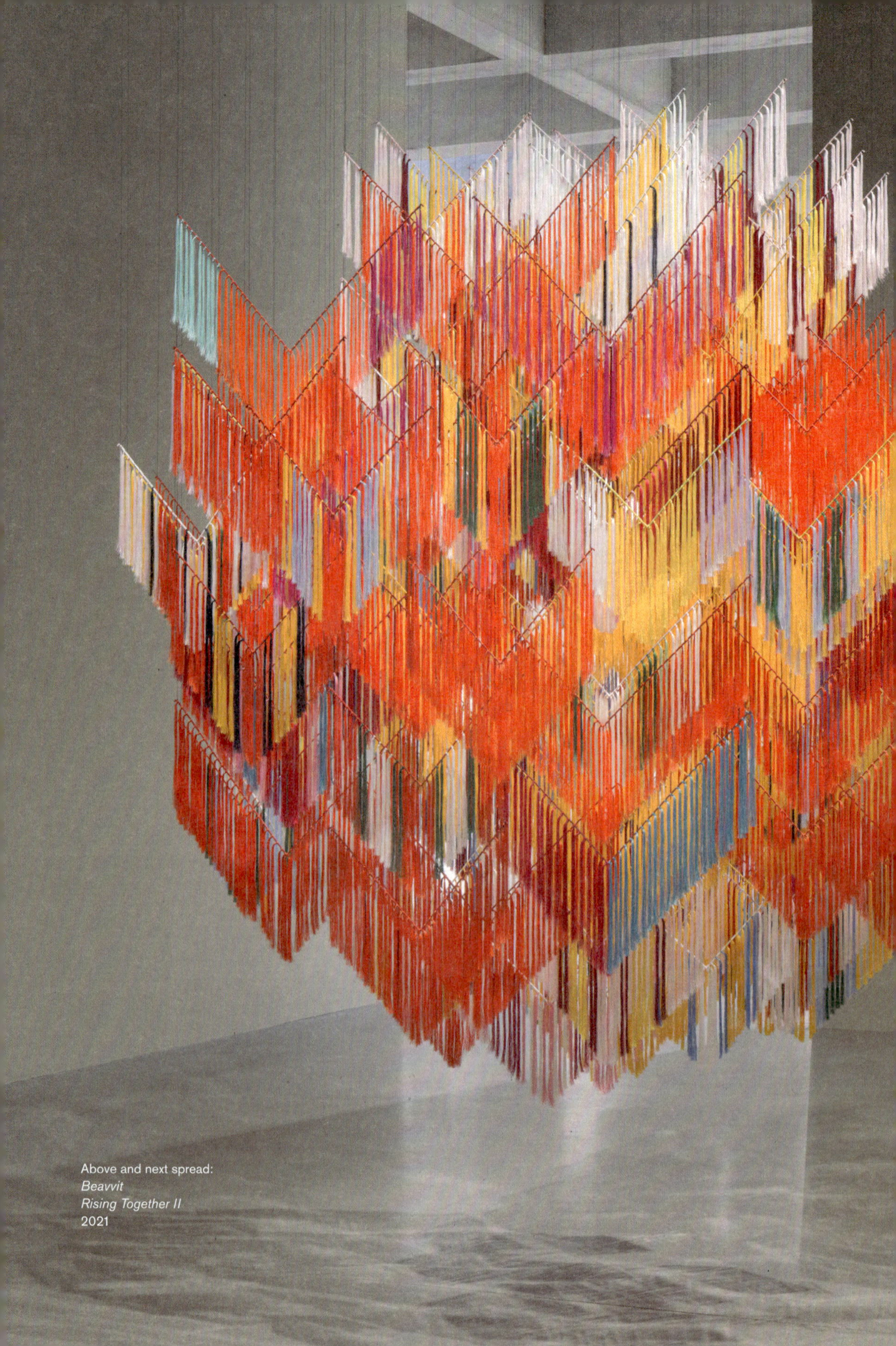

Above and next spread:
Beavvit
Rising Together II
2021

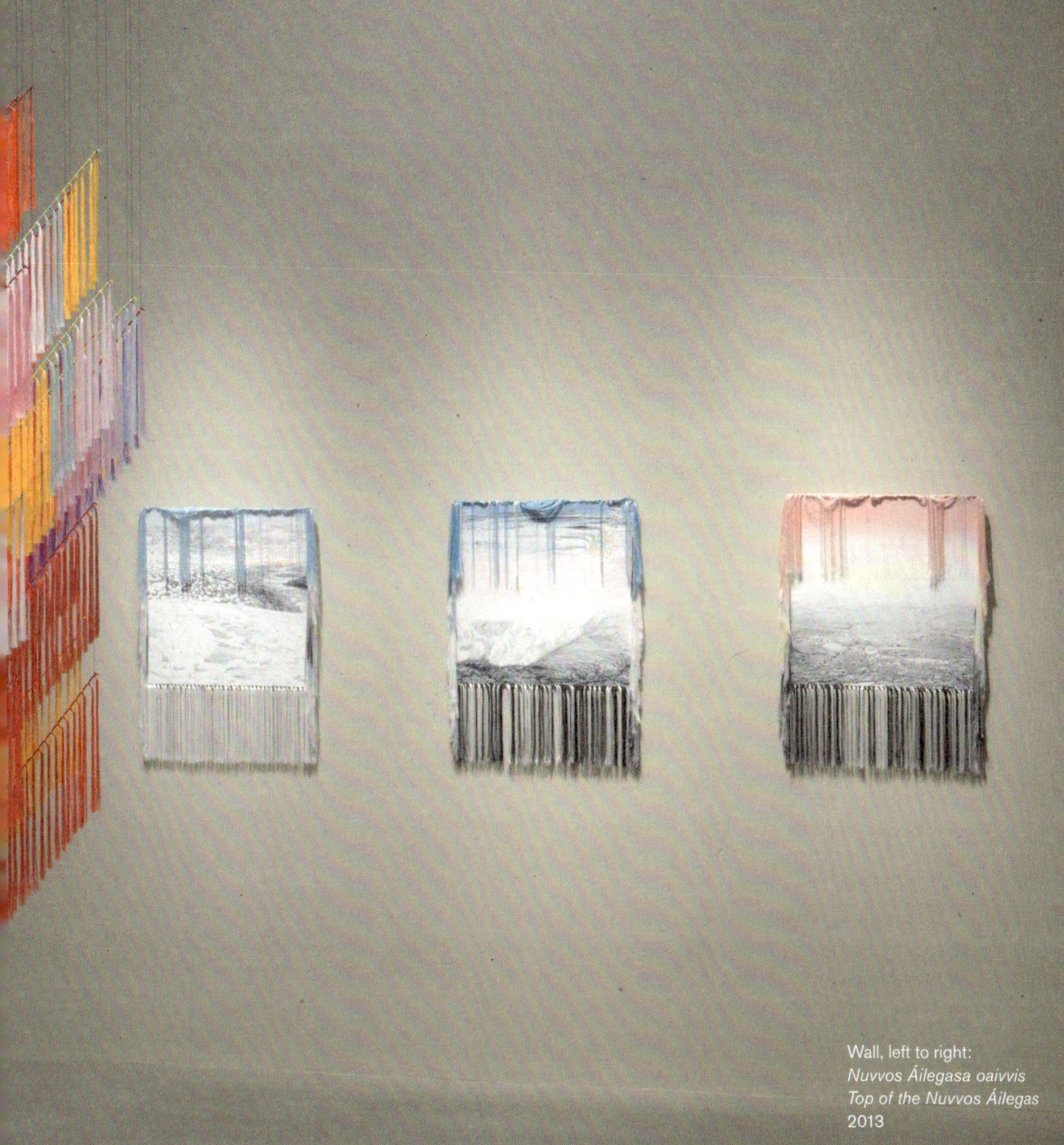

Wall, left to right:
Nuvvos Áilegasa oaivvis
Top of the Nuvvos Áilegas
2013

Nuvvos Áilegas feaskkir
The Corridor of Nuvvos Áilegas
2013

Nuvvos Áilegas, oaidnemeahttun
Nuvvos Áilegas, Fell Unseen
2013

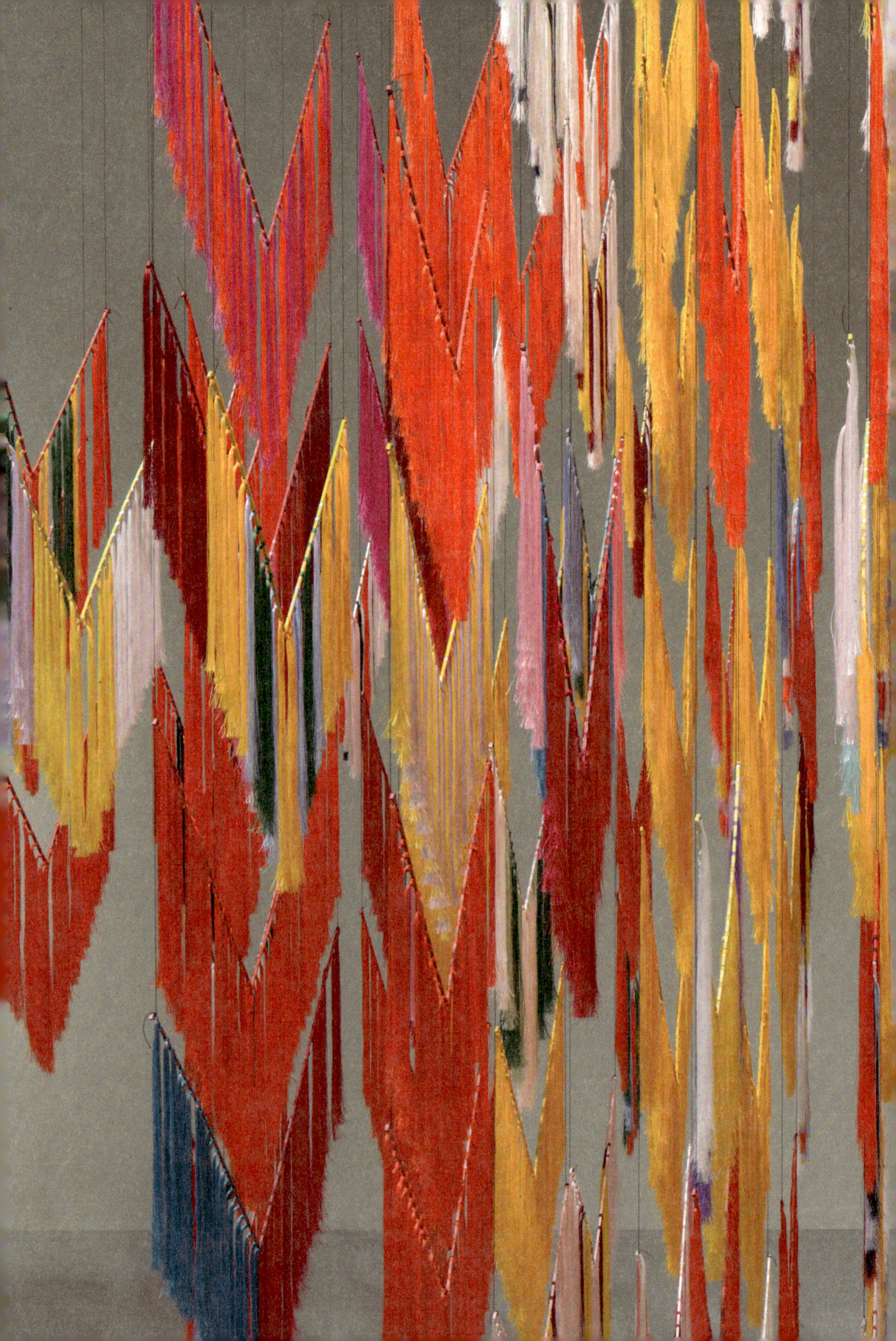

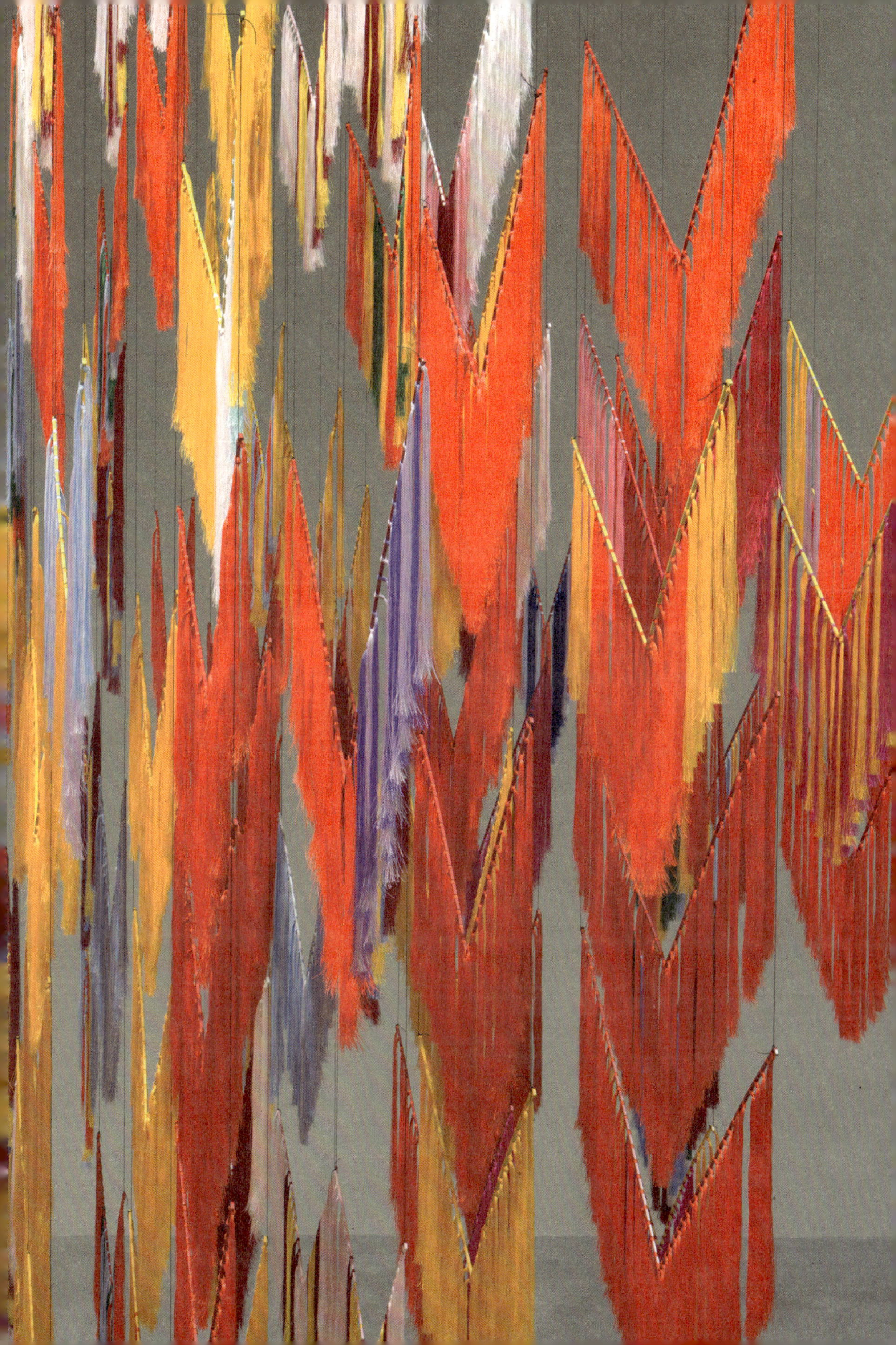

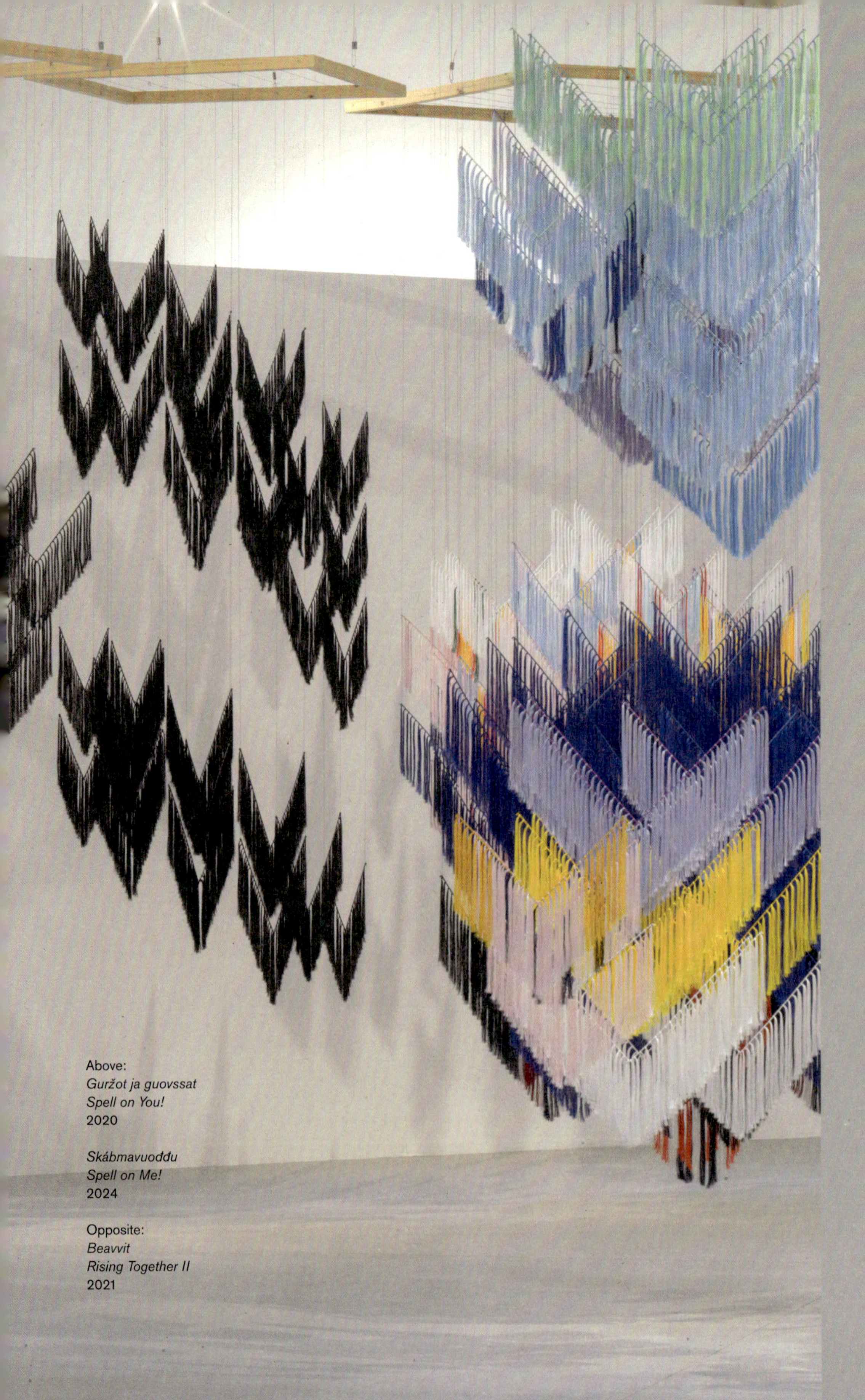

Above:
Guržot ja guovssat
Spell on You!
2020

Skábmavuoddu
Spell on Me!
2024

Opposite:
Beavvit
Rising Together II
2021

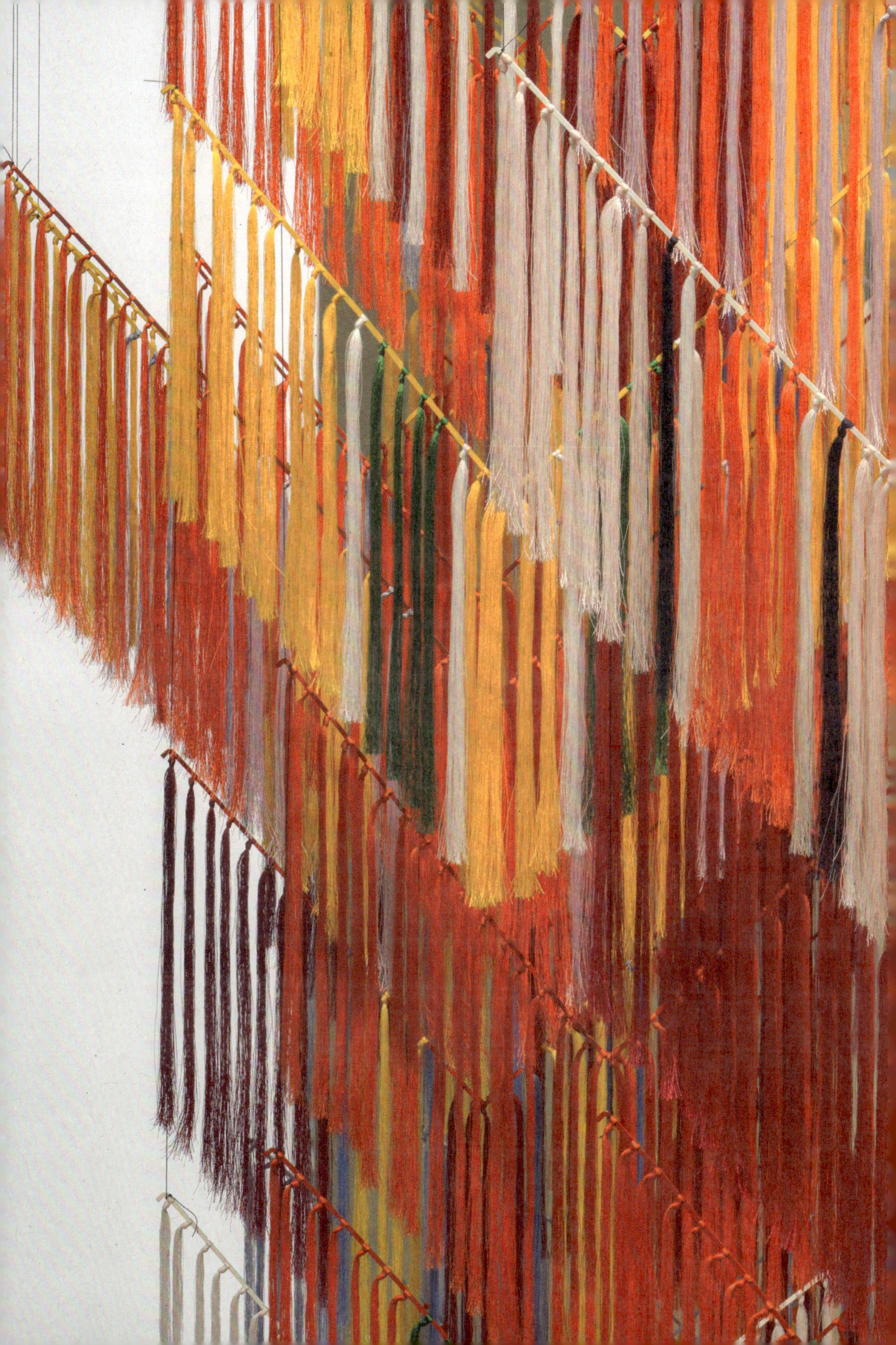

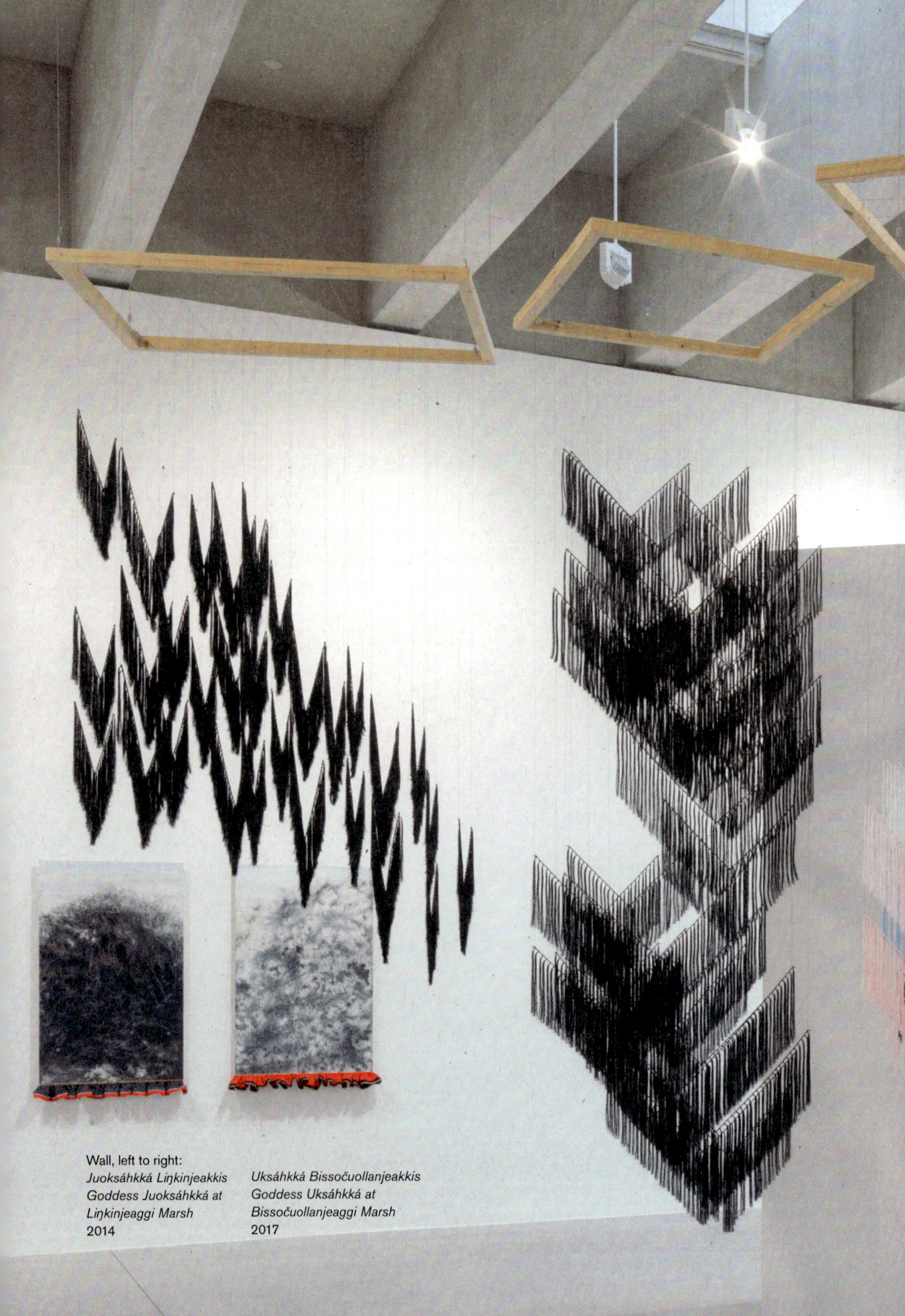

Wall, left to right:
Juoksáhkká Liŋkinjeakkis
Goddess Juoksáhkká at
Liŋkinjeaggi Marsh
2014

Uksáhkká Bissočuollanjeakkis
Goddess Uksáhkká at
Bissočuollanjeaggi Marsh
2017

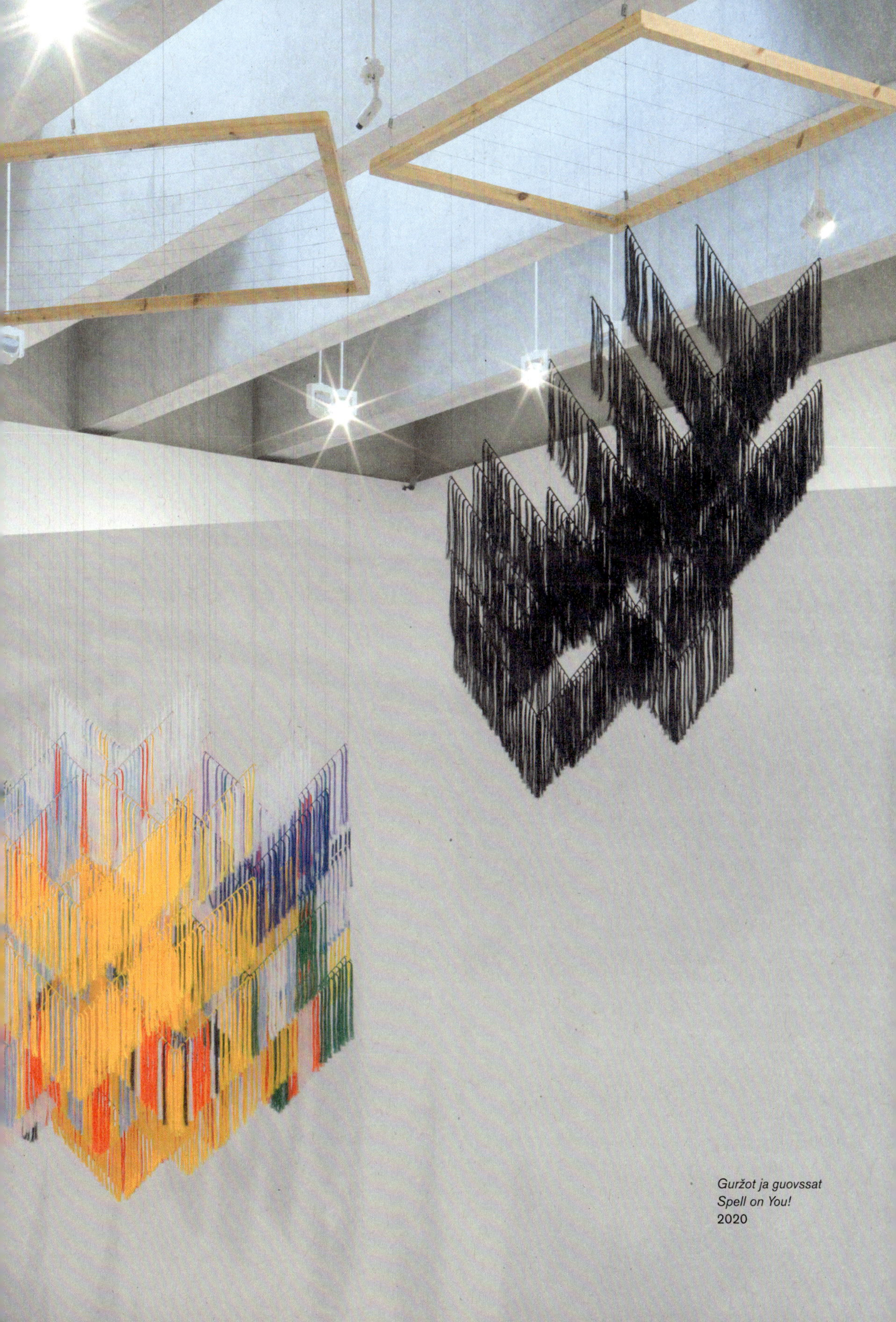

Guržot ja guovssat
Spell on You!
2020

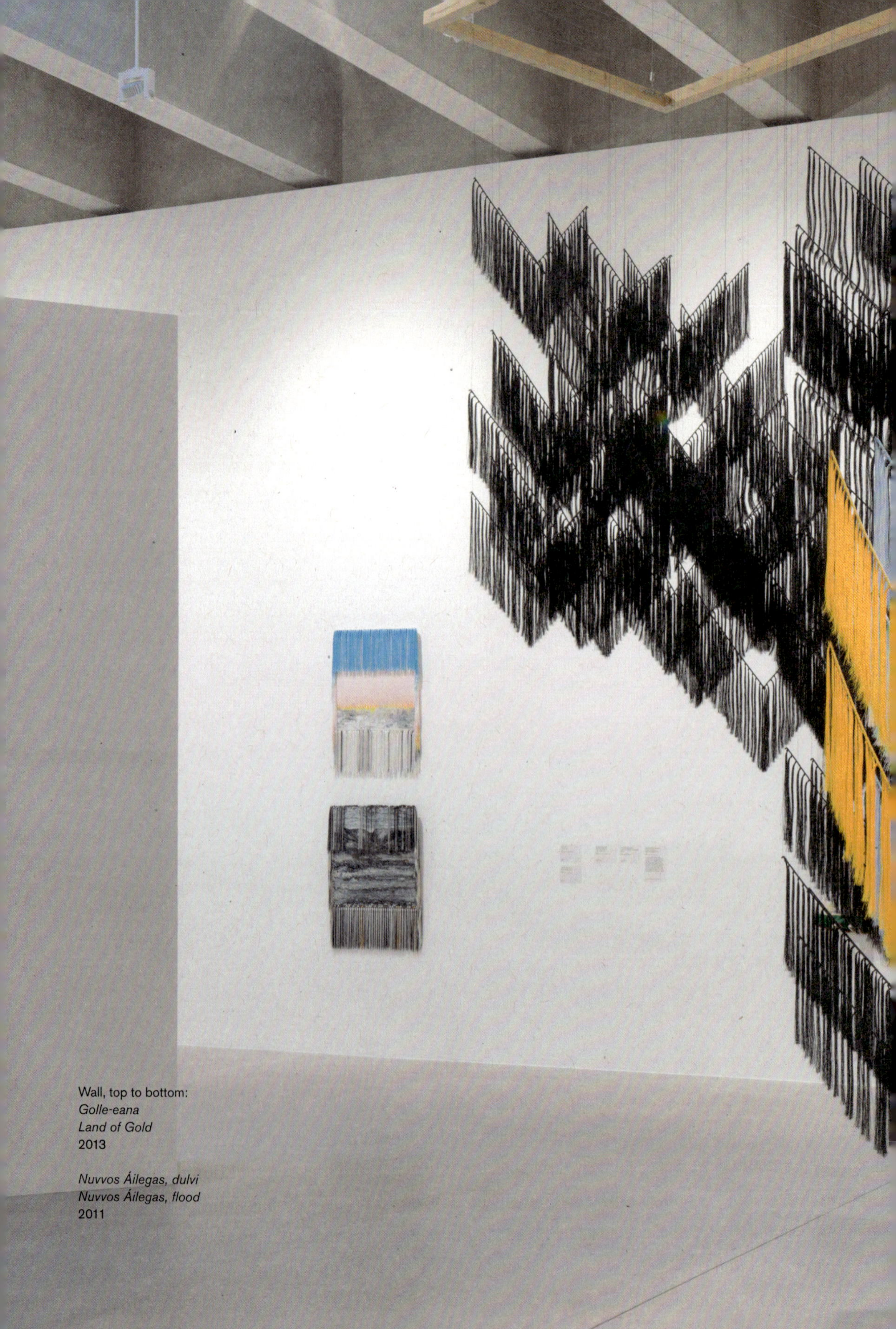

Wall, top to bottom:
Golle-eana
Land of Gold
2013

Nuvvos Áilegas, dulvi
Nuvvos Áilegas, flood
2011

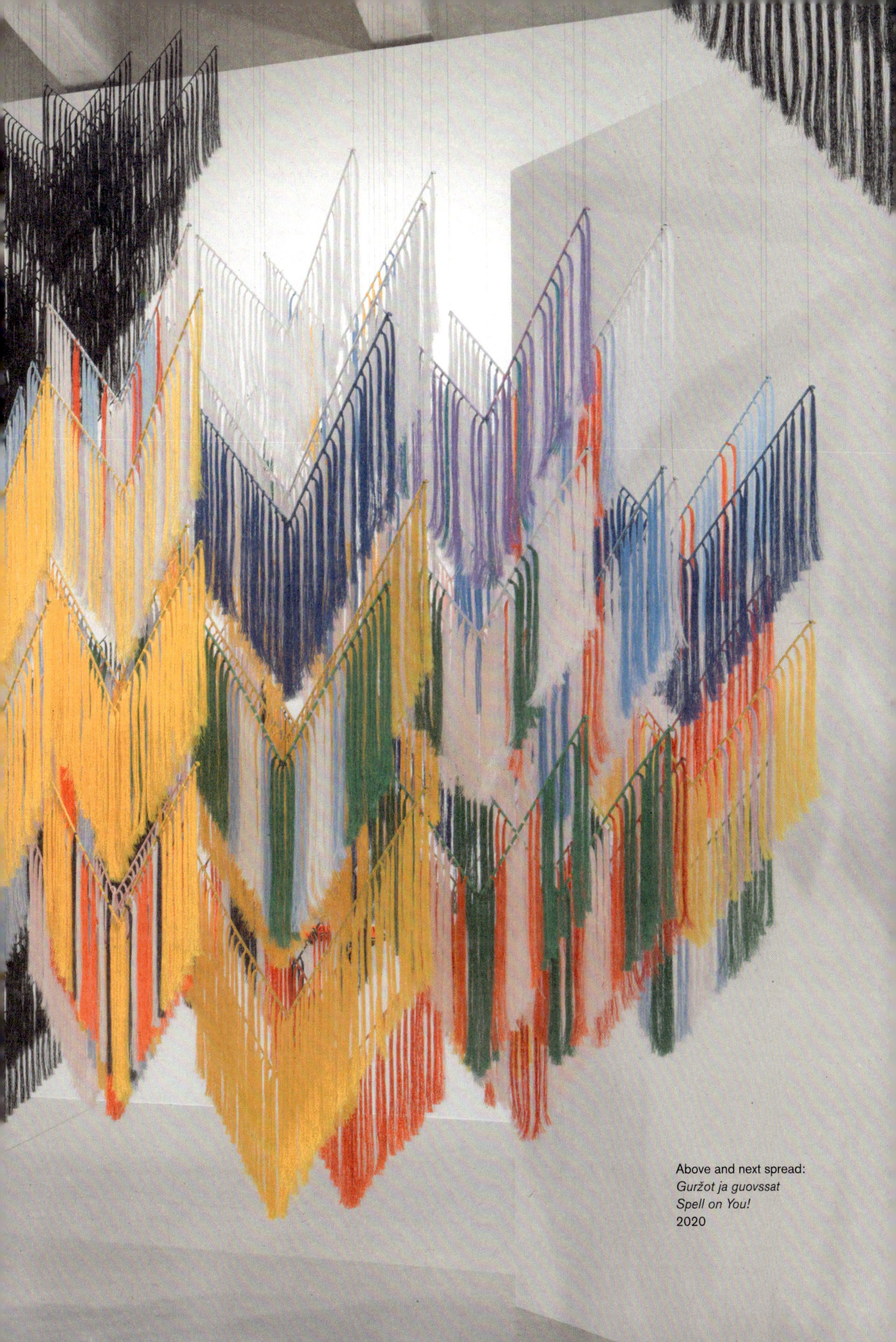

Above and next spread:
Guržot ja guovssat
Spell on You!
2020

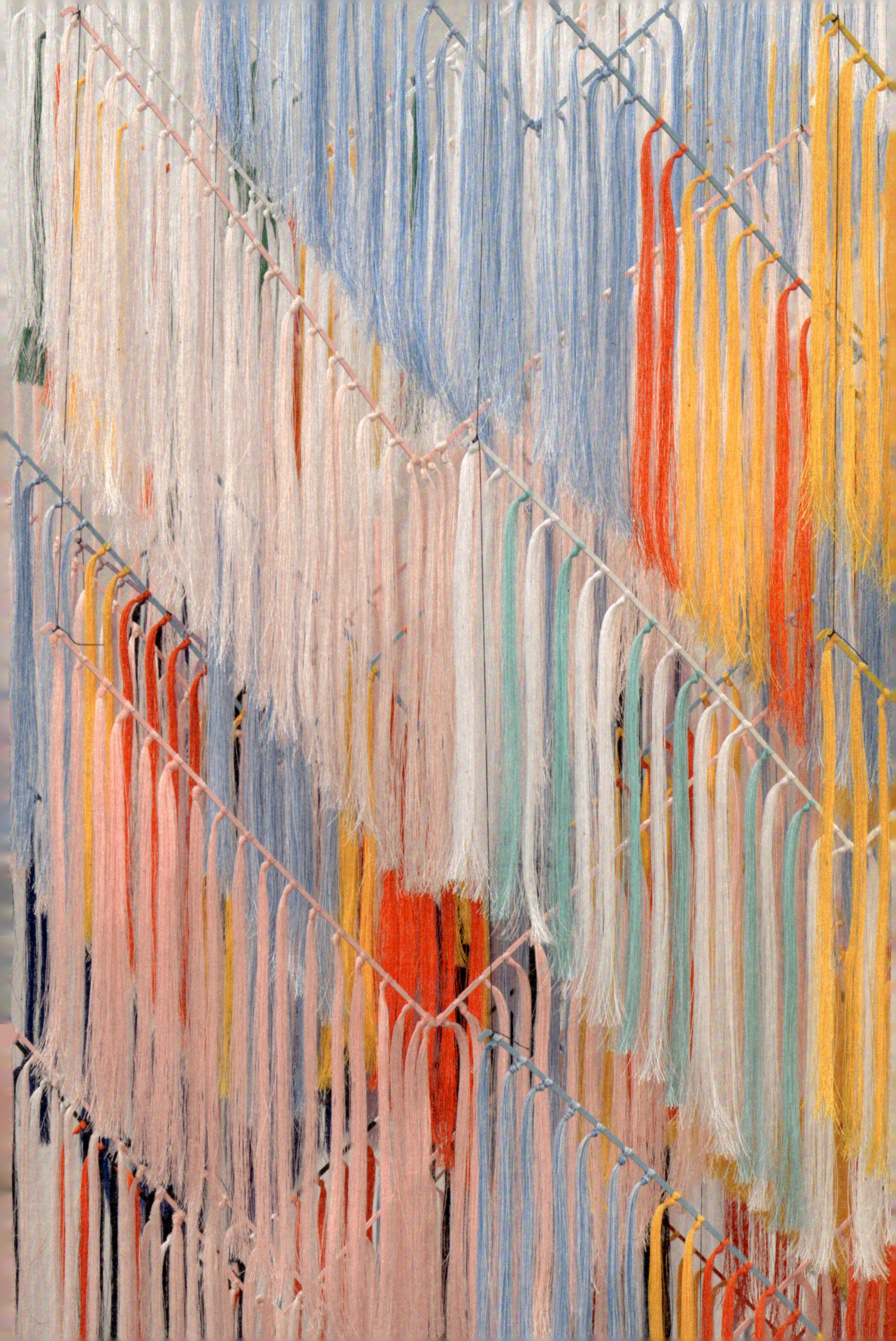

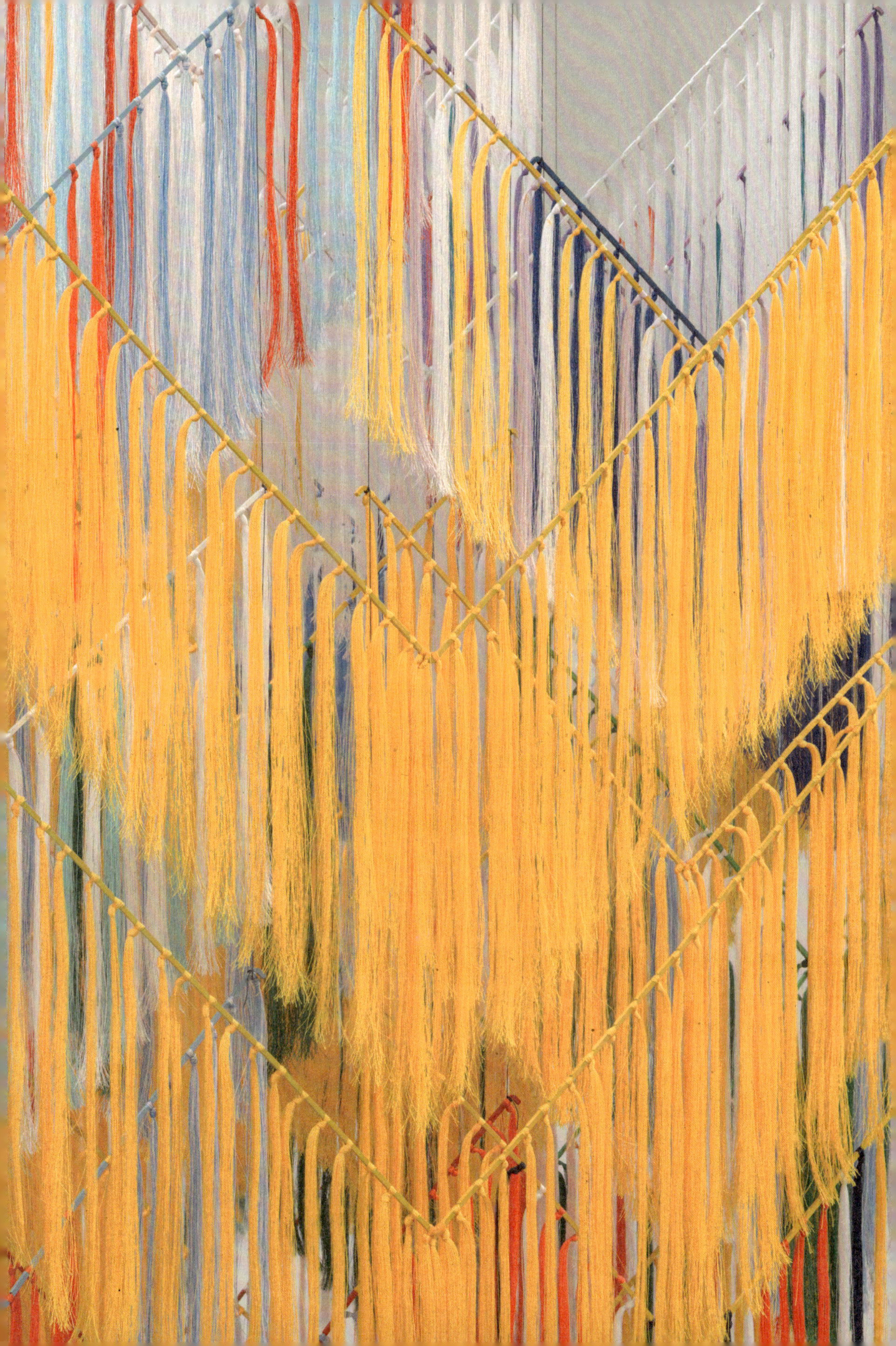

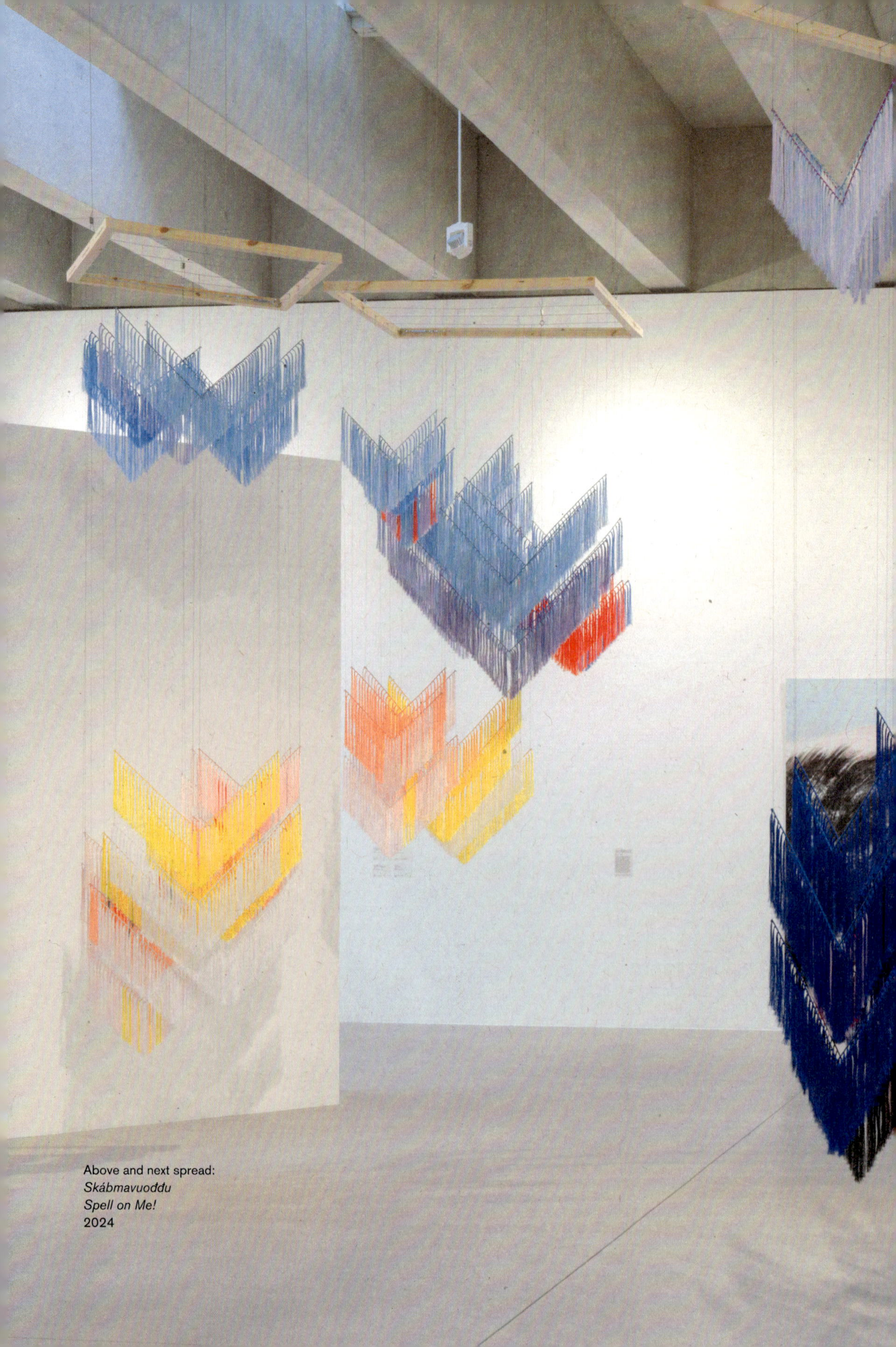

Above and next spread:
Skábmavuoddu
Spell on Me!
2024

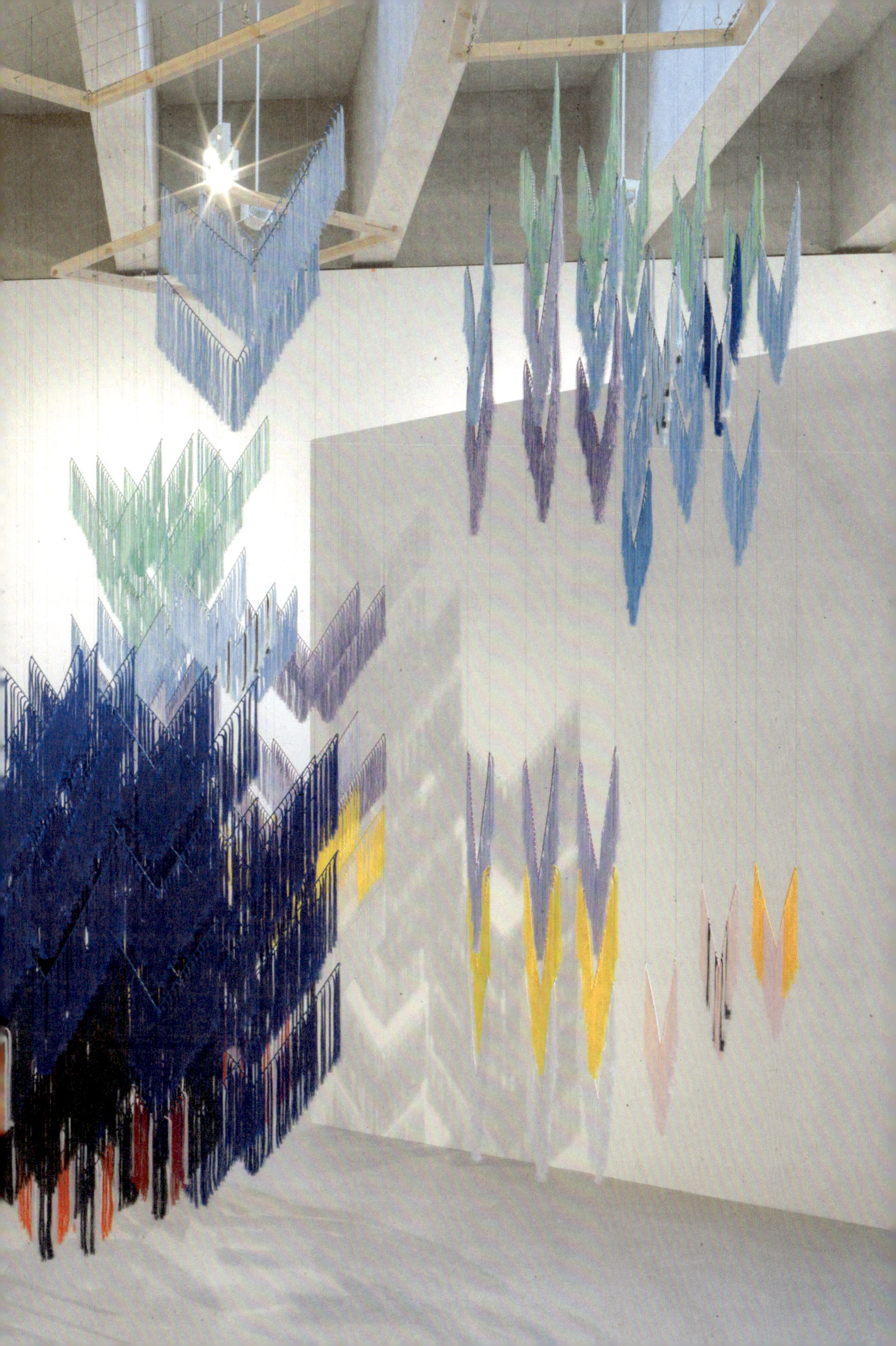

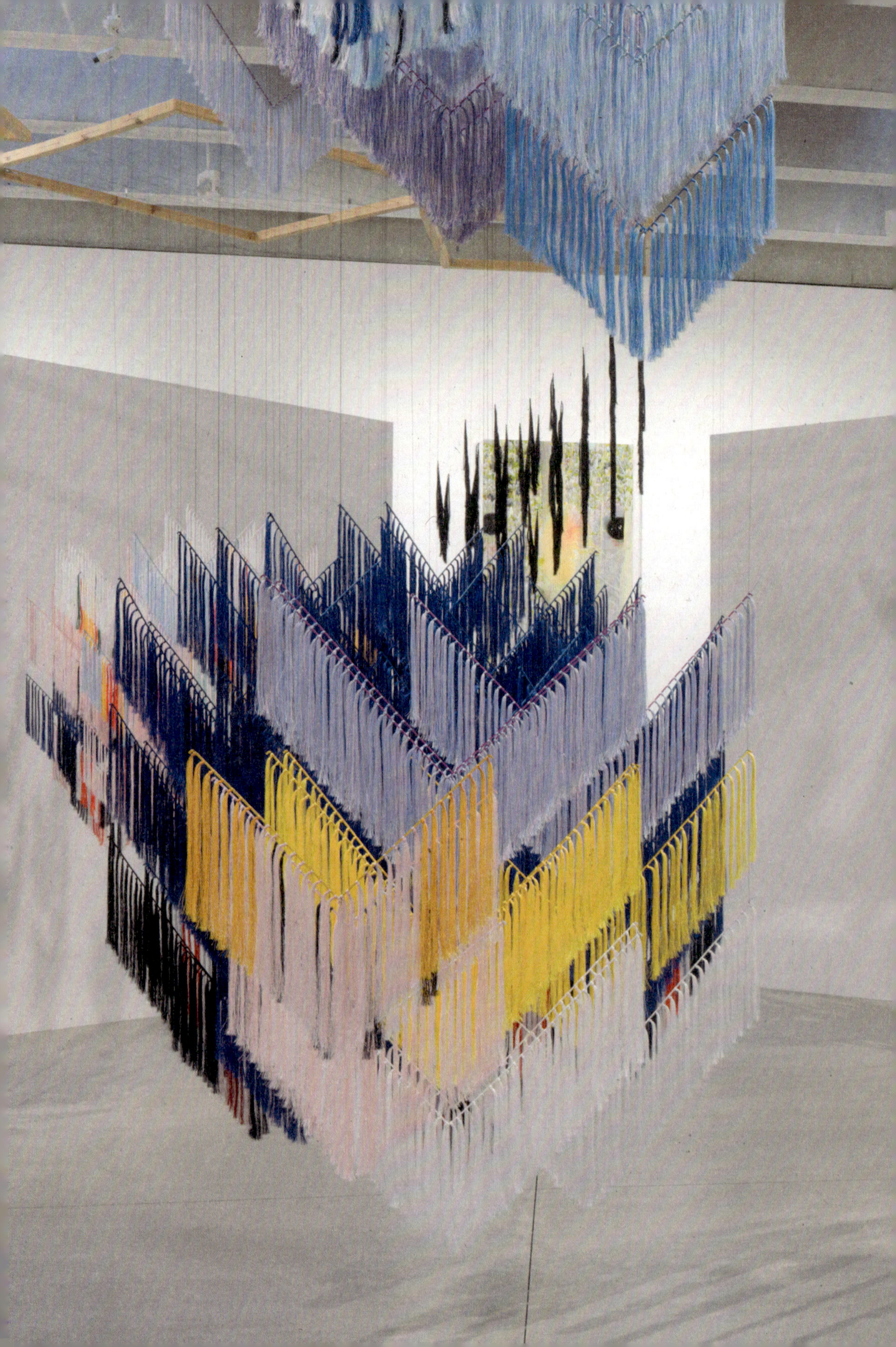

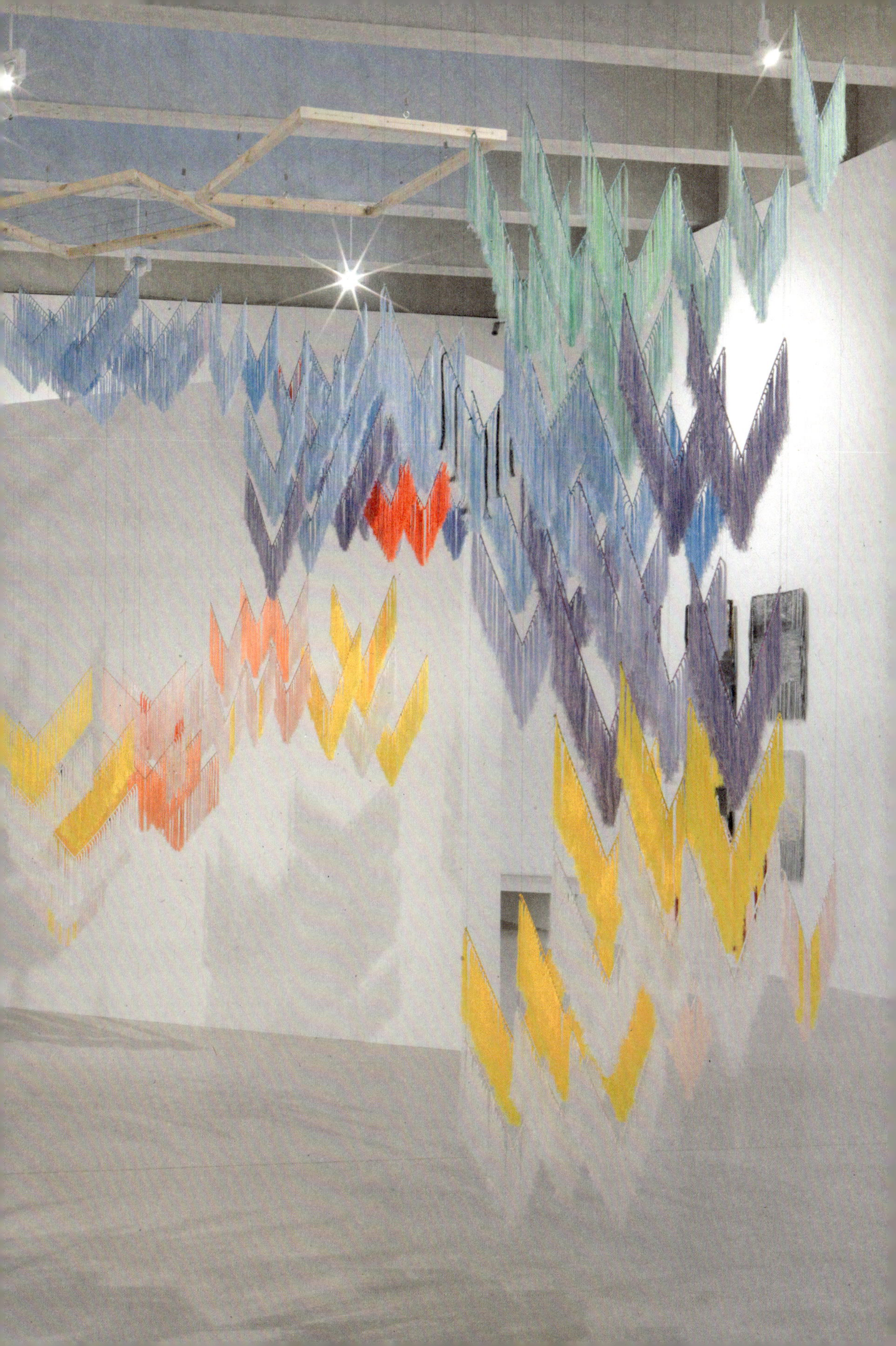

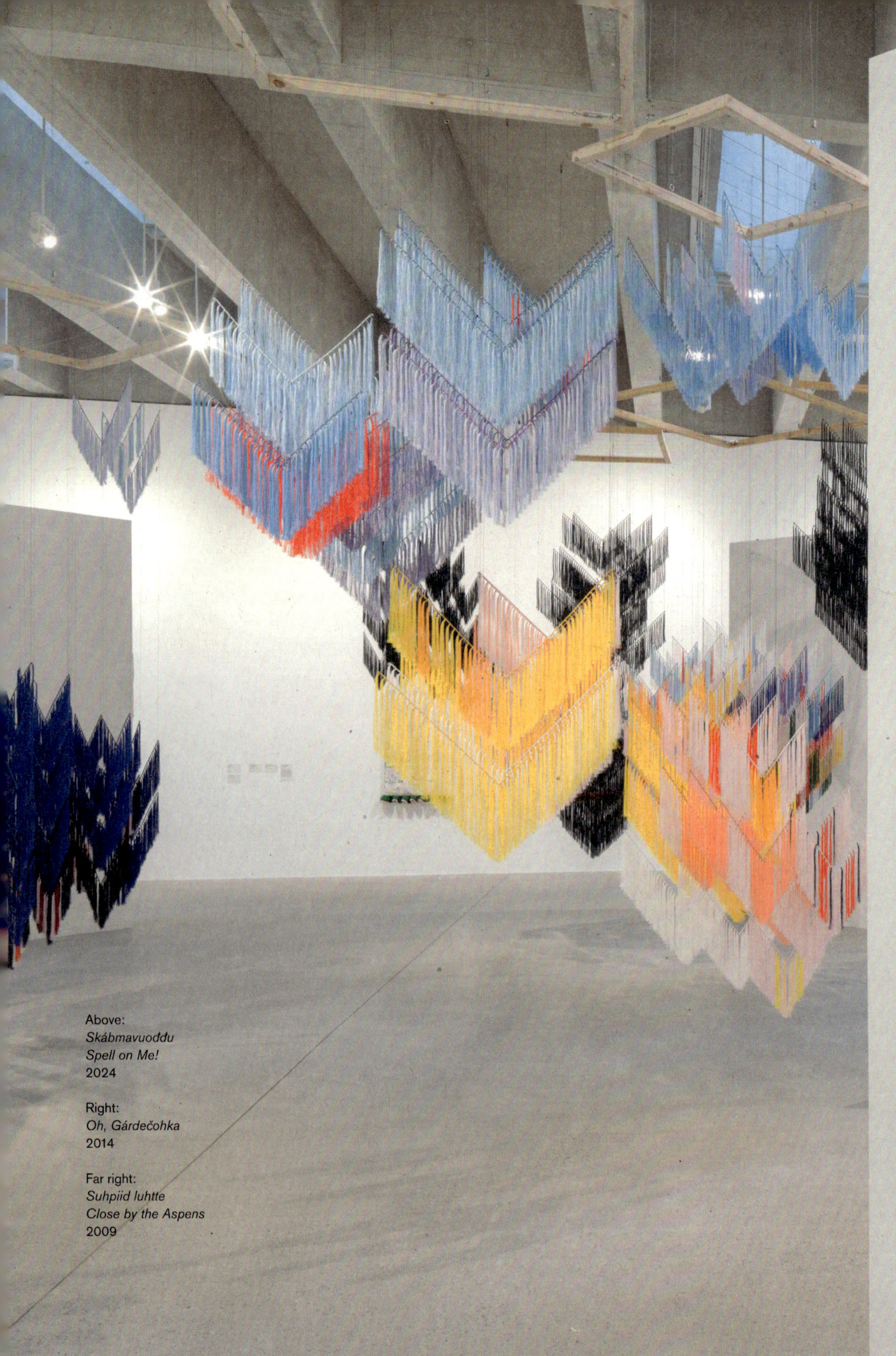

Above:
Skábmavuođđu
Spell on Me!
2024

Right:
Oh, Gárdečohka
2014

Far right:
Suhpiid luhtte
Close by the Aspens
2009

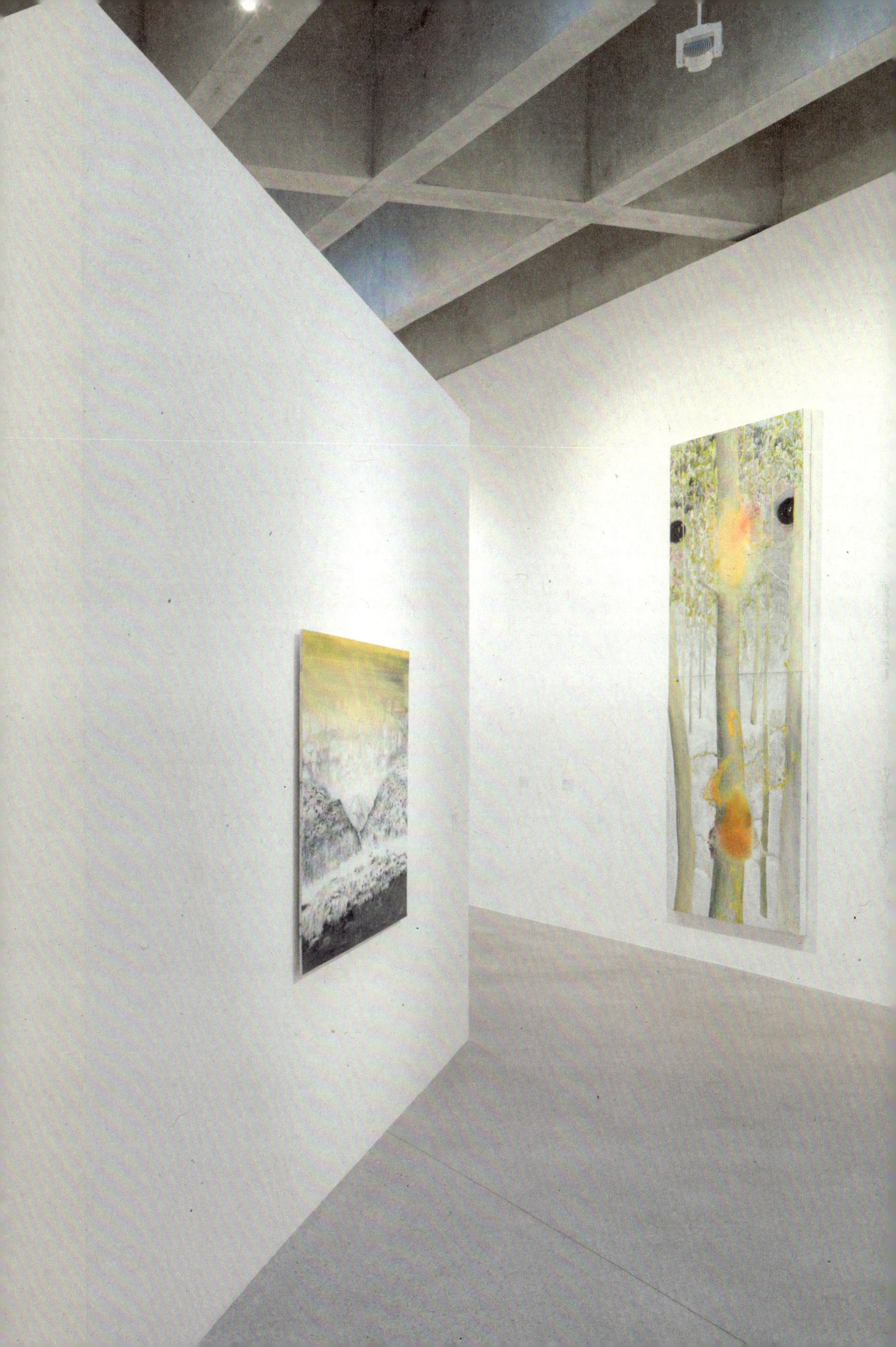

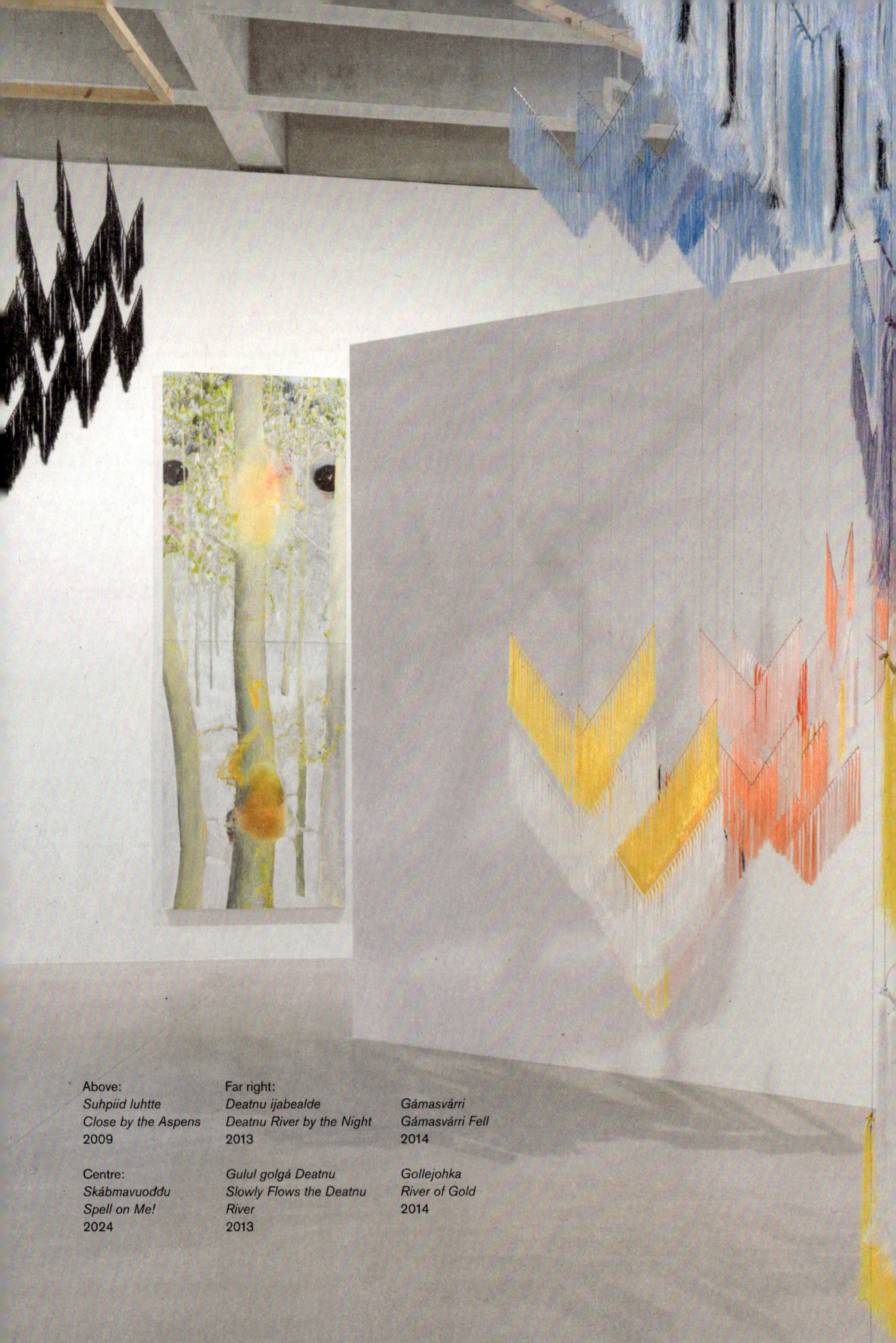

Above:
Suhpiid luhtte
Close by the Aspens
2009

Centre:
Skábmavuođđu
Spell on Me!
2024

Far right:
Deatnu ijabealde
Deatnu River by the Night
2013

Gulul golgá Deatnu
Slowly Flows the Deatnu River
2013

Gámasvárri
Gámasvárri Fell
2014

Gollejohka
River of Gold
2014

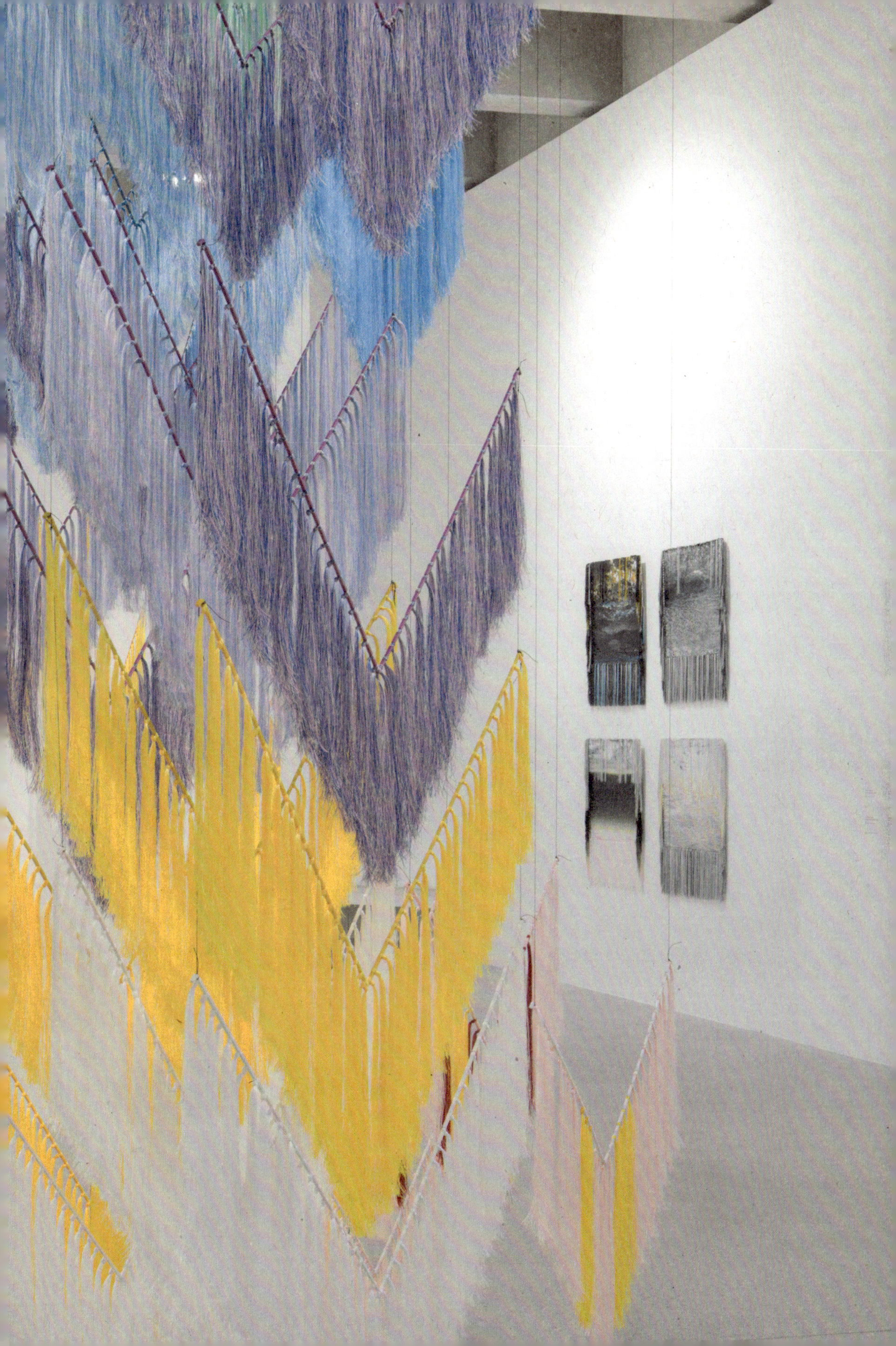

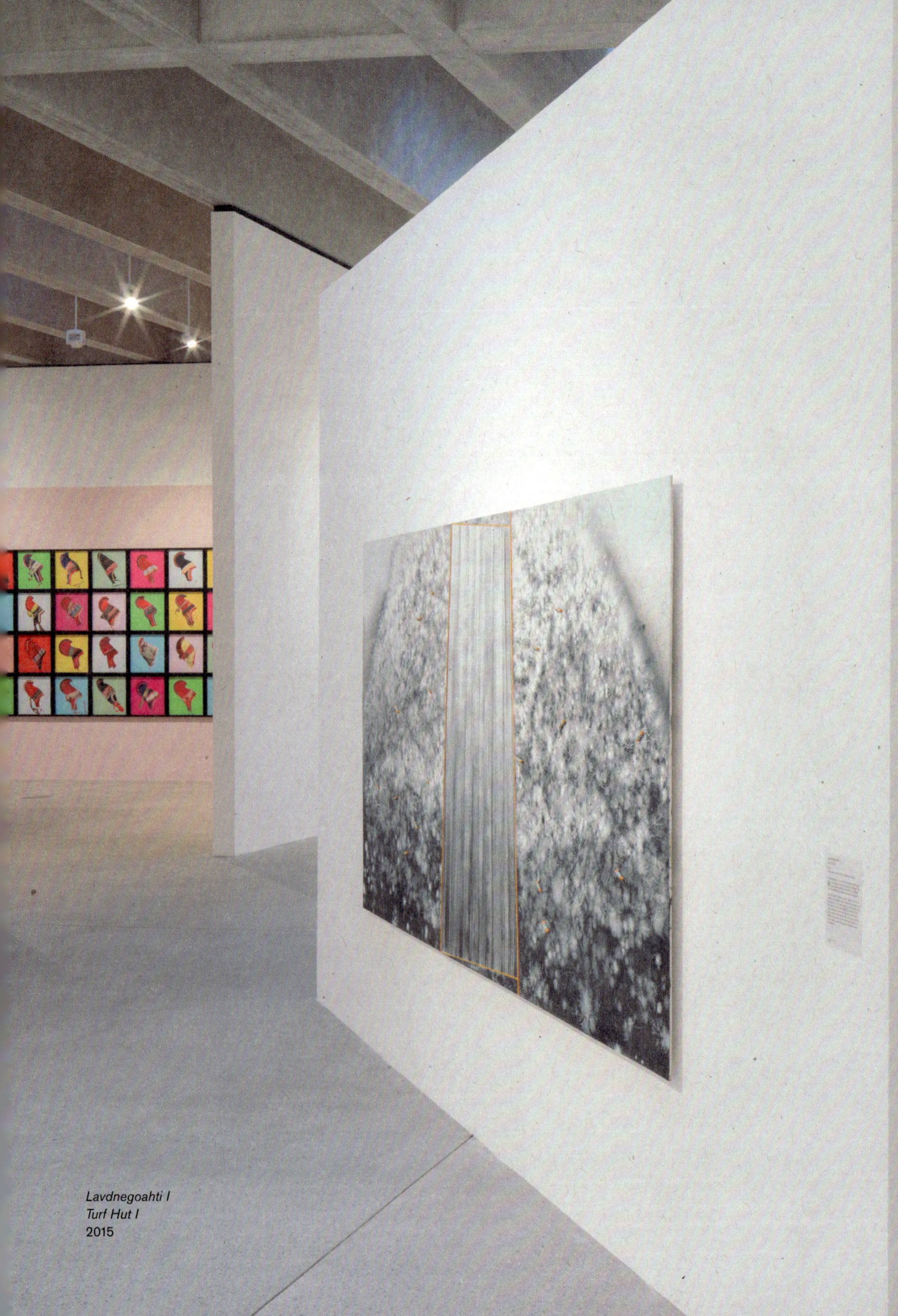

*Lavdnegoahti I
Turf Hut I*
2015

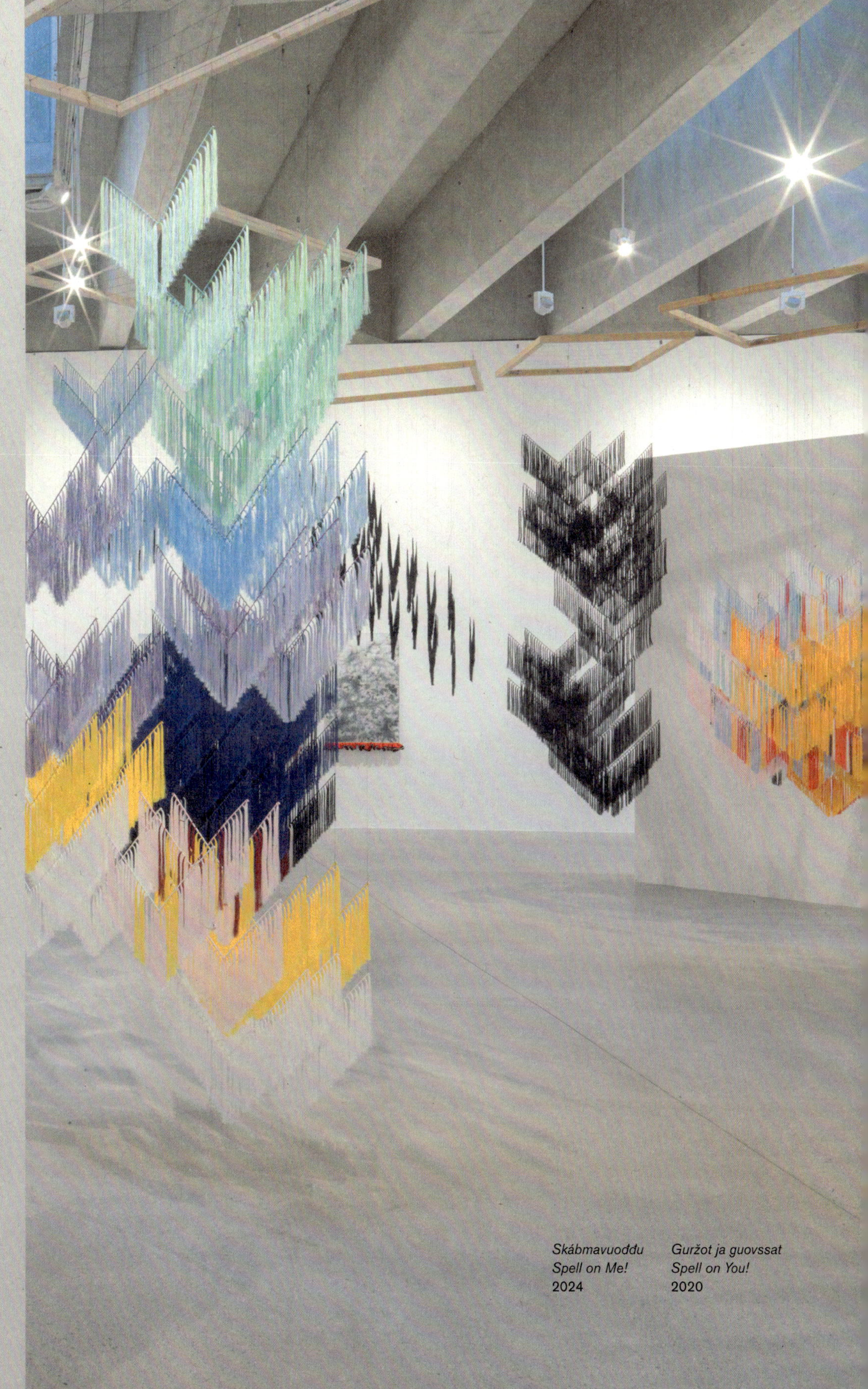

Skábmavuođđu
Spell on Me!
2024

Guržot ja guovssat
Spell on You!
2020

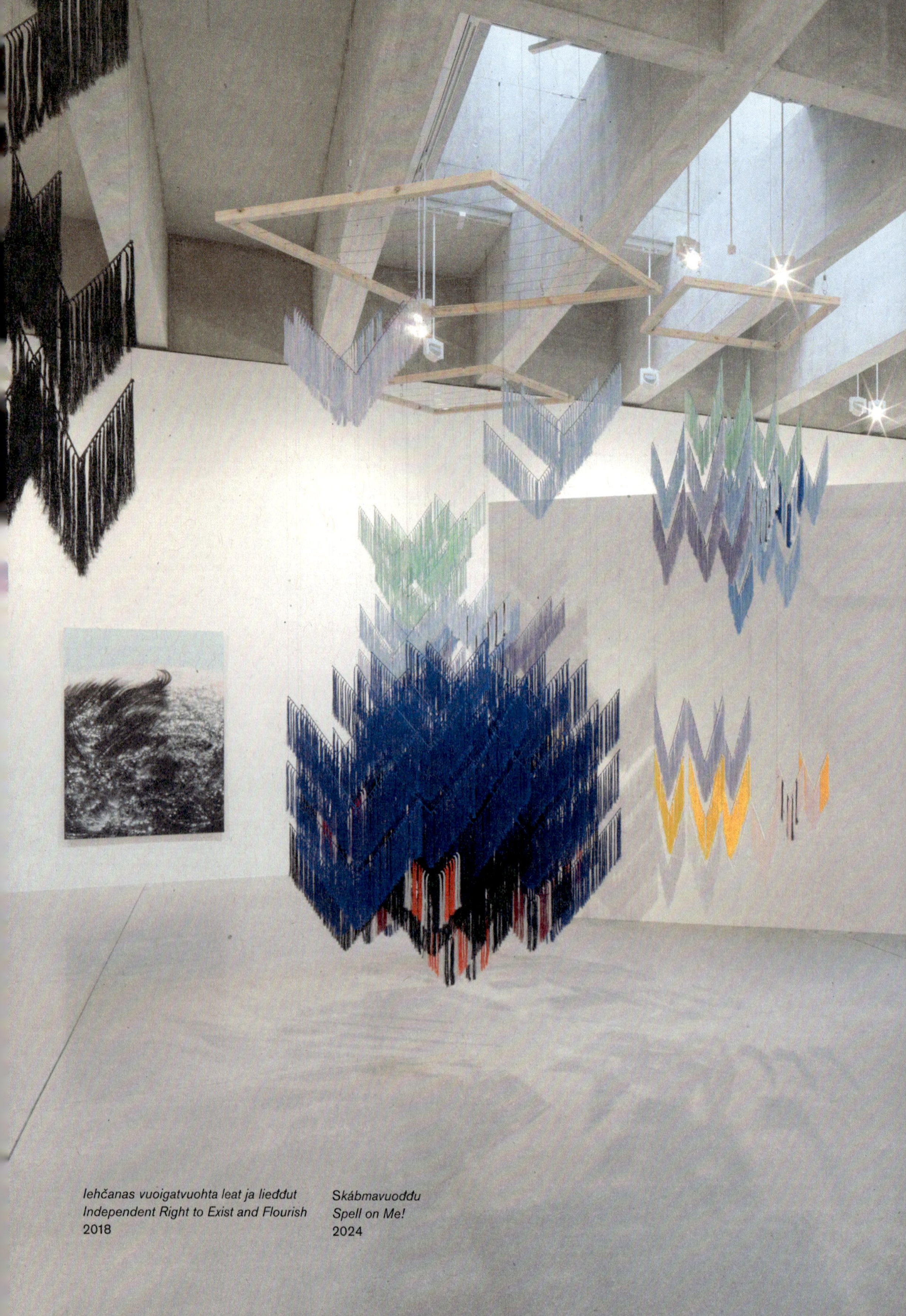

Iehčanas vuoigatvuohta leat ja lieđđut
Independent Right to Exist and Flourish
2018

Skábmavuođđu
Spell on Me!
2024

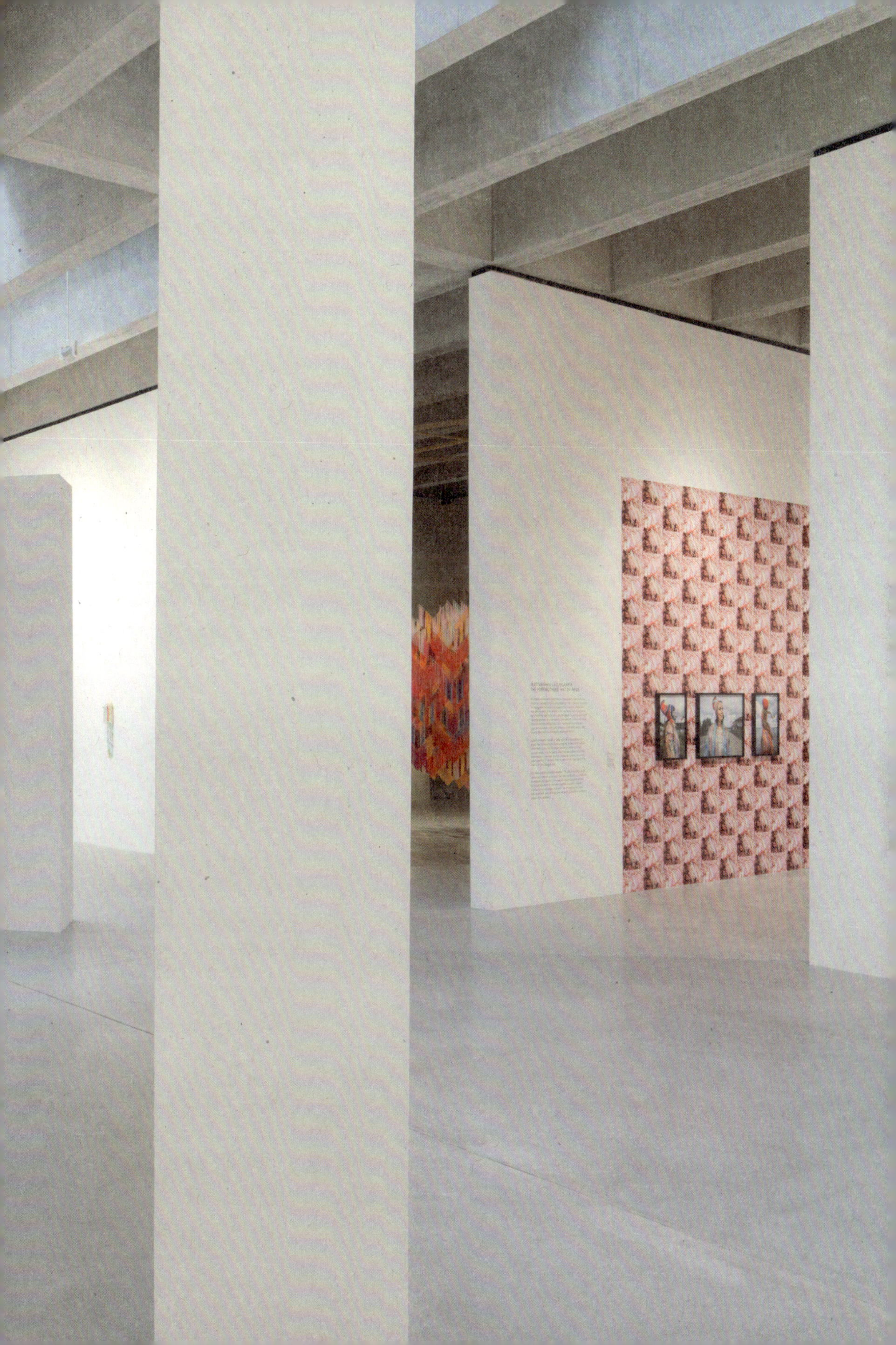

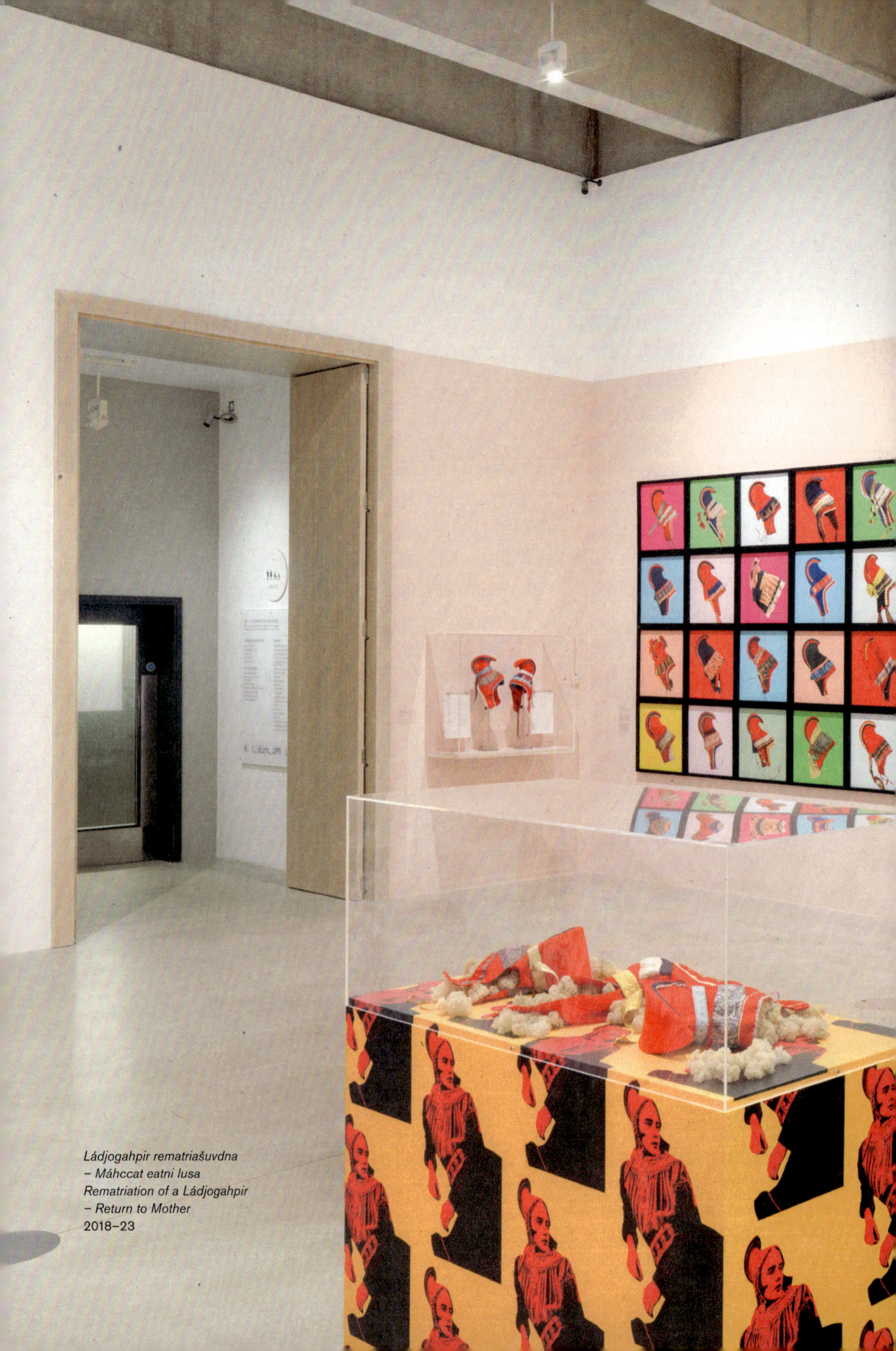

*Ládjogahpir rematriašuvdna
– Máhccat eatni lusa*
Rematriation of a Ládjogahpir
– Return to Mother
2018–23

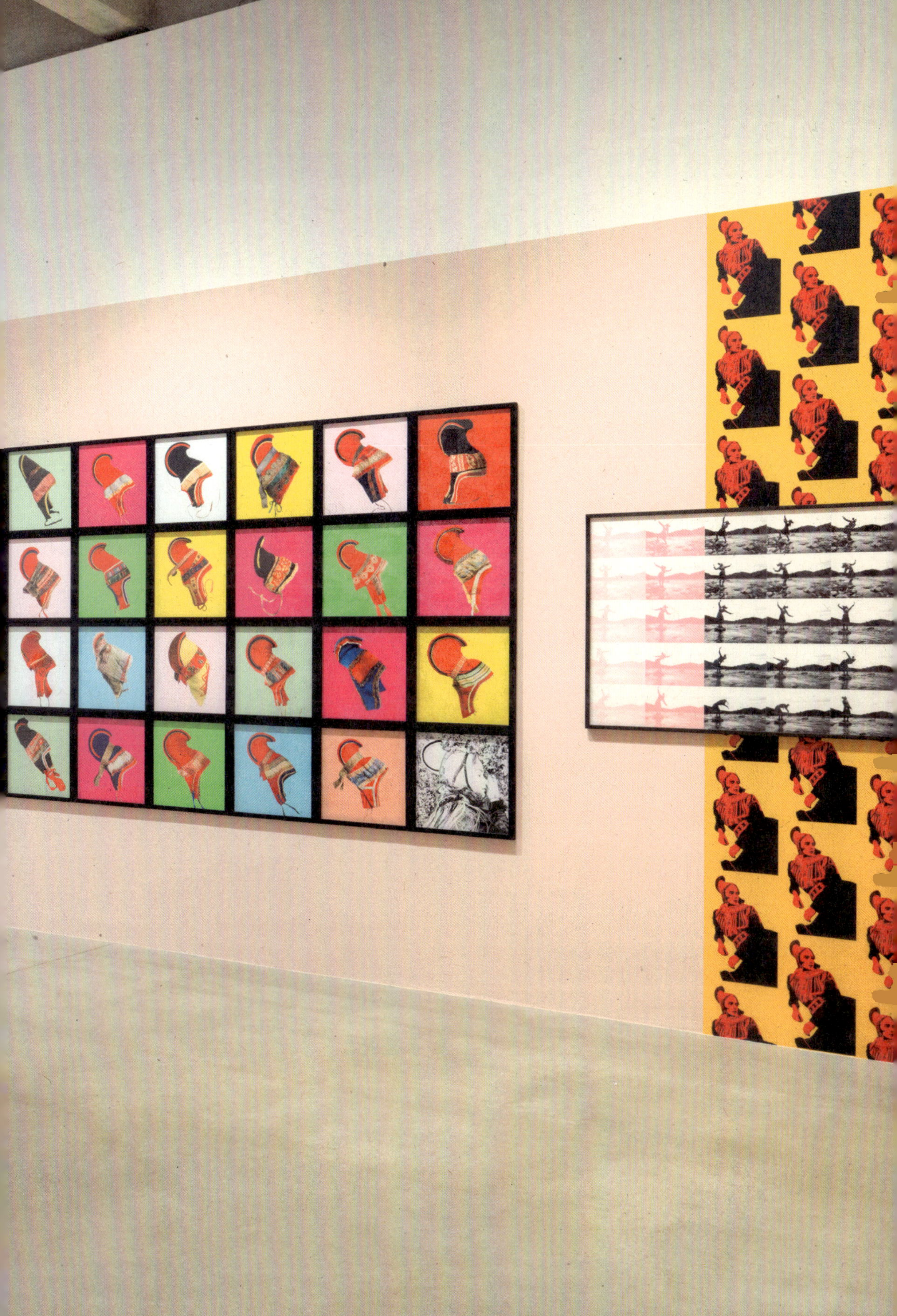

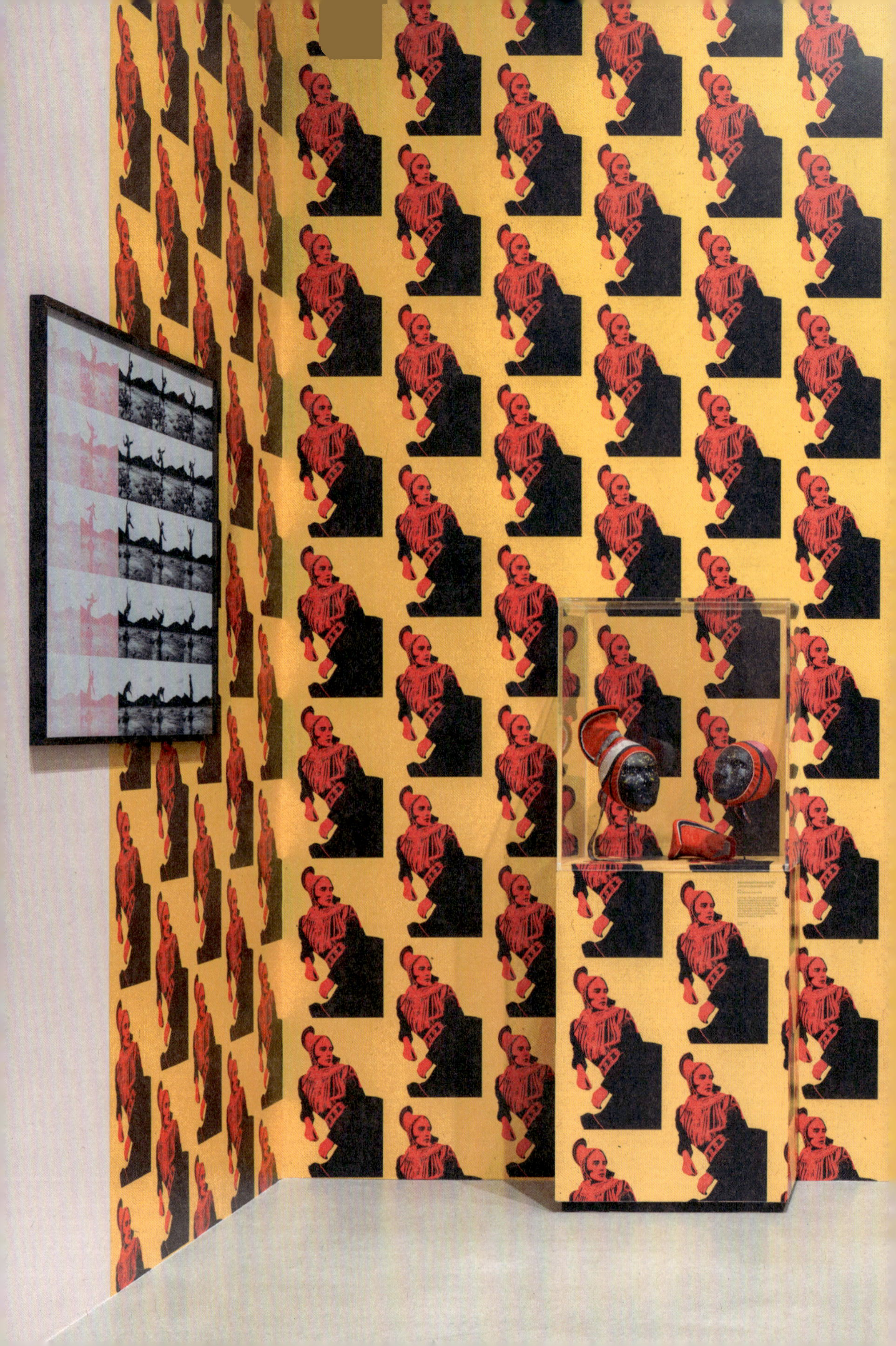

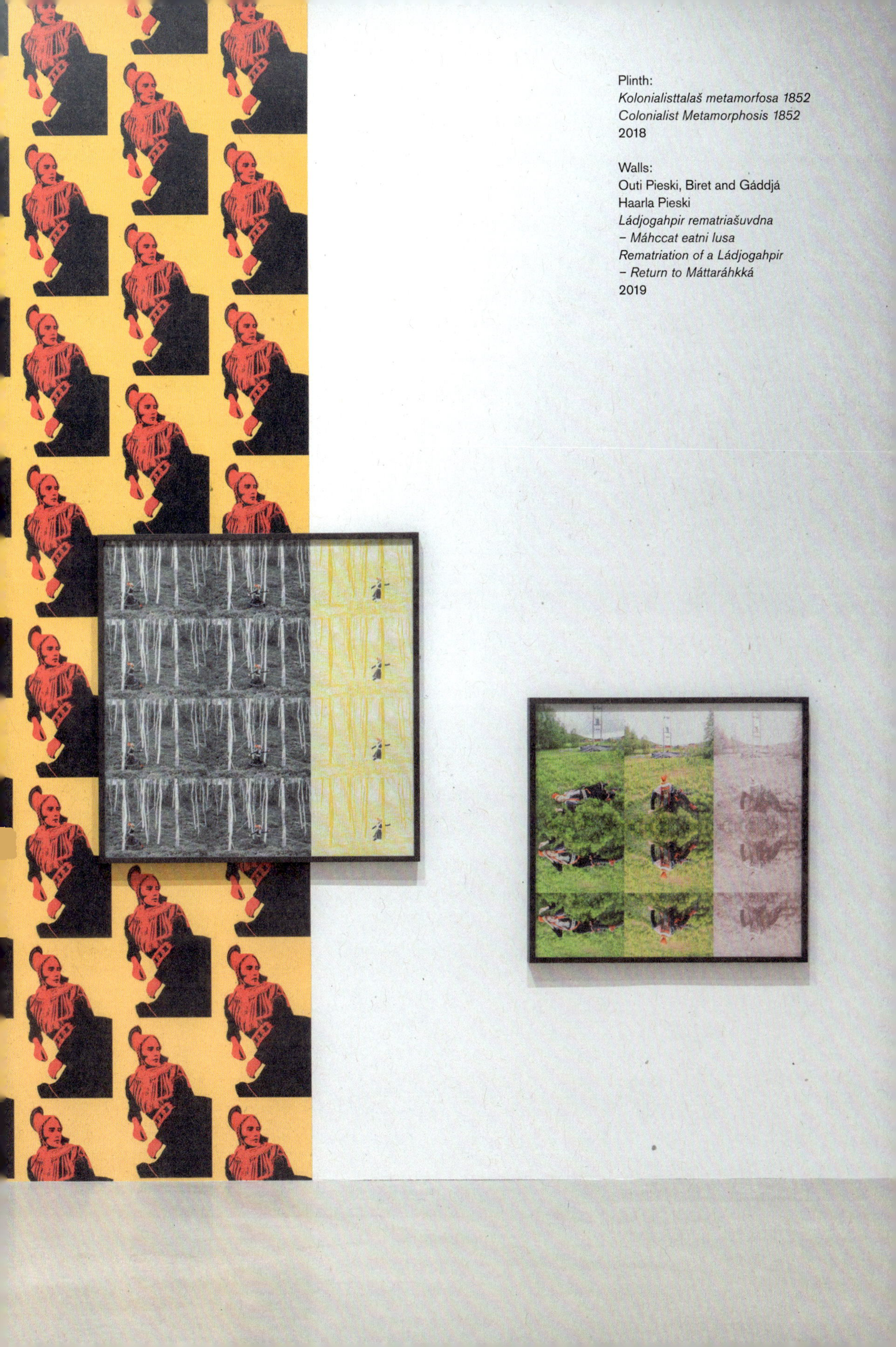

Plinth:
Kolonialisttalaš metamorfosa 1852
Colonialist Metamorphosis 1852
2018

Walls:
Outi Pieski, Biret and Gáddjá
Haarla Pieski
*Ládjogahpir rematriašuvdna
– Máhccat eatni lusa*
*Rematriation of a Ládjogahpir
– Return to Máttaráhkká*
2019

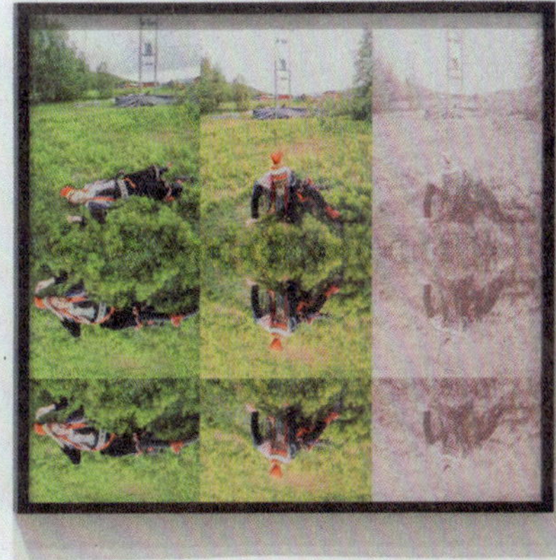

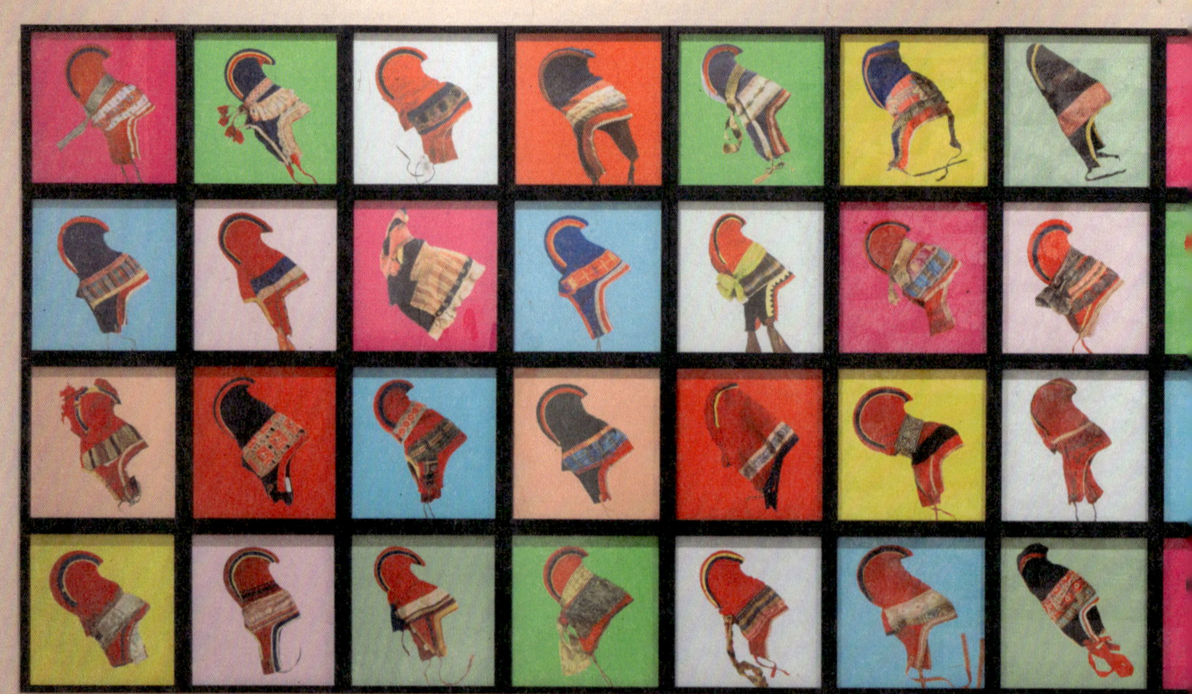

Outi Pieski and Eeva-Kristiina Nylander
47 eanemus ohccojuvvon máttaráhkut
The 47 Most Wanted Foremothers
2019

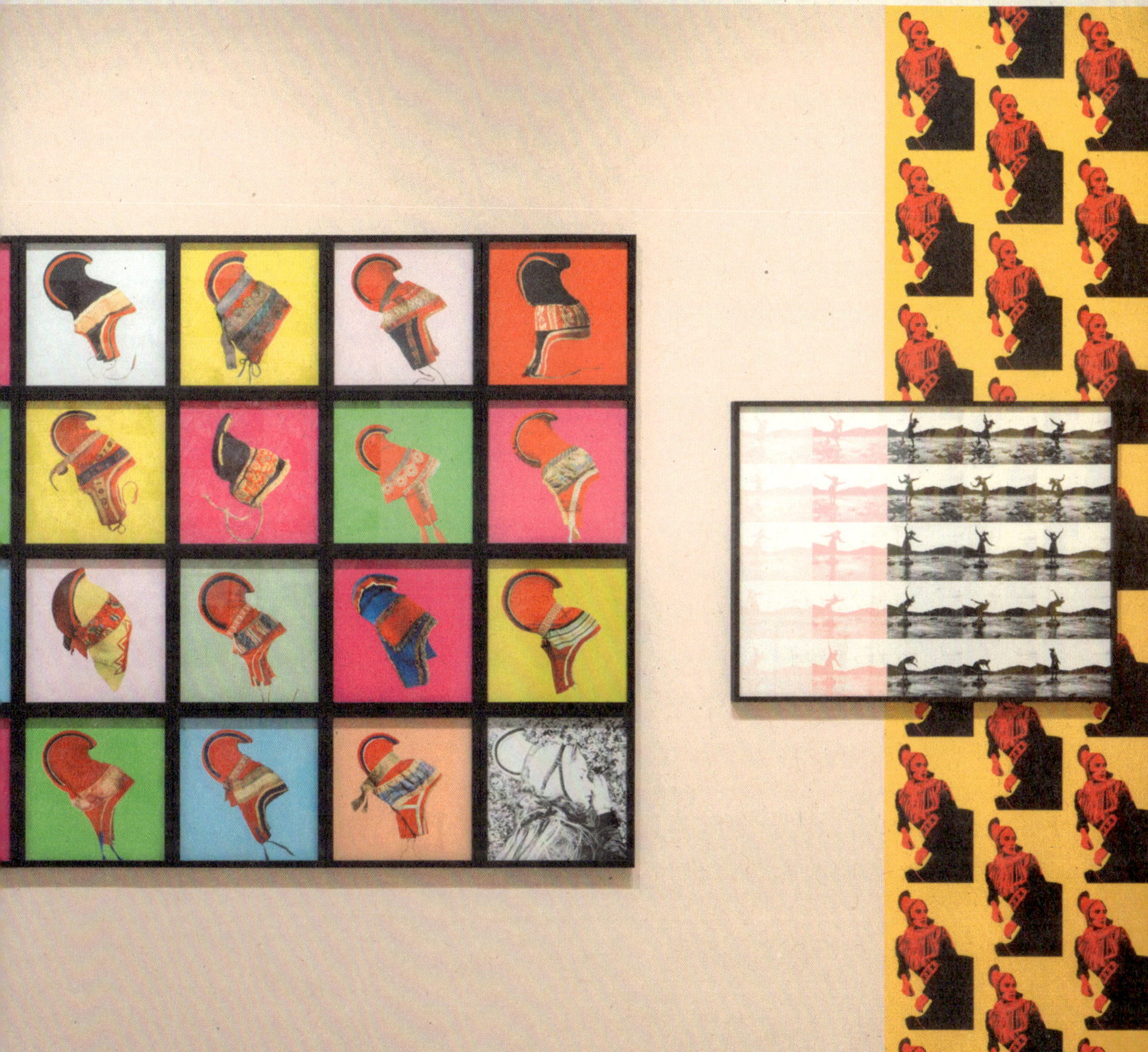

Above and next spreads:
Outi Pieski, Biret and Gáddjá Haarla Pieski
Ládjogahpir rematriašuvdna – Máhccat eatni lusa
Rematriation of a Ládjogahpir – Return to Máttaráhkká
2019

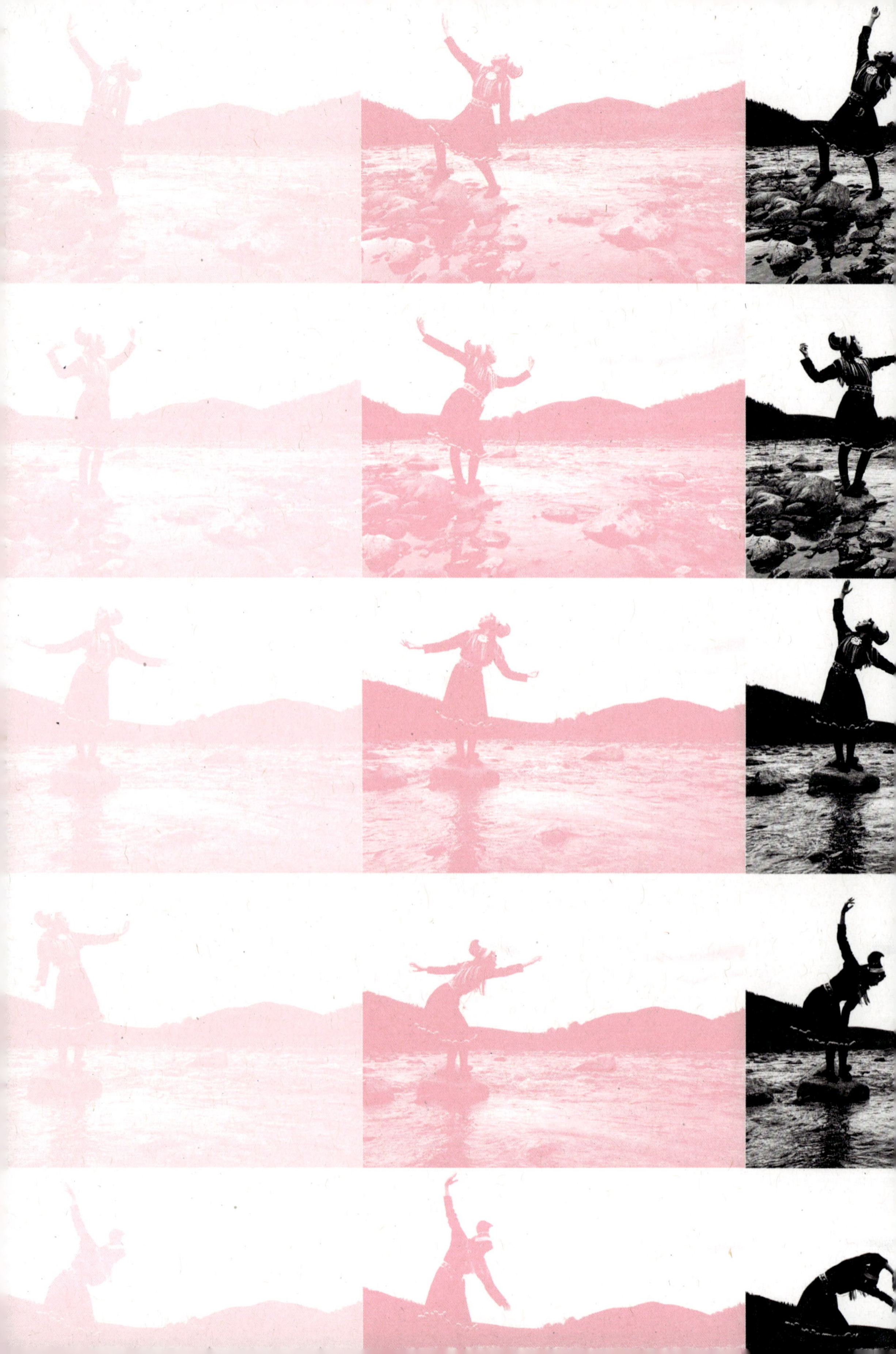

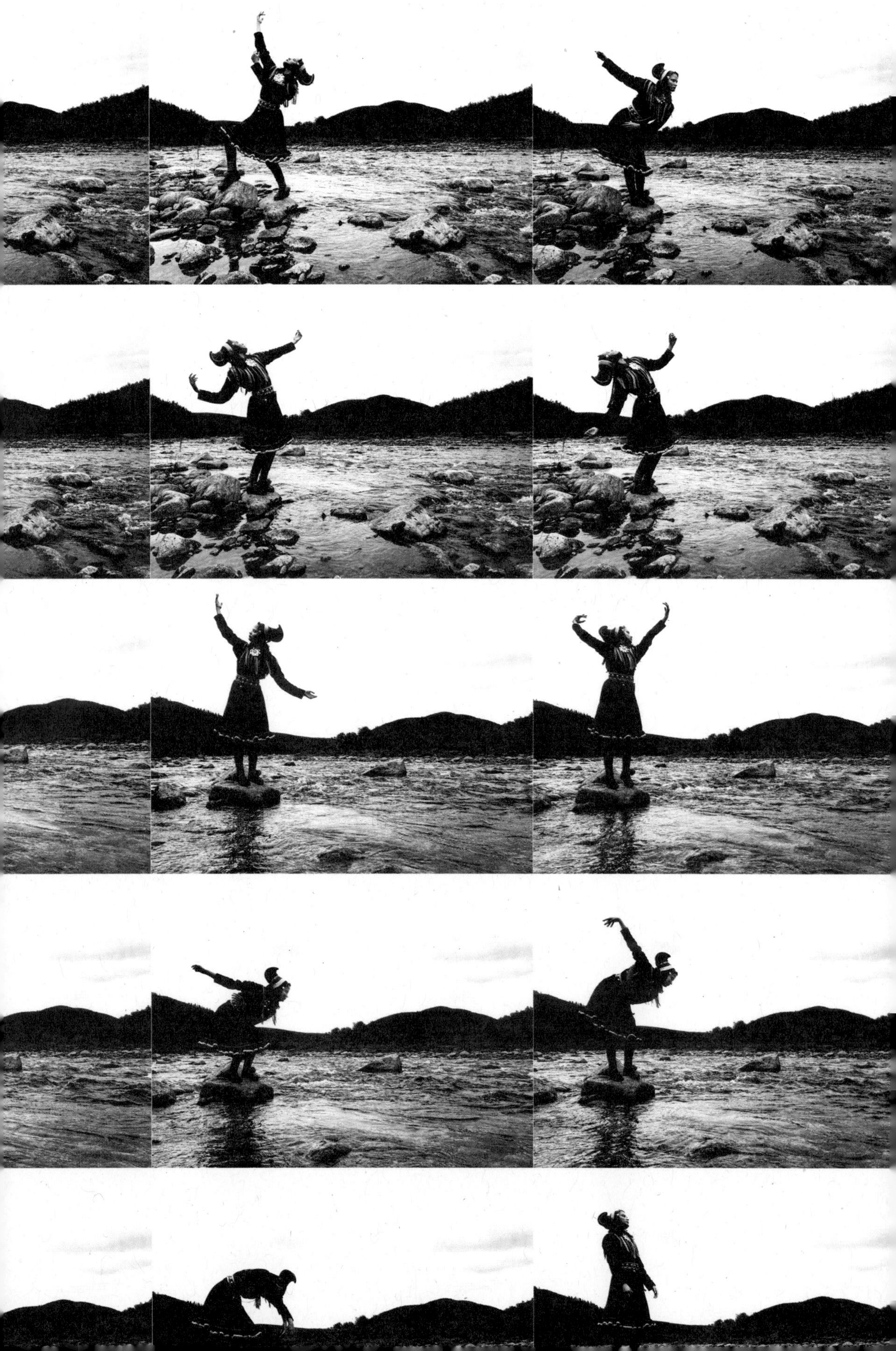

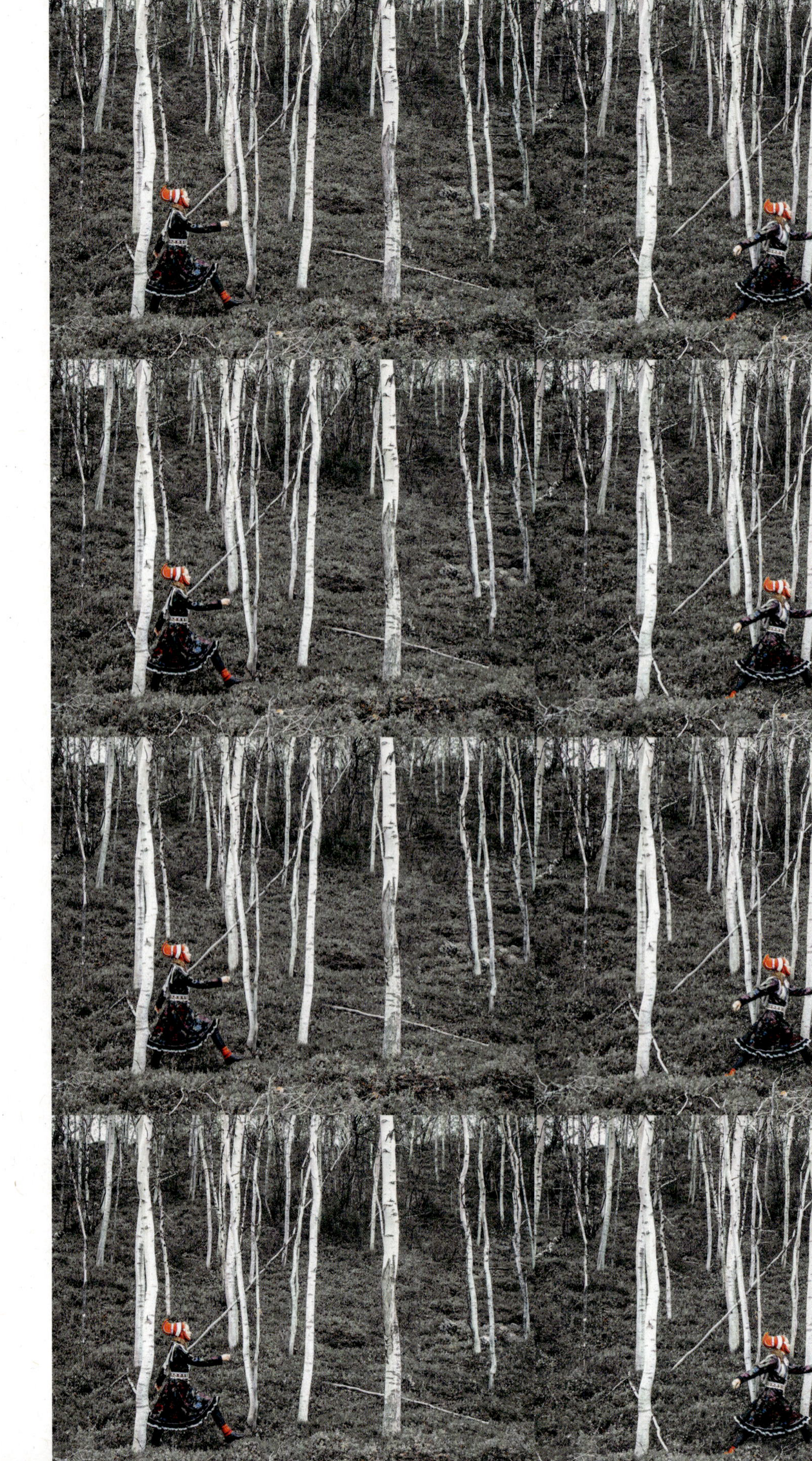

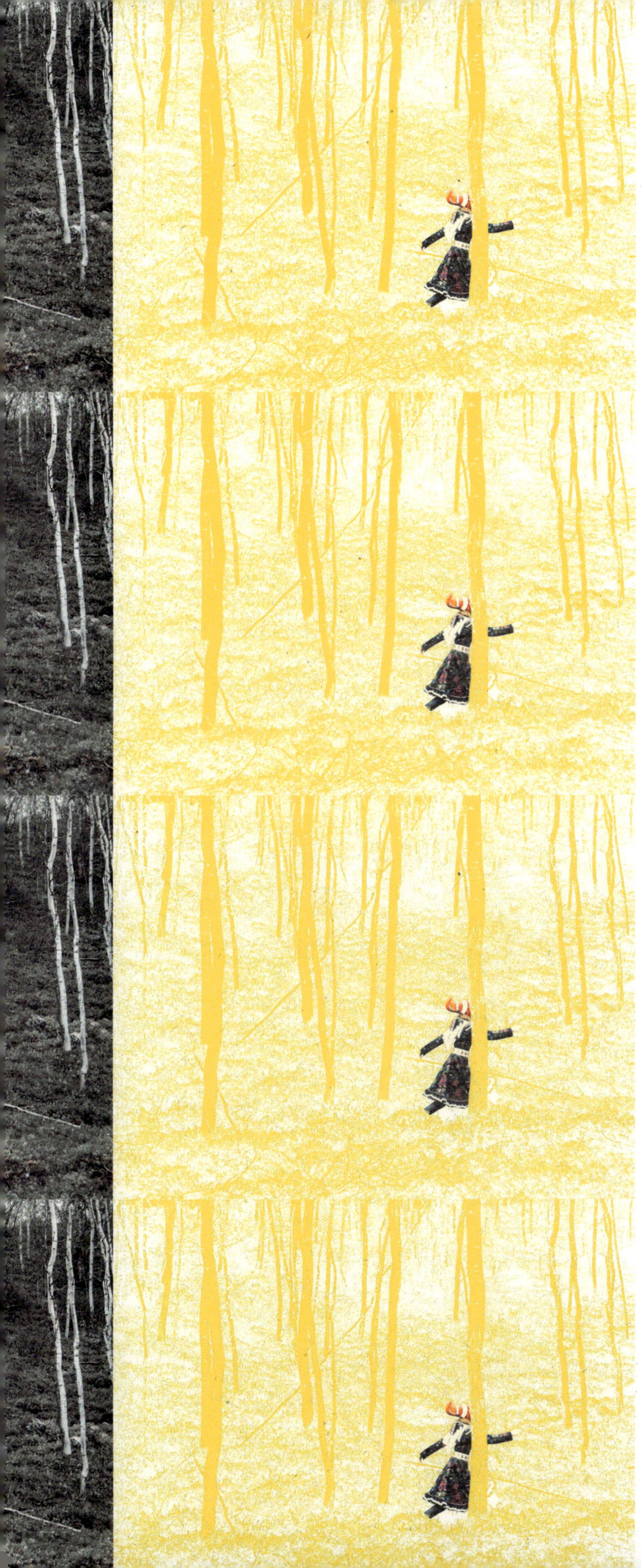

115   Outi Pieski

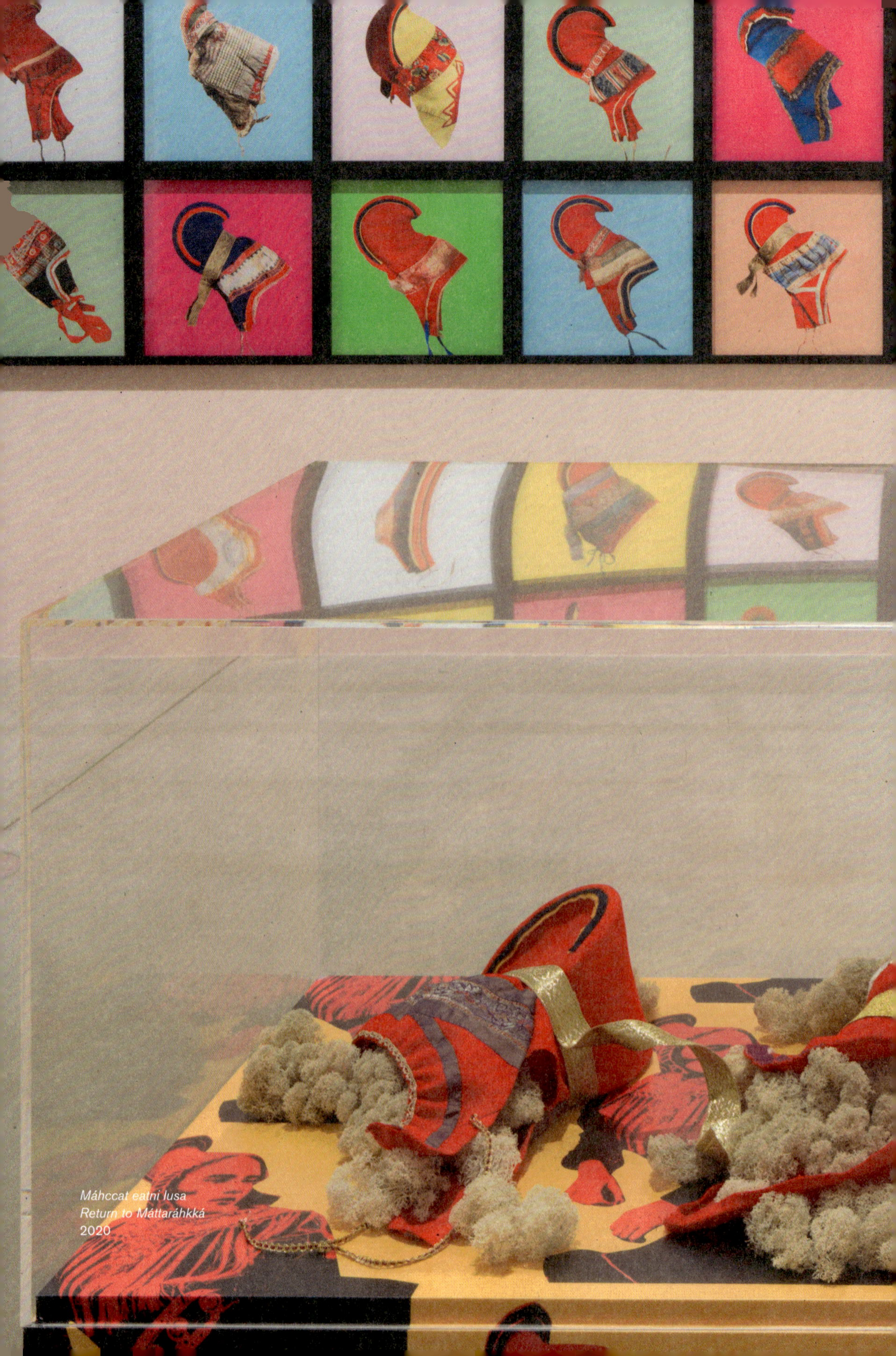

Máhccat eatni lusa
Return to Máttaráhkká
2020

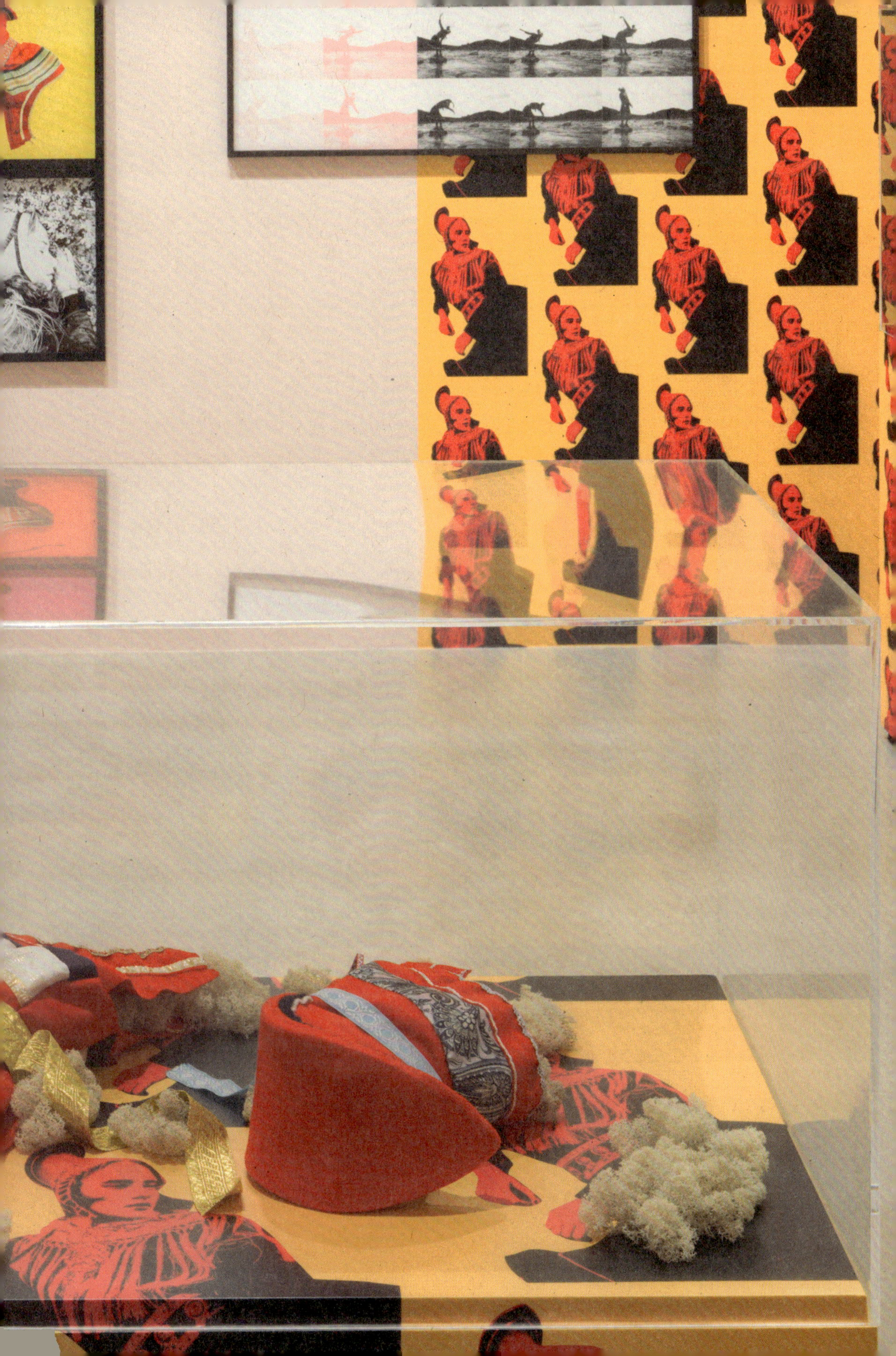

MÁTTARÁHKU LÁDJOGAHPIR
THE FOREMOTHERS' HAT OF PRIDE

On display are elements from Pieski's collaborative project with the
Finnish archaeologist Eeva-Kristiina Nylander. The installation considers
the ládjogahpir, the horned headwear of Sámi women. Pieski and
Nylander researched the demise of the headwear after missionaries
considered the horn to be sinful, and its reappearance as a symbol of
the empowerment of contemporary Sámi women, culture and values.
They documented ládjogahpirat held in European museums and
organised workshops with Sámi women to share skills, values, ideas,
dreams and revive the making and wearing of the hat.

Pauliina Feodoroff: 'Instead of being one monumental piece, this
project has scattered its existence across the borders of the whole
of Northern Sápmi, into the private spaces of women's homes,
women's heads, and the spaces where they go supported by their
headdresses, to meetings, protests, weddings, funerals, festivities,
public speeches. In doing so, they change a bit of every space they
enter with their ládjogahpirat.'

Outi Pieski and Eeva-Kristiina Nylander: 'This way of working can be
defined as craftivism, an activism that uses handicrafts as a medium
to empower participants. Conversations about ládjogahpirat have
led to considerations of colonialism, gender inequality, religion
and traditional knowledge. As a result, the ládjogahpir has been
reassigned with new meanings and recreated as a positive symbol of
today's Sámi resistance.'

Plinth:
Máhccat eatni lusa
Return to Máttaráhkká
2020

Wall:
Portraits of Anni Koivisto,
Anna Näkkäläjärvi-Länsman
and Elle Valkeapää
2019

Plinth:
Litna máttaráhkku
The Light Weight of the Foremother
2021

Lossa máttaráhkku
The Heavy Weight of the Foremother
2021

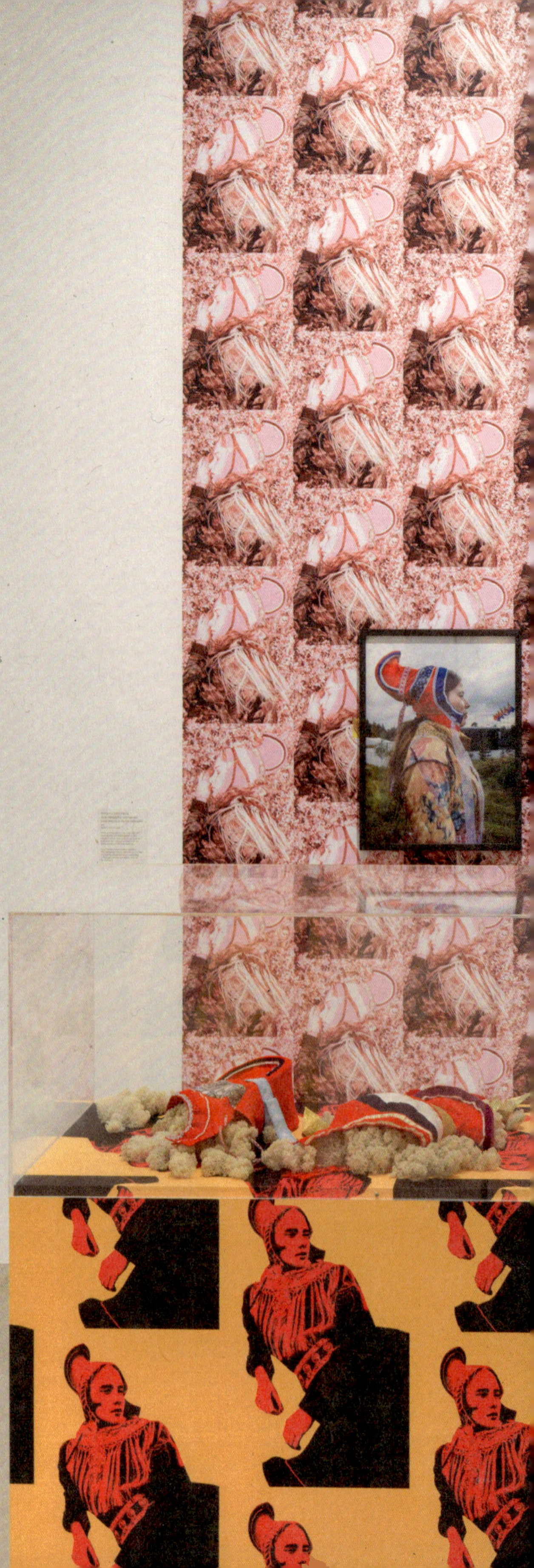

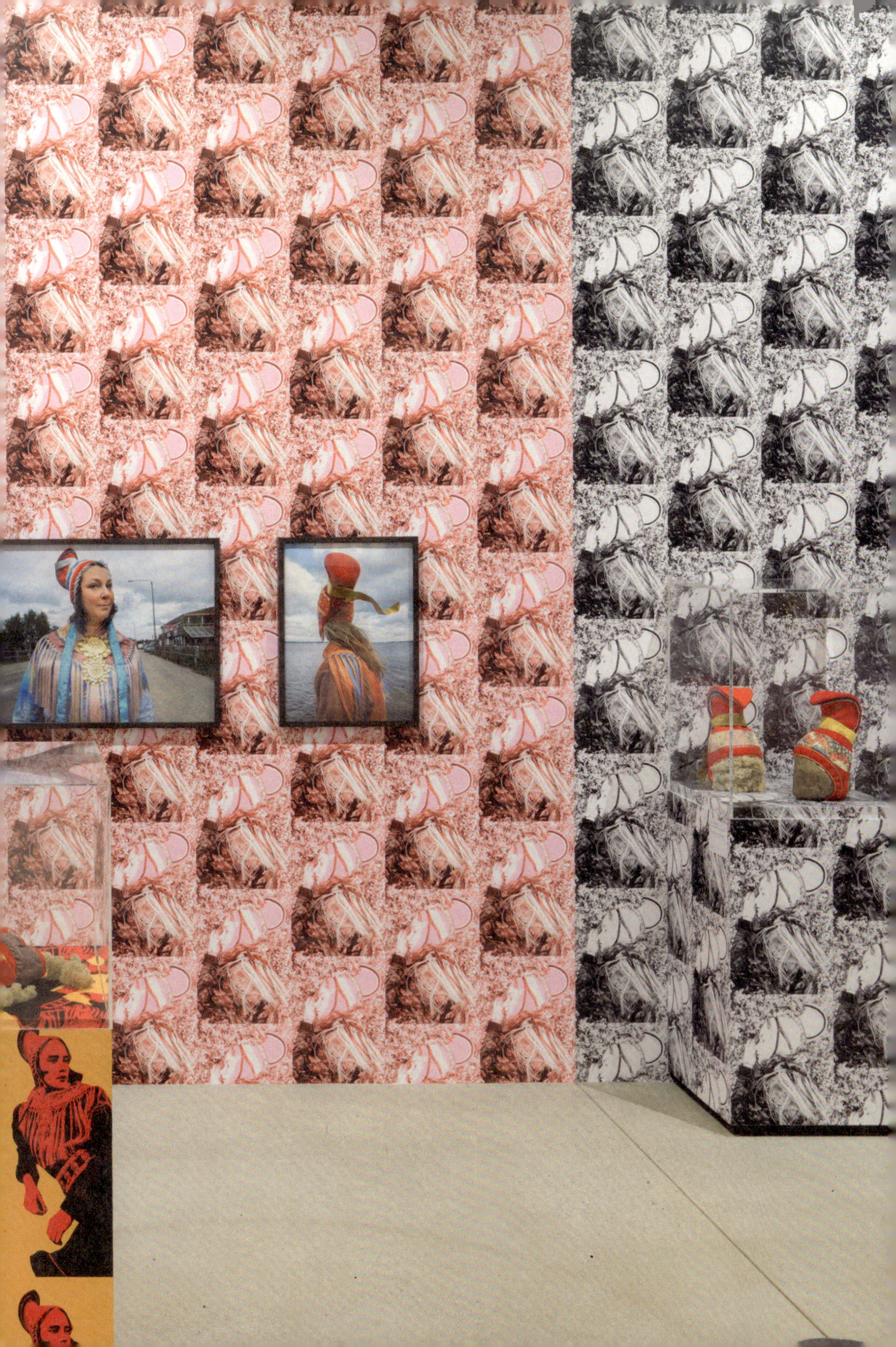

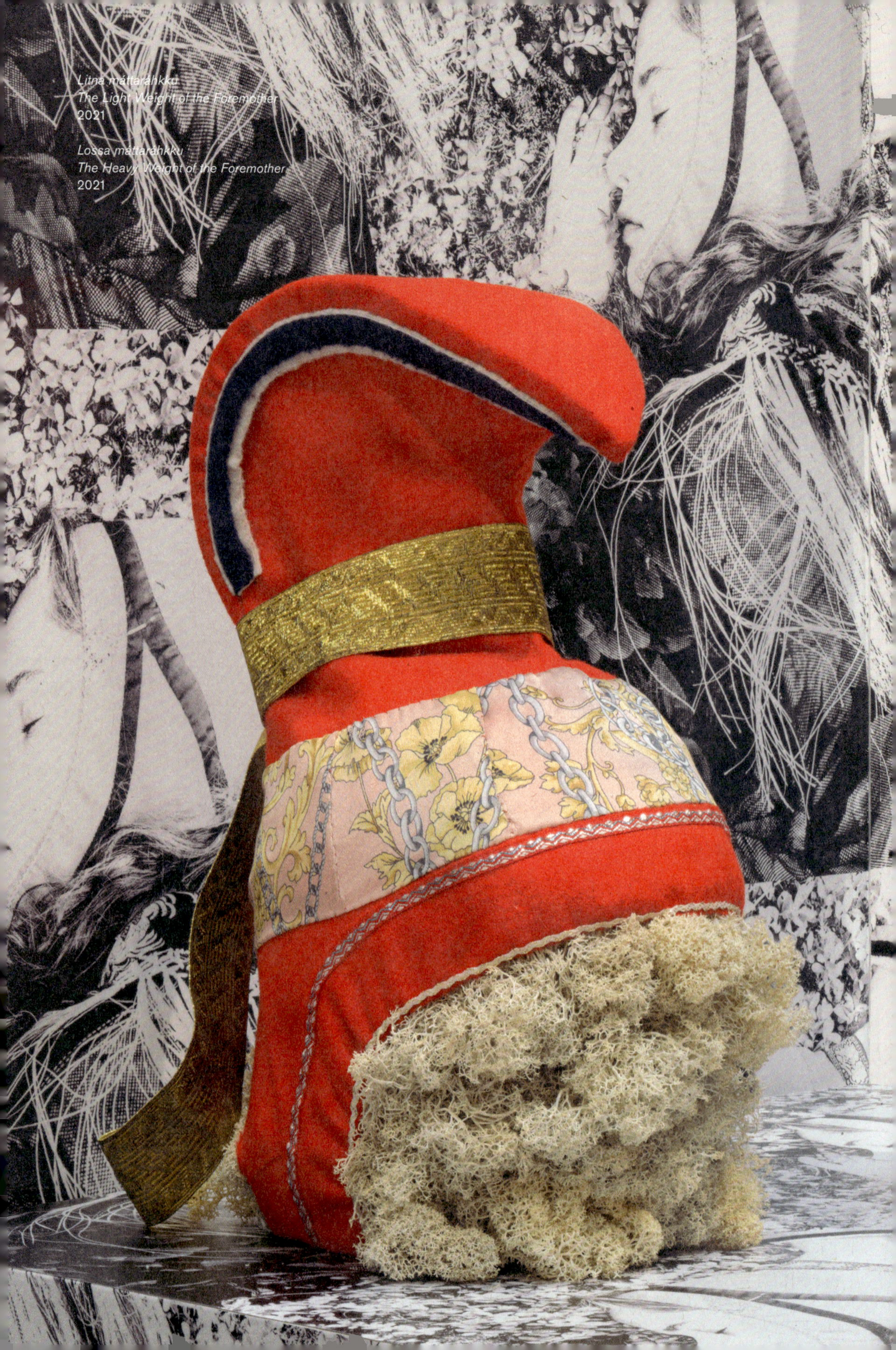

Litna máttaráhkku
The Light Weight of the Foremother
2021

Lossa máttaráhkku
The Heavy Weight of the Foremother
2021

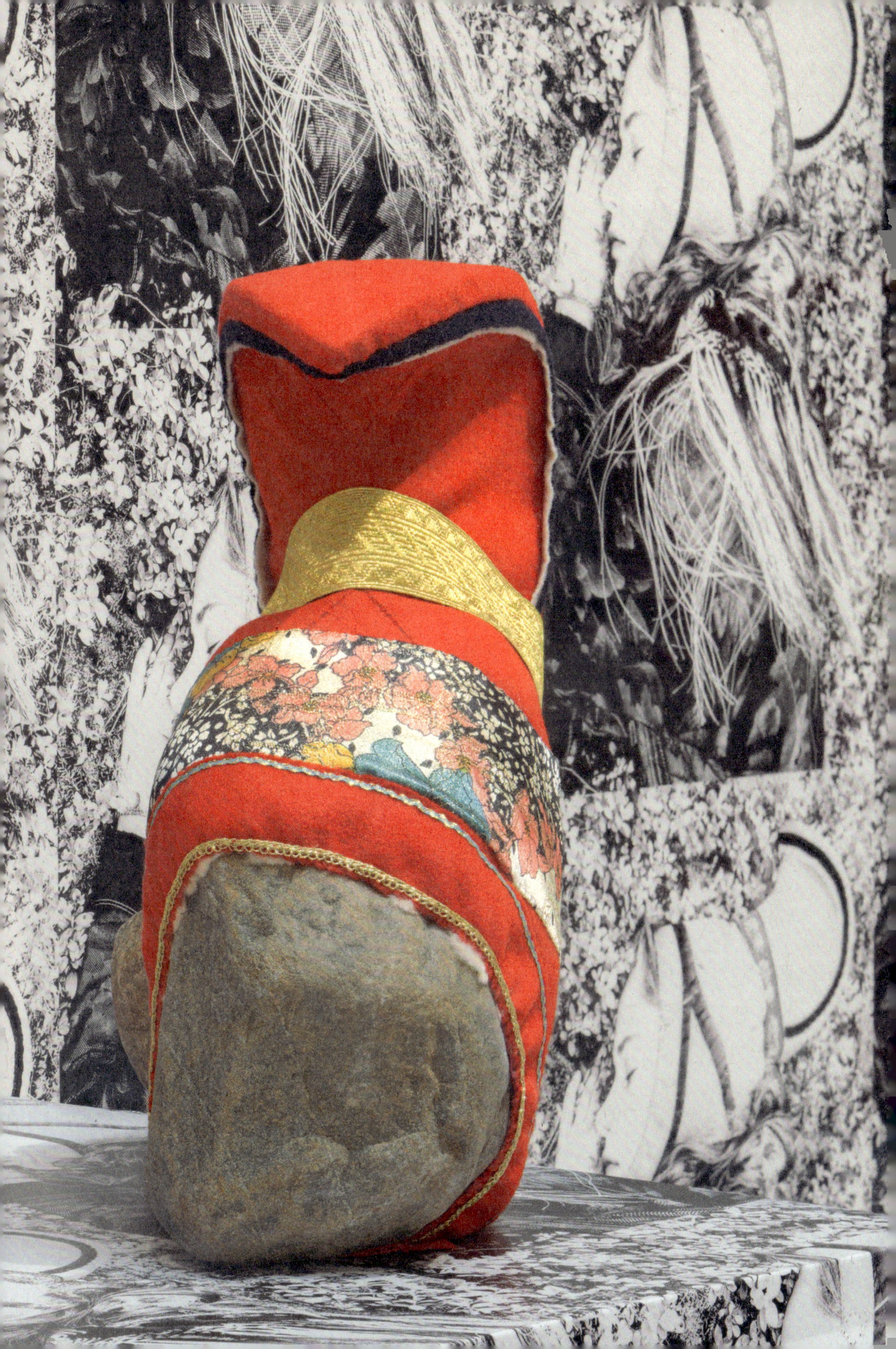

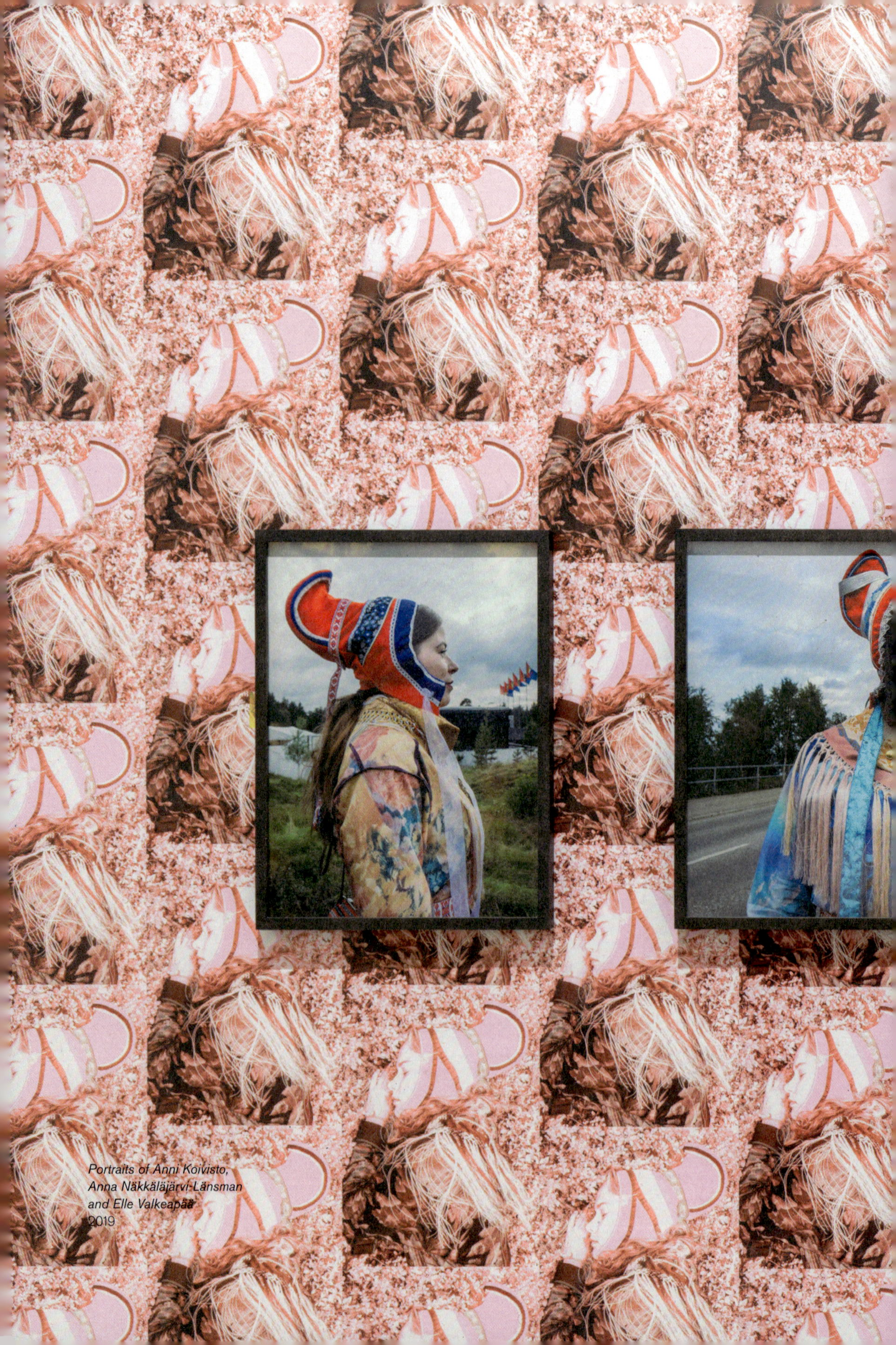

Portraits of Anni Koivisto,
Anna Näkkäläjärvi-Länsman
and Elle Valkeapää
2019

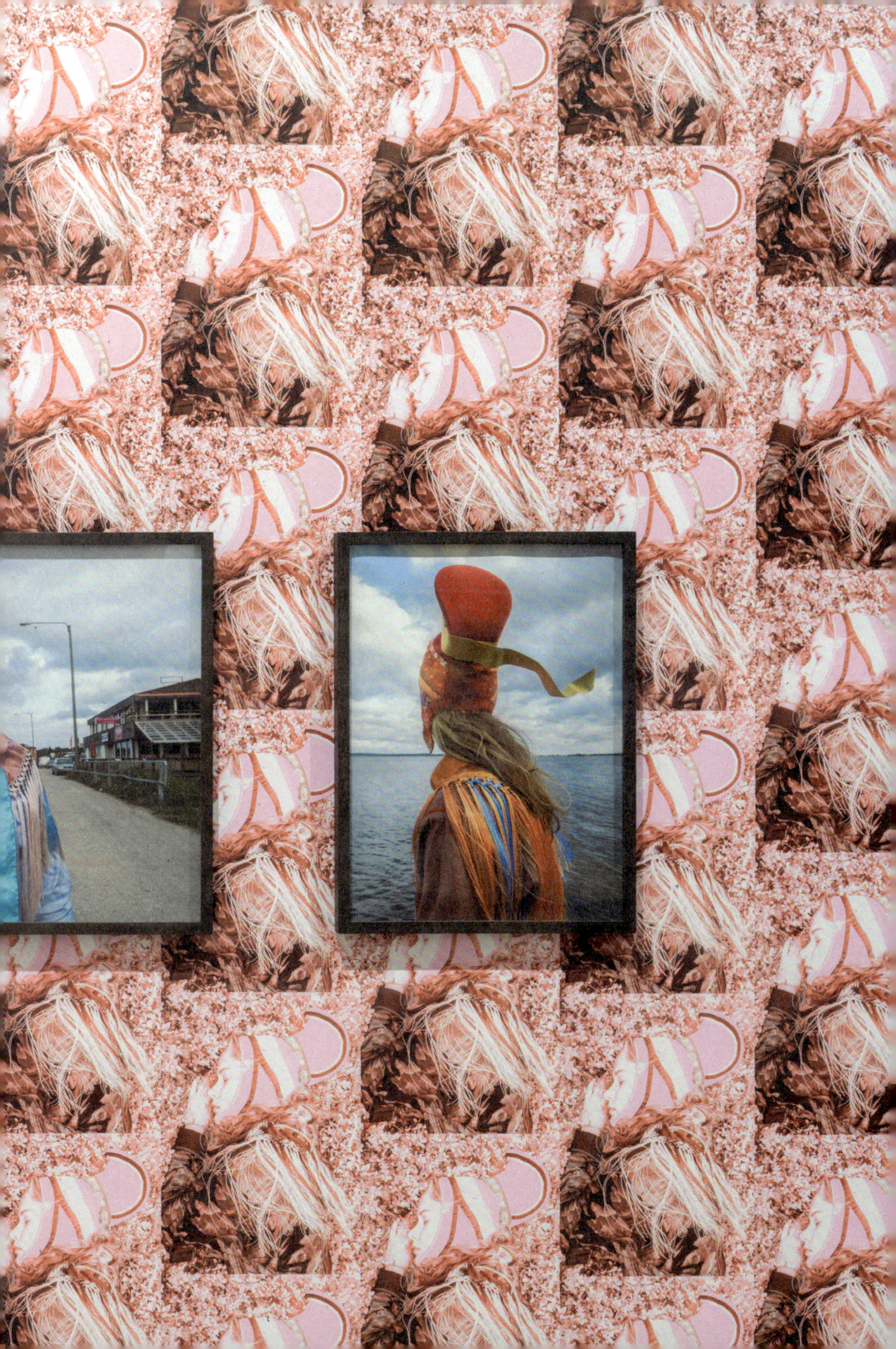

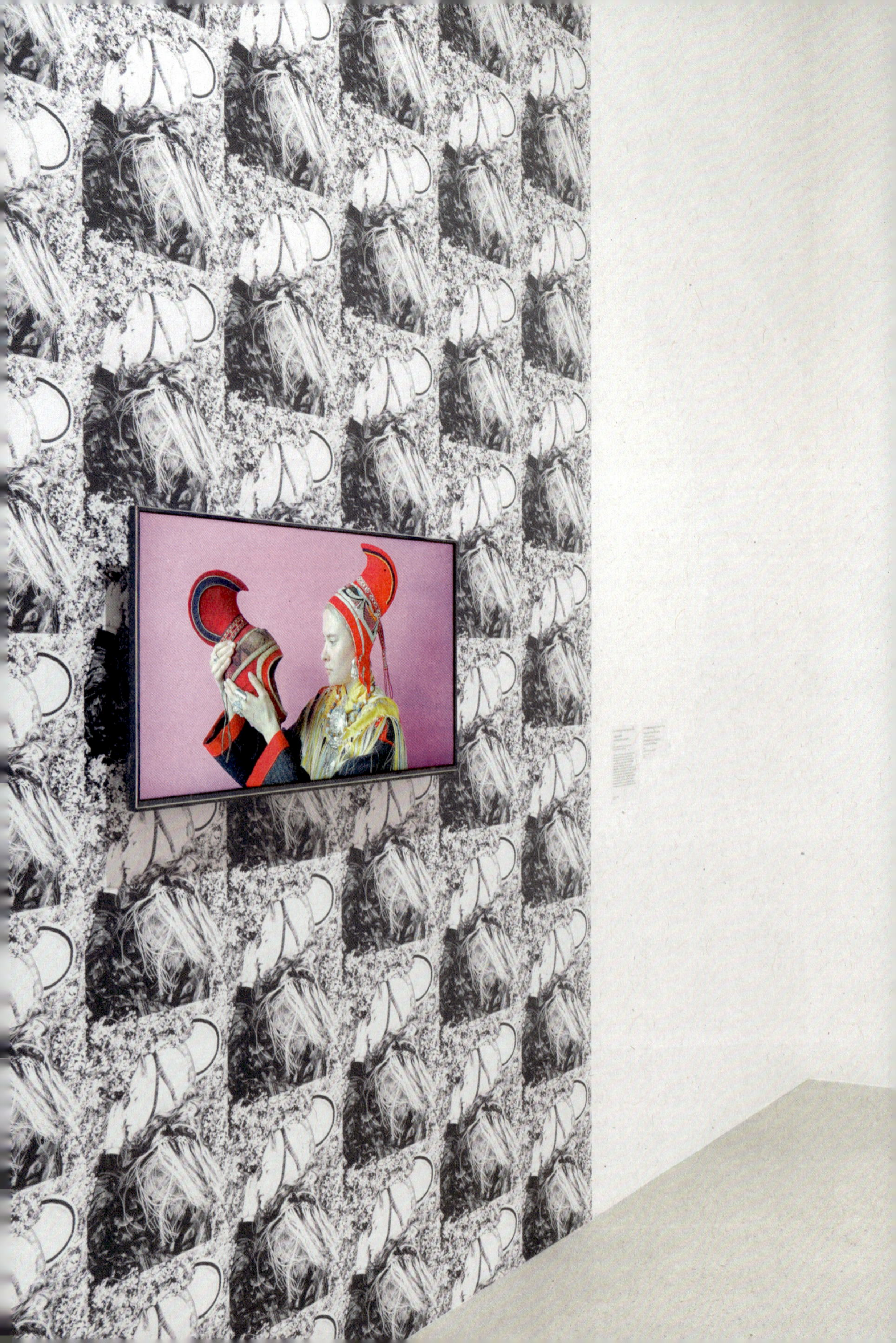

Opposite and next spread:
Outi Pieski and Biret Haarla Pieski
Ceagganaddat
Listening with Foremother
2023

Below:
Subjeavttat dutkamuša vuolde
Subjects of Research
2019

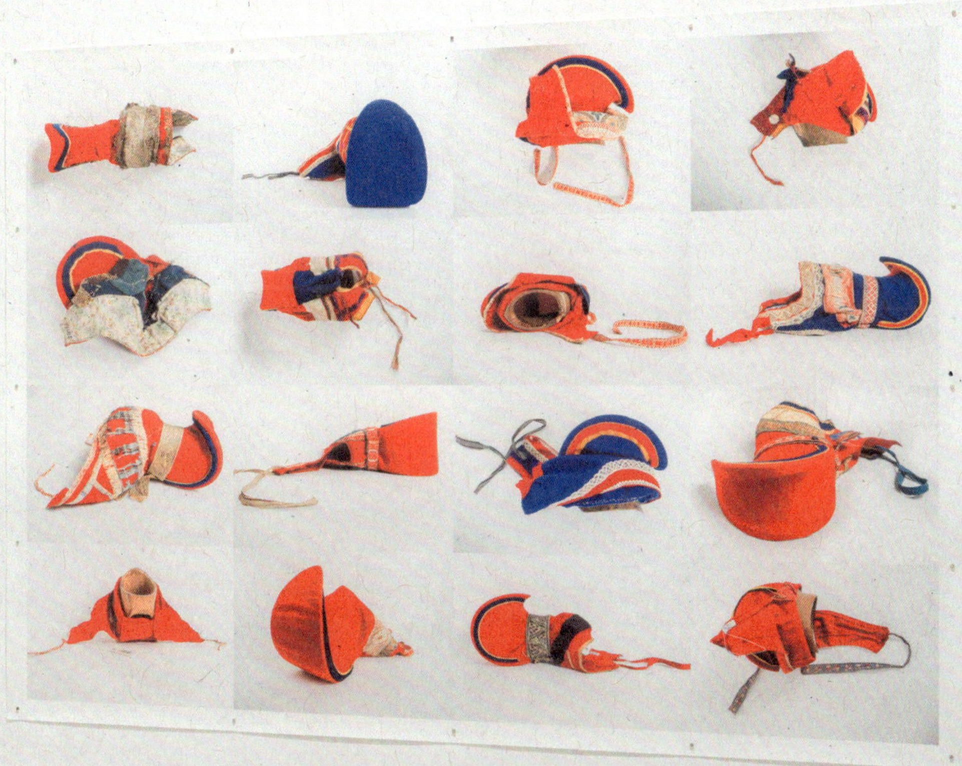

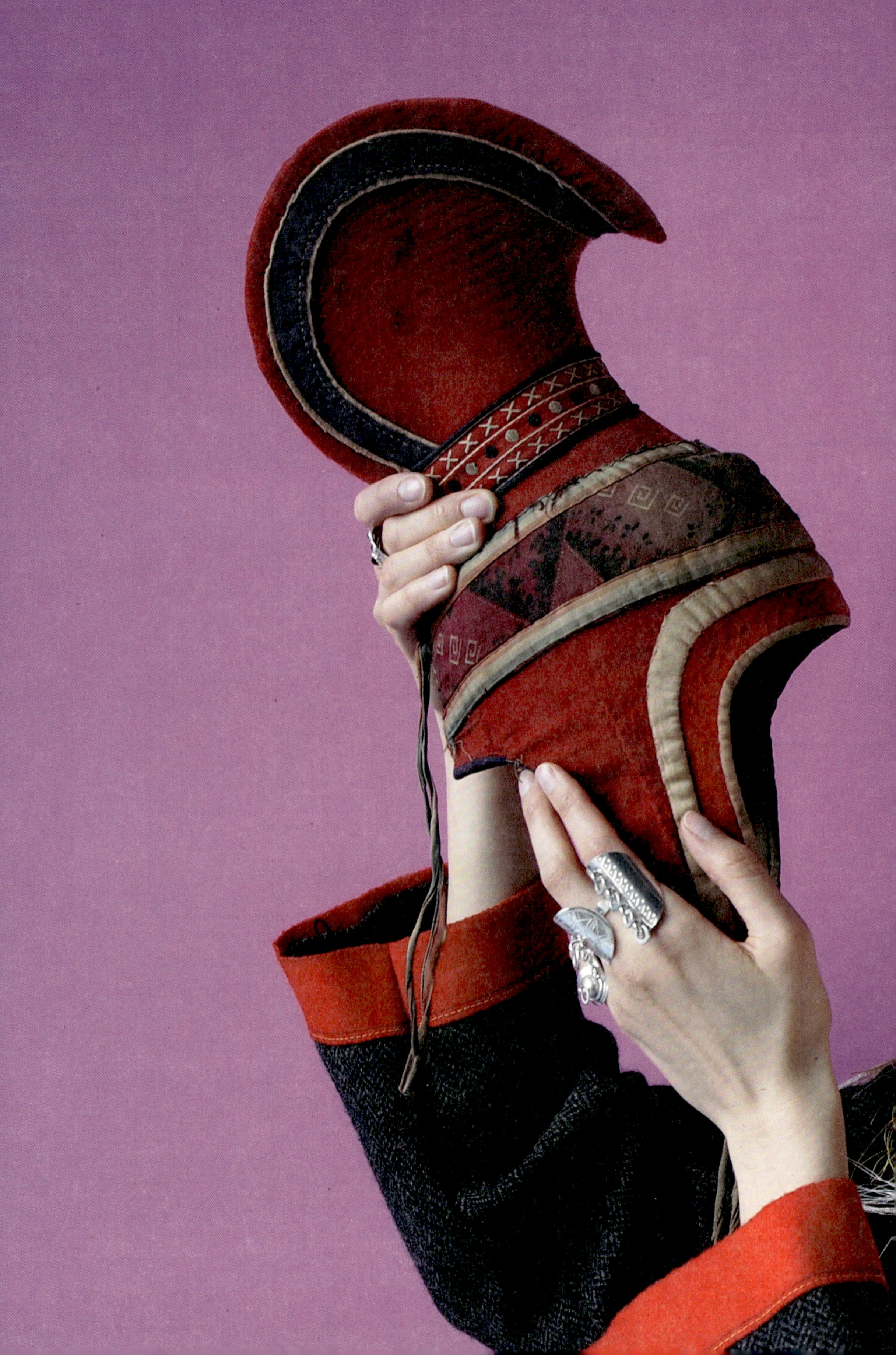

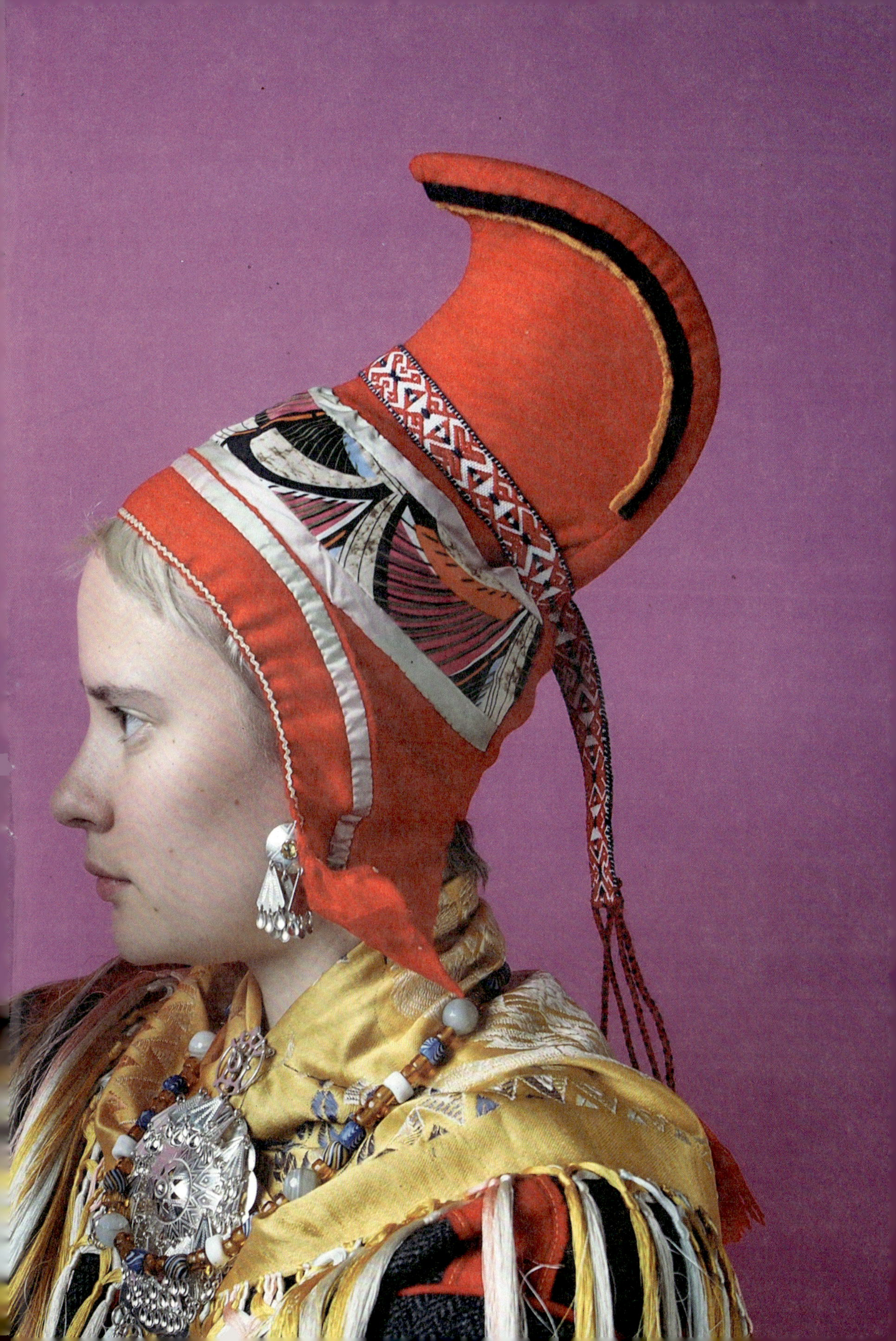

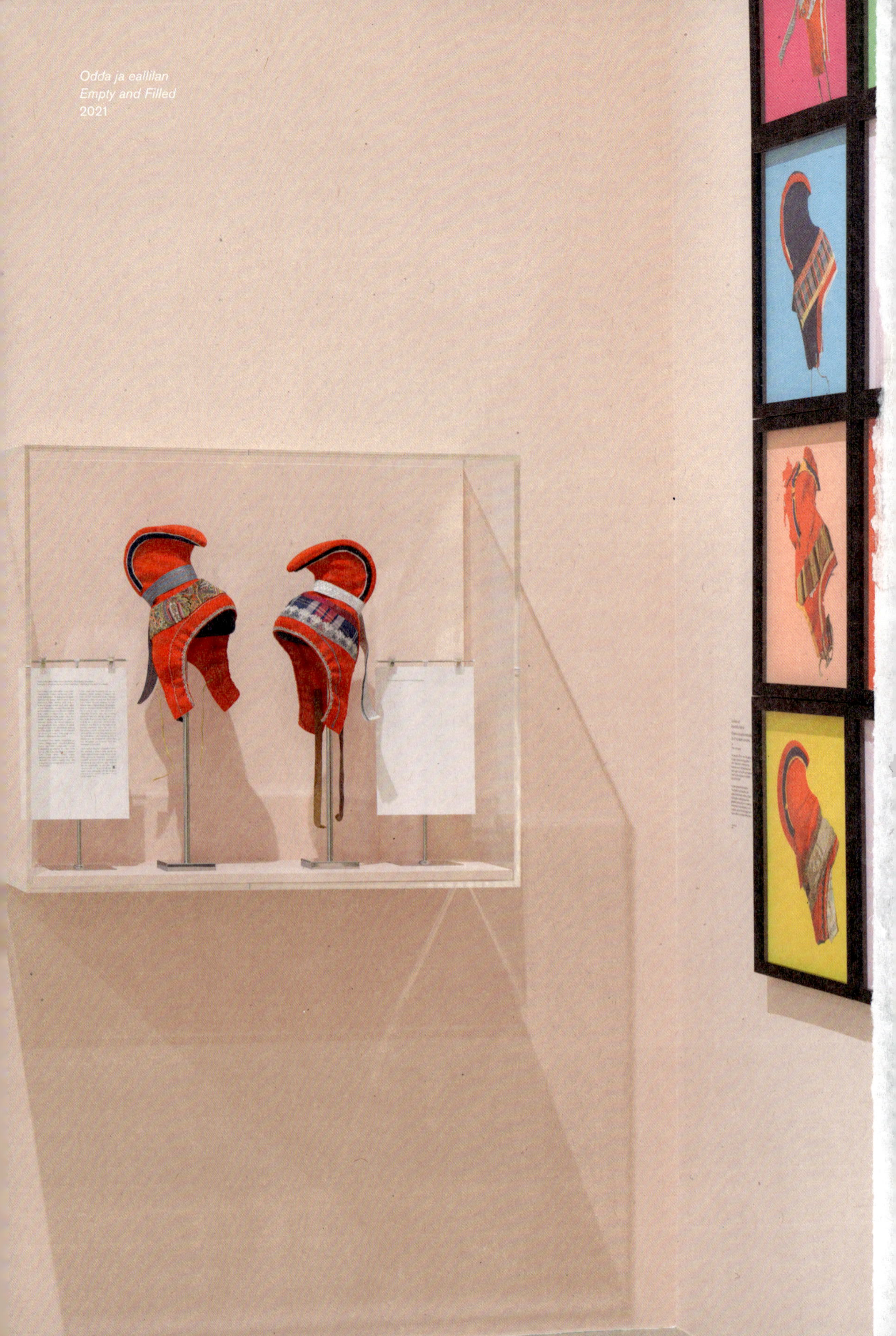
Odda ja eallilan
Empty and Filled
2021